MODERN LEGAL STUDIES

CORPORATE RESCUE: A CONCEPTUAL APPROACH TO INSOLVENCY LAW

AUSTRALIA
LBC Information Services
Sydney

CANADA AND USA
Carswell
Toronto

NEW ZEALAND
Brooker's
Auckland

SINGAPORE AND MALAYSIA
Thomson Information (S.E. Asia)
Singapore

MODERN LEGAL STUDIES

CORPORATE RESCUE:
A CONCEPTUAL APPROACH
TO INSOLVENCY LAW

by

ALICE BELCHER

Senior Lecturer in Law
University of Dundee

LONDON
SWEET & MAXWELL
1997

Published by
Sweet & Maxwell Limited of
100 Avenue Road
Swiss Cottage
London NW3 3PF
(http://www.smlawpub.co.uk)
Typeset by LBJ Typesetting Ltd
of Kingsclere
Printed in Great Britain by
Clays Ltd, St Ives plc

A CIP catalogue record
for this book is available
from the British Library

ISBN 0–421 587504

No natural forests were destroyed to make this product:
only farmed timber was used and re-planted.

ACKNOWLEDGMENTS

I would like to thank my former colleagues at Keele University for their support and encouragement in the early stages of writing this book, particularly Didi Herman and Carl Stychin.

I would like to thank the Law Department at the University of Dundee which provided the supportive atmosphere in which I completed my research and writing.

I would also like to thank the Leverhulme Trust for financial support in the form of a Leverhulme Research Fellowship.

I would like to thank the members of the Modern Legal Studies Editorial Board for encouragement and academic feedback, especially Hugh Beale and an anonymous referee.

Finally, I would like to thank all those who have cheered me on from the sidelines, including Sally, Karen, John, Anne, Eileen and Cecilia.

Alice Belcher
University of Dundee
June 1997

Contents

Table of Cases

Table of Statutes

PART I

CONCEPTS

Chapter 1

Overview

1. Background

It is now more than a decade since the reform of insolvency law edged the United Kingdom towards a "rescue culture". For most of the last decade the subjects of insolvency and business failure have had a place in my portfolio of academic interests. In the late 1980s I was lecturing accounting to management science undergraduates at Keele University. With Sally Wheeler I developed a special integrated course for students taking law and management science which examined the legal and managerial aspects of insolvency. During this period a part of my research efforts were devoted to the prediction of business failure.[1] My interests shifted slightly when I was commissioned to write a paper on the economic implications of attempting to rescue insolvent companies.[2] By the early 1990s I had moved into a law department and developed a final year undergraduate course in the law and economics of insolvency. It was at this point that I decided to write a book on corporate rescue. The book is, in a sense, the product of ten years work and reflection. It approaches its subject matter from many angles (management, accounting, economics and law) because I have approached the subject from all these angles, and I believe that all of them have a contribution to make. Having stated that the book draws on many disciplines, its main focus is the law relating to corporate rescue, but this is also broadly interpreted. For instance, in its treatment of the relevant employment law it goes beyond the boundaries of most insolvency law texts.

---

[1] See Belcher, "Predicting Company Failure" (1991) 7 *Insolvency Law and Practice* 64.
[2] See Belcher, "The Economic Implications of Attempting to Rescue Companies" in Rajak (ed.) *Insolvency Law, Theory and Practice* (1993), pp. 235–249.

The book was written at a time of political uncertainty: the year leading up to the May 1997 general election. In the United Kingdom the Conservatives had been in power since 1979, but the indications were that they would face defeat in a general election. Insolvency laws which had last been reformed in 1985 were being reviewed. Some changes were proposed, and in one area the Conservative government officially announced an intention to legislate. The result of the May 1997 general election, of course, was a massive Labour victory. However, civil servants continue to work on the proposed reforms which may still find their way onto the statute book. Details of the proposals are therefore included in the book.

2. The Scope and Approach of the Book

The approach of the book is to contextualise, analyse and evaluate rather than simply state the law. In broad terms, Part I of the book unpacks the concepts involved in a corporate rescue and Part II of the book investigates the current United Kingdom law. In scope the book limits itself to corporate rescue and the decision possibilities for a company in decline. However, Part II does not confine itself to a statement of corporate *insolvency law*. The approach taken in Part II is one of focussing on the various "players" in a potential rescue and investigating how the law creates opportunities for them or restricts their decisions. The "players" include the company, the directors, secured creditors, unsecured creditors and employees.

In Part I the main aim is to explain the conceptual difficulties surrounding corporate rescue. The first task is to explore the meaning of "corporate rescue," which is done in Chapter 2. The terminology associated with a company's decline then opens the way for the discussion of further conceptual problems, including the concept of distress and the going concern concept.

When the concept of corporate rescue is introduced in Chapter 2, it is argued that rescue should not be confined to legal rescue procedures, but extend to a wider range of measures whether initiated by the company's management or other interested parties. It includes activities relating to marketing and production as well as financial arrangements. Rescue is defined for the purposes of the book as *a major intervention necessary to avert the eventual failure of the company*. The definition is broad enough to encompass both formal and informal rescue activity. Because great importance is placed on

4

the inclusion of the informal, the first basic outline of rescue activities under particular legal regimes embraces both the formal and the informal. The formal rescue regimes of the United Kingdom and the United States are outlined and the informal notions of "turn-around" and "workout" are discussed. The problems of judging the success or failure of a rescue attempt are then acknowledged, and it is concluded that an assessment of success or failure could depend on when it is being evaluated and by whom. Finally, Chapter 2 sets out some specific rescue scenarios and presents some measures of rescue activity. Sell-offs, management buy-outs and take-overs are discussed as possible components of corporate rescue. Some statistics on the use of formal corporate rescue procedures and other indicators of rescue activity such as management buy-outs are also presented and discussed.

The second major concept associated with a company in decline is the concept of distress. In Chapter 3 it is argued that the concept of rescue involves a crisis which usually takes the form of financial distress even if the underlying problem comes from the external environment or poor decisions in other areas of the firm's operations. A basic issue is how to assess whether a company is financially distressed. One definition is based on default. Another way of defining distress is by reference to financial ratios calculated from the company's accounts. The possible effects of distress are also discussed in Chapter 3, and it is argued that distress can be a warning, a hurdle at the entry to a rescue (or insolvency) regime, or a trigger for action by secured creditors, unsecured creditors or the company's management.

One of the most important aspects of distress, in the context of rescue, is that (in the absence of a major intervention) financial distress indicates probable failure. If failure can be predicted, a rescue may be attempted; prediction is, therefore, important to corporate rescue. In Chapter 3 simple definitions of financial distress based on financial ratios are described. The simplest methods of predicting failure employ these relatively crude indicators directly. In Chapter 4 more sophisticated statistical models for the prediction of failure are explained and their limitations noted. Chapter 4 contains technical material which may prove difficult for some readers. The essence of its argument, however, is simple. As statistical models improve and become more widely available, these will be applied. It is, therefore, important to be aware of what they can and cannot achieve.

One definition of a successful rescue is the survival of the company as a going concern, but in order to emerge from a rescue as a going concern the company must keep going during the rescue. This applies whether the rescue attempt is made informally or by using a formal rescue procedure. The concept of the firm as a going concern is, therefore, central to corporate rescue. However, in the field of accounting the going concern concept has a technical meaning. Chapter 5 discusses the going concern concept as employed by accountants and investigates its interaction with insolvency law and rescue scenarios.

Part I closes with a chapter about the design of legal rescue regimes. Chapter 6 includes a taxonomy of possible types of rescue regimes and an assessment of their advantages and disadvantages, mainly in terms of their economic efficiency. Economic models are usually based on the assumption that individual agents make decisions that maximise their own wealth or utility. However, decision making at a time of severe adversity may not follow the pattern of routine decision making, as it is subject to more uncertainty and greater time pressure. The progress of a rescue attempt depends on the decisions made by various parties (agents or stakeholders), and in Part II of the book the law is presented as a framework for the decision making of directors, creditors and employees. Consideration of the decision-making process itself is therefore a vital element in a book that is attempting to assess the law as it is and as it may become. Assumptions about decision making are also vital to the process of law reform. A theory founded on incorrect assumptions about how individuals will respond could lead to policy recommendations with unintended results. The design of a good legal rescue regime is a key issue in the book. Readers are asked to consider the problems of good design only after an introduction to the conceptual and practical problems associated with corporate rescue, and it is only when the problems of good design have been exposed that readers are asked to consider in detail the workings of the law as it is and proposals for its reform.

The aim of Part II of the book is to state the United Kingdom law relating to corporate rescue as it is and as it may become. The approach is to deal with the law as it affects the various players in a corporate rescue. Chapter 7 is about the sort of arrangements that directors may be able to make with a company's creditors. Three types of arrangements with creditors are considered: (a) creditors' schemes of arrangement under section 425 of the Companies Act 1985; (b) company voluntary arrangements under sections 1 through 7 of the Insolvency Act 1986; and (c) non-statutory arrangements or compromises effected by contract or by a consensual agreement between the parties. These types of arrangement can all be proposed by the directors and do not require the company to be under an administration order or wound up. The major problem with these schemes is the lack of a moratorium on the enforcement of claims against the company. This is a problem that may be overcome in the context of small companies if the Insolvency Service's proposals for reform come to fruition, and the proposed 28-day moratorium scheme is described in some detail. Non-statutory arrangements are defined very broadly to include compromises, rescheduling of debt and the raising of extra finance with particular reference to small companies.

Chapter 8 shifts the focus from what the directors can achieve to the power of the secured creditors. Once a company has reached the stage where it is, or is likely to become, unable to pay its debts, the formal rescue regime of administration becomes an option. However, the possibilities open to directors of a troubled company can be very severely limited by the rights of secured creditors. These rights are significant, and the secured creditors can act solely in their own interest in exercising them; they have no duty to take account of the inevitable adverse consequences of their actions on the company. The holders of floating charges over the whole or substantially the whole of a company' s property were put in a strong position by the provisions of the Insolvency Act 1986. They effectively have the power to turn a proposed administration into an administrative receivership. The choice of administrative receiver is theirs, and the administrative receiver acts primarily in their interests.

In Chapter 8 administration is examined as a rescue regime with particular emphasis on the power of certain secured creditors to prevent a rescue attempt via this route. This is another area where the Insolvency Service's proposals for change may have a significant impact. The proposal to reverse the balance of power by giving the 28-day moratorium precedence over administrative receivership has been a cause for concern with secured lenders who have made lending decisions based on their ability to obtain an administrative receivership should the need arise. This aspect of the proposed reforms is therefore examined. The chapter discusses the remedies usually available to secured creditors, with and without the assistance of the court. It covers holders of both fixed and floating charges and includes a short discussion of the "security" afforded by retention of title clauses.

Chapter 9 examines various ways in which suppliers of goods or finance to an ailing company, who would in the normal way become unsecured creditors, can attempt to "jump the queue." The queue in question is the ranking by priority of creditors in a winding up. Queue jumping can be effected either by avoiding the queue altogether or by being at or near the head of the queue when it forms. The main queue-jumping methods discussed in this chapter are the use of the *Quistclose* trust, the idea of statutory super priority, and the retention of title clause. It may be thought that, because queue-jumping techniques only operate on the liquidation of the company, they are irrelevant to corporate rescue. This is far from being the case. The availability of such techniques may influence several decisions that are crucial to the progress of a rescue attempt. A vital loan may only be made if the lender can obtain the "security" of a *Quistclose* trust or the advantage of statutory super priority. Suppliers of goods may only continue to supply the company if they do so from a position of strength, and a retention of title clause may provide or support their bargaining power.

The position of the company's employees is considered in Chapter 10, which sets out the employment issues that arise out of corporate rescue. As stated above, for the purposes of the book rescue is defined as *a major intervention necessary to avert the eventual failure of the company*. A major intervention implies that there will be changes for the company's employees. Three types of changes can be identified: changes in employment contracts; dismissals which result from a reorganisation or redundancy; and changes resulting from the business or part of the business being sold as a going concern. In the first case the individual employee will have the same employer but will be required to work differently or for different hours or pay. In the second case an individual employee who is dismissed may be entitled to some form of compensation. In the third case the employee may have a new employer, but their original employment contract, which would be terminated at common law, may be preserved by the Transfer of Undertakings (Protection of Employment) Regulations. If a company enters a formal rescue regime, the administrative receiver or administrator may seek to rescue the company by continuing to trade. The position of company employees who continue to work for such an office holder has been the subject of an important House of Lords decision and emergency legislation in the form of the Insolvency Act 1994. Overall, the chapter concludes that the key to a successful rescue may lie in consultation and communication with employees. The book has a short concluding chapter which summarises the main points and highlights its unfinished business.

Chapter 2

The Concept of Corporate Rescue

1. Introduction

This chapter introduces the concept of corporate rescue. It is argued that the concept of rescue should not be confined to legal rescue procedures, but extend to a wider range of major interventions whether initiated by the company's management or other interested parties. Having adopted a relatively wide definition of corporate rescue, rescues facilitated by the use of formal legal rescue regimes are distinguished from more informal turnarounds. The discussion then moves on to consider the success of rescue attempts. This is worthy of some attention because it is not at all obvious what constitutes a successful rescue operation. In the final section of the chapter various types of rescue activity are discussed. The chapter concludes with some statistics on the use of formal corporate rescue procedures and other indicators of rescue activity such as management buy-outs both in the United Kingdom and the United States.

2. The Problem of Defining Corporate Rescue

Good management of a company involves not only the running of the company in its present form, but increasingly means the development of the company through time. Management effort in the areas of financial planning, especially in periods of rapid growth in sales, brand maintenance, product development coupled to product lifecycles and the management of research and development activities are vital to this process. Companies are rarely static; they are either adapting to the changing social and economic environment or moving towards distress and failure. If rescue is defined simply as the avoidance of distress and failure, all management activity can be thought of as constant and repeated rescue attempts. This extremely broad definition of what constitutes rescue can be contrasted with a very narrow definition based on legal rescue procedures. Between the two extreme views of rescue as the on-going maintenance of company health, and rescue as the operation of formal legal procedures which offer emergency aid in a situation of imminent failure, there lies a whole spectrum of management activity and outside intervention that could be labelled company rescue. For the purposes of this book a definition encompassing more than the legal rescue procedures but less than all management activity will be adopted. Rescue will be defined *as a major intervention necessary to avert eventual failure of the company.*

The inclusion of informal rescue in the definition is important. First, it accords with the common meaning of a rescue which includes unofficial action by heroic individuals as well as the official action of rescue agencies such as the fire service. Secondly, the costs of using official company rescue procedures are increasingly being compared with the costs of reorganising a company's affairs more informally.[1] Thus a book on corporate rescue must include both the informal and formal options.

A major intervention necessary to avert eventual failure means drastic action at a time of crisis. Coyne and Wright, in their book on divestment and company strategy, make the claim that the strategic response to "normal/ordered" changes in the company's situation or environment should be absorption of the incremental changes, whereas the strategic response to "crisis" conditions should be a structural shift.[2] The definition of rescue adopted here includes the major intervention which would be necessary for a structural shift but does not include the absorption of an incremental change. Nueno, writing about turnarounds, contrasts the features of an urgent turnaround with those of a situation where a turnaround is only advisable. An urgent turnaround implies drastic action, whereas the less urgent situation calls for incremental and progressive change.[3] Only the urgent turnarounds constitute corporate rescues under the current definition. Kharbanda and Stallworthy couple the

---

[1] *See* Chap. 7 for more detail.
[2] Coyne and Wright (eds.), *Divestment and Strategic Change* (1986).
[3] Nueno, *Corporate Turnaround: A Practical Guide to Business Survival* (1992), p. 160.

concept of rescue activity with the idea of distress. They write about "strategies for rescuing companies in distress."[4] This linkage is discussed further in Chapter three, which explores the concept of distress.

3. Formal and Informal Rescue Activity

The inclusion of both formal and informal rescue activity within the ambit of this book has already been explained. In this section some of the terminology of corporate rescues of both sorts is explained. Formal rescue regimes in the United Kingdom and the United States are described first. The less formal concepts of turnaround and workout are then considered.

FORMAL RESTRUCTURING

In the United Kingdom formal corporate rescue procedures are available under the Insolvency Act 1986 and are called insolvency procedures. In the United States the corporate rescue procedure is found in Chapter 11 of the 1978 Bankruptcy Code and is called bankruptcy. Rescue under these procedures is an alternative to liquidation. In the United Kingdom liquidation is also an insolvency procedure under the 1986 Act. In the United States the procedure for a liquidating bankruptcy is found in Chapter 7 of the Bankruptcy Code. The U.K. and U.S. rescue procedures will now be summarised.

United Kingdom Procedures

United Kingdom insolvency law is ideologically a creditor-oriented regime. This orientation has been shifted slightly by the innovations now contained in the Insolvency Act 1986, but the contrast with the debtor-oriented bankruptcy code in the United States remains marked. The main objective behind most of the U.K. insolvency procedures is the repayment of creditors. Within this objective the

---

[4] Kharbanda and Stallworthy, *Takeovers, Acquisitions and Mergers: Strategies for Rescuing Companies in Distress* (1988).

maintenance of the priority of the creditors' claims is also extremely important. The system is also one in which weight is given to the deterrence and punishment of misconduct by the directors, particularly the squandering or misapplication of assets that could otherwise be used to repay creditors. The U.K. formal rescue procedures are administration, receivership and formal arrangements with creditors. These all involve a major intervention due to a financial crisis of some sort, but they fall short of liquidation.

Administration orders

The Cork Report on Insolvency Law and Practice made several proposals designed to facilitate and encourage more corporate rescue in the United Kingdom. Many of its recommendations were implemented in 1985 and are now contained in the Insolvency Act 1986. A completely new rescue procedure was introduced, called administration. An administration order can only be granted if the company is or is likely to become unable to pay its debts.[5] The court must also be satisfied that the administration order is likely achieve one of four specified purposes. The first possible purpose is clearly a corporate rescue; it is "the survival of the company, and the whole or any part of its undertaking, as a going concern." The next two possible purposes are forms of arrangement with creditors. The final possible purpose is "a more advantageous realisation of the company's assets than would be effected on a winding up."[6]

When an administration order is granted, an administrator is appointed and takes charge of the company. The administrator must be a qualified insolvency practitioner[7] and is usually an accountant. The effect of an administration order is a moratorium on all actions by creditors. The administrator draws up a plan setting out how the stated statutory purpose is to be achieved. The administrator's proposals must then be put to a creditors' meeting. Administrators are given very wide powers designed to enable them to run the business whilst proposals are being drawn up and voted upon. They are given a general power to "do all such things as may be necessary for the management of the affairs, business and property of the company."[8] They are also given specific powers which include: the

---

[5] s.8(1)(a) of the Insolvency Act 1986.
[6] s.8(3) of the Insolvency Act 1986.
[7] s.230(1) of the Insolvency Act 1986.
[8] s.14(1) of the Insolvency Act 1986.

power to raise or borrow money; the power to carry on the business of the company; the power to establish subsidiaries of the company; and the power to transfer to subsidiaries of the company the whole or any part of the business and property of the company.[9] The take-up of the new procedure was somewhat disappointing.[10] Directors can apply for an administration order, but if one is granted they immediately lose charge of the management of the company. Creditors can apply for an administration order, but a receivership may be a more attractive option for them. These two factors may explain the disappointing numbers of administration orders in the years since their introduction.

Receiverships

A receiver is a person appointed to take possession of property which is the subject of a charge and to deal with it primarily for the benefit of the holder of the charge. Historically, the function of a receiver was to receive income or realise property, not to rescue the business. Another major change in the law following the Cork Report was the designation of certain receivers as *administrative receivers*. Administrative receivers were given new powers and responsibilities which it was hoped would promote more company rescues. An administrative receiver has most of the powers of an administrator and, like an administrator, must be a qualified insolvency practitioner. The basic position of a receiver was not, however, changed. In particular, a receiver appointed under the terms of a debenture still has a primary duty to realise the debenture holders' security rather than a general duty to the company. An administrative receiver is "a receiver or manager of the whole (or substantially the whole) of a company's property appointed by or on behalf of the holders of any debentures of the company secured by a charge which, as created, was a floating charge."[11] The legislation is worded so that if a debenture holder with the right to appoint an administrative receiver wishes to do so, that right prevails over any application for an administration order. The advantage of appointing an administrative receiver (who owes a primary duty to the debenture holder and is chosen by the debenture holder) rather than an administrator (who owes a wider duty to the company), means that an administrator is very unlikely to be

---

[9] See Sched. 1 to the Insolvency Act 1986 for a full list of powers.
[10] This is substantiated and discussed further in section 5 below.
[11] s.29(2) of the Insolvency Act 1986.

appointed where there is a floating charge over the company's assets. The numbers of administrative receiverships have been consistently high since the passing of the new legislation.[12]

Arrangements with creditors

The new insolvency legislation also introduced a new procedure for making a binding compromise with the company's creditors called the company voluntary arrangement (CVA). The existing procedure has been described as "complicated, time-consuming and expensive to operate."[13] Both procedures are now available, but the earlier version found in sections 425–427 of the Companies Act 1985 is hardly ever used. Part I of the Insolvency Act 1986 contains the provisions for company voluntary arrangements. This was another procedure that was intended to encourage more corporate rescue; however, the numbers of CVAs have been very small. Directors can remain in control while a CVA proposal is drawn up; however, the procedure does not include an automatic moratorium on actions by creditors. If a CVA is coupled with an administration order, a moratorium can be obtained, but the directors must lose control of the company to the administrator. There are only a few insolvency practitioners who have actively promoted CVAs and gained experience of the procedure over the last 10 years. From the practitioner's point of view, the fees available for CVAs are relatively small and the time needed to see a CVA from start to finish is relatively long compared with a quick liquidation. The small number of CVAs has led to proposals for reform. There has been a consultation process and the previous government indicated its intention to legislate in this area. Details of the current and proposed schemes appear in Chapter 7 of this book.

United States Procedures

In the United States, firms filing for bankruptcy can liquidate under Chapter 7 or reorganise under Chapter 11 of the 1978 Bankruptcy Code. Chapter 11 is, therefore, the U.S. rescue procedure. It allows firms to remain in operation while a plan of reorganisation is worked out with creditors. The motivation behind the Chapter 11 provisions

---

[12] See below.
[13] Farrar, Furey, Hannigan and Wylie, *Farrar's Company Law* (1991), p. 675.

of the 1978 Code is to increase the possibilities for firms to emerge from the reorganisation process as going concerns. Congress viewed the role of reorganisation as one of "providing a breathing space to save the jobs of supposedly viable firms that are in temporary financial distress."[14] Although the motivations for the U.K. and U.S. rescue procedures may sound similar, Chapter 11 is distinctive in several ways. When an administration order is granted, control of the company passes to the administrator who, as stated above, must be a qualified insolvency practitioner. On entering Chapter 11 control passes to the "debtor in possession," which has been described as a "quasi-trustee in bankruptcy."[15] What is unique about Chapter 11 is that it allows the company's existing management to become the debtor in possession. Franks and Torous claim that "in the majority of cases previous managers retain control"[16] although "occasionally the bankruptcy court appoints a trustee to oversee the firm's operations if management is guilty of fraudulent behaviour."[17] Westbrook states that "the pre-petition management of the debtor will generally remain in control throughout the proceeding."[18] In relation to public companies Gilson has reported that old management is most often ousted *during* the Chapter 11 process,[19] but *entry* into Chapter 11 does not require existing management to relinquish their control of the company. Another distinctive feature of Chapter 11 is that, although it is a "bankruptcy" proceeding, there are no conditions for entry and in particular there is no requirement for the company to be insolvent or even heading for insolvency. Rather than having to establish grounds for entry into the rescue procedure, management is entitled to use Chapter 11 "as a matter of right."[20]

Chapter 11 affords protection by establishing a moratorium. Any acts to collect against the debtor or its property are automatically stayed by the filing of the Chapter 11 petition.[21] Actions to lift the

---

[14] Franks and Torous, "Lessons from a Comparison of U.S. and U.K. Insolvency Codes" (1992) 8 *Oxford Review of Economic Policy* 70 at 75.
[15] Westbrook "Chapter 11 Reorganisation in the United States," Chap. 21 of Rajak (ed.), *Insolvency Law: Theory and Practice* (1991). This provides a longer introduction to c.11 especially written for the European reader.
[16] Franks and Torous, *op. cit.*, at 77.
[17] *ibid.* at 76.
[18] Westbrook, *op. cit.*, p. 347.
[19] Gilson, "Management Turnover and Financial Distress" (1989) 25 *Journal of Financial Economics* 241.
[20] Westbrook, *op. cit.*, p. 351.
[21] 11 U.S.C. para. 362(a).

automatic stay will succeed unless the court finds that the debtor has offered "adequate protection" for the property interest in question. For instance, adequate protection for landlords usually consists of the promise to make periodic payments.[22] Under Chapter 11 a reorganisation plan must be formulated. For an initial period[23] the debtor in possession has the exclusive right to propose a plan and extensions to that period are frequently granted.[24] The making of a plan involves allocating creditors to classes. There are no statutory rules for the establishment of classes[25] and so there is the potential for the proponent of the plan to engineer the classes and thus manipulate the outcome of the voting on the plan. Reorganisation by the approval of a plan has been termed the "unanimous consent procedure" or UCP,[26] but it is only unanimous in that each class of creditors and equity must consent to the plan. Within each class of creditor a strict majority in number and two-thirds by value is all that is required for consent. For equity the required voting margin is at least two-thirds in amount.[27]

It can be seen that the debtor in possession is in a strong position. The threat of a "cramdown" under paragraph 1129 of the Bankruptcy Code also operates to the advantage of the debtor in possession. This comes into play if a reorganisation plan is voted on but the consent of all the classes of creditors and equity is not obtained. As long as one class of creditors has approved the plan, the bankruptcy court can confirm that plan, or a modified version of it, subject to certain rules of priority which depend on whether it is secured or unsecured creditors who are dissenting.[28] The basis of these rules is that a dissenting class must be treated fairly and equitably.[29] White states:

> "If no reorganisation plan is adopted using either the UCP or cramdown, then sometimes managers will voluntarily sell the firm as a going

---

[22] Westbrook, *op. cit.*, p. 348.

[23] 11 U.S.C. para. 1121(c) gives the debtor 120 days to file a plan and a further 60 days for acceptance.

[24] Franks and Torous, "An Empirical Investigation of U.S. Firms in Reorganization," (1989) 44 *Journal of Finance* 750; and White, "The Corporate Bankruptcy Decision," (1989) 3 *Journal of Economic Perspectives* 139.

[25] 11 U.S.C. para. 1122.

[26] White, *op. cit.*, at 139.

[27] *ibid.*

[28] Westbrook, *op. cit.*, p. 362.

[29] White, *op. cit.*, at 40. Some authors claim that the rules for cramdown are those of absolute priority as in liquidation, but Westbrook points out that this usage is "somewhat inexact"; Westbrook, *op. cit.*, p. 362.

concern on the open market. . . . This liquidating reorganization is similar to a chapter 7 liquidation, except that the firm is sold as a going concern. . . . Finally, if no progress is being made towards completion of the chapter 11 reorganization, then normally some creditor petitions the bankruptcy judge to order a shift of the firm's bankruptcy filing to a chapter 7 liquidation."[30]

The advantages of the U.S. procedure have been summarised by Westbrook as the better preservation of the value of the company (because the current management, however flawed, will do a better job than a newly appointed outsider) and the encouragement of early filing (because management do not lose control of the company by filing a Chapter 11 petition).[31] The disadvantages of Chapter 11 have been pointed out by Franks and Torous, who describe the U.S. procedure as lengthy and expensive.[32]

TURNAROUNDS

A turnaround candidate has been defined as "a company or business entity faced with a period of crisis sufficiently serious to require a radical improvement in order to remain a significant participant in its major industry.[33] Thus, a turnaround involves reversal; a dramatic and sustained improvement in the company's performance is evidence of a successful turnaround. However, "turnaround" does not include all dramatic and sustained improvements; technically, it is used in a narrower sense which means reversal *at the point of crisis*. A turnaround event occurs when the very existence of the company is threatened.[34]

A turnaround can be contrasted with a "sharpbend." "Sharpbenders" have been defined as companies characterised by "a period of stagnation or decline relative to competitors in their industries followed by a dramatic and sustained improvement which resulted in their outperforming their rivals."[35] For sharpbenders there is no

---

[30] White, *op. cit.*, at 140.
[31] Westbrook, *op. cit.*, at 351.
[32] Franks and Torous (1992), *op. cit.*, at 80.
[33] Zimmerman, *The Turnaround Experience: Real-world Lessons in Revitalizing Corporations* (1991), p. 22.
[34] *ibid.* p. 19.
[35] Grinyer, Mayes and McKiernan, *Sharpbenders: The Secrets of Unleasing Corporate Potential* (1988), p. 1.

trauma of an impending financial collapse; for turnaround candidates survival is at stake and major change is therefore forced upon the company. The definition of rescue adopted in this book includes turnarounds but not sharpbends. Turnaround is a very general concept and encompasses various types of rescue activity. Some writers explicitly recognise different types of turnaround, such as the marketing turnaround, the financial turnaround and the operations turnaround.[36] Goldston states that different types of turnaround may be appropriate depending on which aspect of the firm has "fallen from grace thus holding back the entity from realizing its full potential."[37] The importance of matching the type of turnaround to the cause of decline is also emphasised by Hardy: "If the underlying cause is a structural shift in markets, the response should be strategic turnaround, which involves changing the product/marketing mix. If decline relates to internal efficiency, the organisation should seek ways of increasing revenue, cutting costs, and decreasing assets, *i.e.* engage in an operating turnaround."[38]

In his case studies of 16 turnarounds, Zimmerman concentrates almost exclusively on the manufacturing and production aspects of turning a business around. In this context he finds that the most successful turnaround agents were production people or engineers who had extensive experience in the industry in question.[39] For Zimmerman:

"Recovery has to be accomplished by actual improved performance on the part of the firm itself, without the benefit of legal restructuring, such as bankruptcy. Formal restructuring procedures such as bankruptcy occasionally permit the company to become better off by exporting problems to other parties (unsecured creditors, lenders, governments, investors or employees) who must involuntarily assume the debts the firm is obliged to pay but cannot. In a scientific sense these are not turnarounds, they are restructurings. What societies need are turn-arounds that operate in a positive sum game rather than the shifting of obligations within a zero sum game—recoveries which make the firm better off without making someone else worse off."[40]

---

[36] Goldston, *The Turnaround Prescription: Repositioning Troubled Companies* (1992), p. x.
[37] *ibid.*
[38] Hardy, *Strategies for Retrenchment and Turnaround: The Politics of Survival* (1989), p. 136.
[39] Zimmerman, *op. cit.*, p. ix.
[40] *ibid.* p. 26.

This is a very negative view of formal legal rescue procedures. If formal rescue procedures can preserve more companies as going concerns they can be part of a positive sum game. However, writers on turnaround as corporate strategy have a tendency to focus on operational and marketing issues,[41] and this preoccupation means that, although they mention the financial aspects of a turnaround, discussions of financial problems and problem solving are notably lacking in this literature. For at least one writer the separation of financial restructuring and turnaround activity is complete: in his book, which purports to be a prescription for conducting a successful turnaround, Goldston, despite paying lip-service to the idea of a "financial turnaround," states: "*After* companies have been scaled down, restructured, or moved into prepackaged bankruptcy, the only way for anyone to make any money on the newly acquired equity in the company is by performing a 'turnaround'."[42]

Goldston's thinking is not in accordance with this book's approach to the concept of corporate rescue. The definition of corporate rescue as major intervention means that *all* major changes are included in rescue activity, whether they are in the form of financial restructuring or shifts in production or marketing strategy. The advantage of an approach that embraces all rescue activity is that the contribution of all the possible "turnaround agents" can be recognised. Strategic approaches to turnaround do not usually mention insolvency practitioners as turnaround agents. Goldston sees a "turnaround team" as a necessity: "every troubled company must have a select group of individuals spearheading the effort to reverse the fortunes of the firm."[43] The company's management are seen as the most obvious core of the team, with consultants also being possible as members. In general, this literature treats "facilitators" with caution. Nueno points out that "working with facilitators is more difficult than working with [fellow] executives because there is no permanent link, there is virtually no hierarchical relationship and they resist control."[44] In a financial crisis, however, the decision to call in an investigating accountant may not be in the hands of the management. Management may prefer not to have to work with an outsider, but may have one forced upon them. In an informal rescue situation a bank lender

---

[41] Corporate strategists also write in a style which is usually prescriptive and makes heavy use of jargon.
[42] Goldston, *op. cit.*, p. 187 (emphasis added).
[43] *ibid.* p. 30.
[44] Nueno, *op. cit.*, p. 132.

may require the company to allow an insolvency practitioner to investigate and make reports. Insolvency practitioners who undertake corporate rescue work are increasingly being asked to work with companies for longer periods without any official appointment as administrator or administrative receiver to suggest ways in which the company can be turned around. The label "turnaround doctor" has been applied to insolvency practitioners involved in this type of work.[45]

WORKOUTS

A workout is the restructuring of the terms of a company's debt contracts to remedy or avoid default achieved by private renegotiation with its creditors outside formal bankruptcy or insolvency proceedings. In the United States private workouts are now fairly common. Gilson, John and Lang reported in 1990 that nearly half of the firms in default avoid formal bankruptcy proceeding by either resolving the default or restructuring debt through a private workout.[46] Since 1990 various factors have combined to make workouts slightly less popular in the United States. In the United Kingdom a small number of very large companies have restructured their debt through a sort of private workout brokered by the Bank of England and called the London Approach. The experience of workouts in the United States and the development of London Approach in the United Kingdom are discussed in more detail in Chapter 7 of this book.

4. Successful Rescue

Having adopted a convenient but imprecise definition of corporate rescue, it is necessary to consider what might constitute a successful rescue. The two issues that are discussed in this section are *what* counts as success and *when* should success be judged?

The first problem in the definition of success concerns the degree of success that can be achieved. Partial rescue is a term which is

---

[45] Flood and Skordaki, *Insolvency Practitioners and Big Corporate Insolvencies*, ACCA Research Report No. 45 (1995), p. 16.
[46] Gilson, John and Lang, "Troubled Debt Restructurings: An Empirical Study of Private Reorganization of Firms in Default" (1990) 27 *Journal of Financial Economics* 315.

sometimes used, but there may in fact be no such thing as a completely successful rescue. Following a completely successful rescue the company should, perhaps, be left in a healthy position, pursuing the same economic activities at the same level with the same management and workforce. But this is incompatible with the definition of corporate rescue adopted in this book. If a company finds itself in need of a major intervention to save it from failure, then the process of rescue must involve a radical change in management, workforce, financing arrangements or the scope or level of its activities. This change will undoubtedly mean that a loss is incurred by someone; management, employees, shareholders, secured creditors, ordinary creditors, the government and the national economy are all possible losers. All rescues can then be seen as, in some sense, partial.

On the other hand, liquidation need not mean complete failure. In terms of the company itself, liquidation clearly means failure. However, there are various scenarios that in economic terms would be successful rescues of the economic activity, output, jobs, etc., associated with the company, but involve the death of the company itself as a legal persona, for instance the liquidation of the company where most or all of the assets are sold off to be used as before, perhaps by the same workers. Another form of death for a company could be a take-over. Companies which are taken over maintain their legal existence as separate entities but often lose their corporate identity in becoming part of the parent enterprise.

There is evidence that the managers of companies in financial distress focus almost entirely on avoiding the immediate threat of failure,[47] but, in the context of the economy as a whole, stability and sustainability may also be valued and sought after. A successful rescue should bring about not only survival in the short-term but also sustained economic activity in the longer term. It can be seen from the above that the way in which success is defined is linked to the question of when the success or failure of a rescue attempt should be judged. If a company is rescued by being taken over, this may seem successful immediately after the take-over but appear less successful if the company is later liquidated or sold off or has its activities cut drastically by its new parent company. In considering the success of turnarounds Zimmerman states that "the endurance of the recovery should also be considered in determining whether success or failure

---

[47] Nelson, *Corporations in Crisis* (1981).

has been achieved. A turnaround of a year or so is not much of a turnaround."[48] This question of when to look for the success or failure of the attempted rescue is one aspect of the messiness inherent in the real world which makes attempts to design a good legal framework for rescue attempts difficult.

A final point about defining success is that success or failure may depend on the standpoint of the person questioned. Success for debtholders may be the return of their capital, but this is likely to be coupled with failure from the point of view of managers or employees who lose their jobs. A company in financial difficulty and needing to repay specific creditors may restructure by closing down part of its business. If the creditors exit with their capital and the possibility of re-investing, but some employees exit with very little money and almost no hope of new employment, it may be hard to assess the overall success or failure of the rescue. Although it has been argued that liquidation need not necessarily mean the end of the underlying economic activity of the company, in practice it usually does. Whilst it is acknowledged that the exit from many rescue attempts is directly into liquidation, it was decided that the process of liquidation should not form a part of this book, which is conceptual rather than procedural and is about successful rescue rather than failure.

5. Types of Rescue Activity

So far in this chapter rescues have been described in various imprecise ways. First, the concept of rescue was defined as a major intervention necessary to avert eventual failure of the company. This was a deliberately wide and inexact definition adopted so as to include a range of scenarios for the affected company. Secondly, whilst considering the success of rescue attempts, the consequences of a rescue were considered and it was stated that even a successful rescue must involve a radical change in management, workforce, financing arrangements or the scope or level of the company's activities. The essence of a rescue in the context of the economy must be that some of the company's economic activity lives on. This means that the liquidation of the company may not be a failure if some of its operations are transferred intact to another concern.

---

[48] Zimmerman, *op. cit.*, p. 22.

In this section some specific rescue scenarios are set out and some measures of rescue activity are presented. It should be noted that for most of these scenarios a crisis is not the only possible catalyst, and this makes the counting of rescue attempts difficult. Also, the individual possibilities for major intervention which are described here are not discrete alternatives; each may be part of a rescue operation or could constitute the whole of what is necessary for the rescue.

RESTRUCTURING

Restructuring is one way in which a company can adapt to a changing environment. Environmental changes requiring a response from the company include: change in the product market; change in technology; threatened intervention by government and regulators; and threatened action by suppliers or competitors. Responses to change that are gradual and orderly can be distinguished from those that are responses to crises and therefore come under the umbrella of "rescue". Various forms of restructuring can be identified, but the forms that are most often encountered in rescue situations are closing down parts or selling off parts of the business. In a financial crisis, closing down a part of the business that is a financial drain can save the rest. A sell-off can have an even more positive effect if it raises much-needed cash immediately.

RETRENCHMENT

Retrenchment refers to activities that reduce the scope or scale of an organisation's operations. This sort of activity has also been referred to as downsizing, resizing, cutbacks and rationalisation. Insofar as retrenchment is necessary for the survival of the operation, it is a rescue activity. Hardy states: "Many organizations are phasing out only part of their operations in order to protect the larger entity. . . . Retrenchment must, in these circumstances, be considered as an investment in survival."[49]

Retrenchment can be organised outside a formal rescue regime or can be part of a formal plan or proposal within a rescue regime. The

---

[49] Hardy, *op. cit.*, p. 1.

economic arguments for closure of a particular plant or site of operation may be strong and retrenchment can appear as a relatively easy solution; however, retrenchment may have political costs, which should be taken into account. Hardy' s case studies of retrenchment provide some illustrations of how it can be managed so as to accommodate both economic and political pressures.[50] Resistance to the changes required for retrenchment may come from managers, workers and the community, with the most important group often being the employees. The ability to maintain high levels of morale, motivation and commitment within the company is crucial. Thus, successful retrenchment may depend on recognising turnaround as a political as well as an economic problem and effectively managing both the economic and the political pressures involved.

SELL-OFFS

The act of divestment involves the sale of a discrete business. A crisis is often, but not always, the trigger for a divestment. If the board are still in control—that is, no receiver has been appointed and no legal rescue regime has been entered—management may be able to choose a core of activity which it wants to continue and divest the company, or more likely the group, of other activities in order to be able to concentrate effort and resources on the chosen core. For a sell-off to be effected in these circumstances, a turnaround in the core activities must be thought to be feasible and the business to be sold off must itself be attractive enough to find a buyer. Both parts of the business could then be rescued. The crisis itself may be in the core activities or in the business that is targeted for the sell-off. When the crisis is in the main activities, this core may be rescued by the release of resources through the disposal of a subsidiary activity. The resources obtained are likely to include financial benefits, but the release of management time and technical support may also be important to the rescue of the core. If the problem is in the subsidiary activity, it may be that this is still saleable; this is particularly likely if the problem in the subsidiary is not impending collapse but the ability to sustain future growth. Sell-offs can also occur in the context of legal rescue regimes.

---

[50] *ibid.*

It is usual for sell-offs to be in the form of a subsidiary company.[51] Where the management of a parent company forms a new subsidiary for the purpose of the sell-off and transfers relevant assets to it, the process is called a *hive down*. When finance for the purchase of the business is largely in the form of loans, the deal is called a *leveraged buy-out*. A *management buy-out* (MBO) is a sell-off where the existing management are the purchasers. Management buy-outs are often financed heavily by loans and so are both MBOs and leveraged buy-outs. Columns (1) and (2) of Table 2.1 reveal the scale of divestment activity in the United States and the United Kingdom.[52] Numbers of sales of U.K. subsidiaries include sales to established parent companies and sales in which the subsidiary becomes an independent concern, as in a management buy-out. Sales to established companies are sometimes called parent-to-parent divestment.[53] Most of the sell-offs recorded in columns (1) and (2) will probably have occurred as part of a rescue attempt. Although divestment can be an orderly strategic response to a changing environment, Coyne and Mills claim that it is crisis conditions that produce most of the possibilities for divestment.[54] The statistics in Table 2.1 do not reveal anything about the success or failure of the rescue attempts behind the sell-offs. If there is an attempt to save a core of activities through divestment, the success or failure of the rescue could focus on that remaining core, but an overall evaluation of success or failure could include both the core and subsidiary businesses. If the sell-off occurs in the context of a legal rescue regime, it could be that the part that is sold off is the only part to be rescued, but even that could be seen as a successful rescue if the alternative is the liquidation of the whole business. An assessment of the level of success achieved must involve following up the businesses which have been sold off. There has been some empirical work in the United Kingdom on the outcome of management buy-outs. The MBO is a special form of sell-off and merits some separate discussion.

---

[51] The assets of the business can be sold and the business continued by the purchaser, but the taxation implications of this method of acquiring a business can be complex.

[52] Numbers of U.K. MBOs are difficult to obtain; the figures in this table are rather old but allow a comparision of sell-off activity and MBOs.

[53] See Thomas, "Parent-to-parent Divestment," Chap. 2 of Coyne and Wright (eds.), *op. cit.*

[54] Chapter 1 of Coyne and Wright (eds.), *op. cit.*, p. 10.

Table 2.1—Sell-offs and Management Buy-outs in the United States and the United Kingdom

Year	U.S. Divestures[a]	U.K. Sales of Sub-sidiaries[b]	U.S. MBOs[c]	U.K. MBOs (1st Measure)[d]	UK MBO's (2nd Measure)[e]
1980	700	101	49	100	107
1981	800	125	82	170	124
1982	850	164	117	180	170
1983	900	142	139	195	205
1984	850		128	180	210
1985	1200			150	229

Sources:
[a] Ravenscraft and Scherer, *Mergers, Sell-offs & Economic Efficiency* (1987); these are approximate figures.
[b] *Business Monitor.*
[c] and [e] Wright, Coyne and Mills, *Management Buy-outs* (1987).
[d] Kharbanda and Stallworthy, *Takeovers, Acquisitions and Mergers: Strategies for Rescuing Companies in Distress* (1988).

MANAGEMENT BUY-OUTS

Columns (3) to (5) of Table 2.1 concern management buy-outs. To the extent that sell-offs or divestures take the form of management buy-outs there is some double counting in columns (1) and (3) of Table 2.1 for the United States and columns (2) (4) and (5) for the United Kingdom. One of the problems encountered in attempting to count the number of MBOs in the United Kingdom is that many deals are completed with a minimum of fuss and publicity. Also, "some financiers are reluctant to give details of buy-outs which they have supported."[55] The difficulties can be seen in the differences between the two U.K. measures given in columns (4) and (5). The level of MBO activity is estimated to be continuing at the rate of about 200 per year. The numbers in column (5) were generated as part of a detailed survey of U.K. MBOs conducted by Wright, Coyne and Mills. They found that about 60 per cent of the MBOs were divestments by parent companies, about 5 per cent were of individual

[55] Coyne and Wright (eds.), *op. cit.*, p. 144.

companies in receivership and a further 14 per cent were where the parent company was in receivership. The survey was conducted some time after the buy-outs had been completed and included information about employment. In 44 per cent of the MBOs employment was reduced, producing an 18 per cent fall in total full-time employment immediately after the buy-out, most of this coming from buy-outs from receivership. However, by the time of the survey employment had risen overall by 11 per cent from its time-of-buy-out level. The survey reveals that a small number of both customers and suppliers were lost at the time of the buy-out, but remaining relationships were reported as being better than before. The authors noted that "in buy-outs from receivership, a policy of nurturing key suppliers and customers before the crash is often a crucial element in a successful restart."[56] The estimated failure rate of MBOs was one in eight. These numbers give some indication of what has occurred in MBOs which have gone ahead; the difficulty in drawing conclusions from this sort of evidence, particularly for the purposes of policy recommendations, is that any extra buy-outs which can be encouraged using policy incentives will be those at the margin and therefore less likely to succeed.

One rationale for management buy-outs is that the current management team is being prevented from being as efficient as it could be and that becoming owner/managers will provide the incentives and opportunities necessary for the current management to perform well enough to save the company. In 65 per cent of MBOs in the Wright, Coyne and Mills survey there was no change in the management team. Freedom to act and to exercise judgment coupled with renewed motivation have often been given by management teams as reasons for the pursuit of a buy-out.[57] However, there are those who believe MBOs from a surviving parent company should not occur. If the management team is good enough to run a successful business, they are valuable employees who should be retained within the firm. If they are not that good, a parent company which is itself continuing to trade would not want to tarnish its own reputation by setting a management team on the road to disaster.[58] There is also the problem of the conflict of interest which is inherent in a management buy-out, expressed by Peck as follows: "Managers

---

[56] *ibid*. p. 90.
[57] *ibid*. p. 142.
[58] *ibid*. p. 149.

have a fiduciary duty to maximise share value. Yet, they also have an incentive to sell the firm to themselves as cheaply as possible."[59]

One way in which management may try to lower the price of their company is to manipulate reported profits, prior to making their offer, by using discretion in the drawing up of accounts. Evidence from U.S. buy-outs on this question is equivocal. Perry and Williams analysed 175 MBOs and found evidence of the manipulation of earnings.[60] An investigation by DeAngelo where the sample of MBOs included a larger proportion of distressed companies, however, found no evidence of earnings management in the run up to a buy-out.[61] One explanation for these results is that management has less room for manoeuvre in times of adversity.

The first step in a management buy-out is usually for the management team to consult an accountant or a financial institution to act as intermediary and conduct a preliminary assessment of the proposed deal. If the result of the initial investigation is positive, informal discussions with the management of the parent company will take place. This may happen before entry into a legal rescue procedure. A proposal could also be made when the company is in the hands of a receiver or administrator, in which case there may be less need for secrecy and consultation with intermediaries before the initial approach, as management would have little to lose. If the initial approach is received favourably, detailed negotiations will follow. In the United Kingdom the bargaining process may be entirely secret if it occurs outside a legal rescue regime. Within a rescue regime the desire to sell off part or all of the business becomes public knowledge. In the United States no management buy-outs are conducted in secrecy; sales must be made public and third parties are invited to bid.[62] The management team will need to obtain sufficient financial backing for the deal, and in practice this may act as the filter which stops weak managers becoming purchasers. Important components of the deal which have to be decided are the form of ownership transfer and the financial arrangements for the purchase. Most management teams want to own the majority of shares, if not a

---

[59] Peck, "The Influence of Professional Investors on the Failure of Management Buyout Attempts," (1996) 40 *Journal of Financial Economics* at 268.

[60] Perry and Williams, "Earnings Management Preceding Management Buyout Offers," (1994) 18 *Journal of Accounting and Economics* 157.

[61] DeAngelo, "Accounting Numbers as Market Valuation Substitutes: A Study of Management Buyouts of Public Stockholders," (1986) 67 *The Accounting Review* 77.

[62] In the United States MBOs are often contested.

controlling interest, in the newly acquired company. The purchase is usually financed by a small proportion of money put up by the managers themselves—10 per cent is a typical amount—and a large proportion is put forward by financial institutions. If management are to hold the majority of shares but provide only a small proportion of the purchase price, the deal has to be heavily financed by loans. This means that the newly acquired company is often very highly geared and therefore burdened with inescapable loan interest payments. Despite these burdensome arrangements, as stated above, only one in eight buy-outs have been observed to fail.

In a management buy-out the key to the successful rescue of the business activity is obviously the quality of the management team. However, in many instances of distress, management is the problem rather than its solution. Inadequate management and management problems have been cited as significant causes of corporate decline in several studies.[63] In many cases it may be that current management has to be replaced to facilitate the rescue. One mechanism for replacing an inefficient management team with a more efficient one is a take-over.

TAKE-OVERS

Take-overs are relevant to corporate rescues in three ways. In two of them they are the solution and in the third they are the cause of the problem:

(1) The business may be rescued by being the subject of a take-over.

(2) The business may be rescued by making an acquisition, in particular an acquisition of a firm in the same or a related industry.

(3) The business may be in need of a rescue attempt because of a bad decision to make an acquisition.

All take-over activity will not constitute rescue activity as defined earlier in this chapter. Whilst take-overs are major interventions, they

---

[63] See Slatter, *Corporate Recovery* (1984), p. 26, where the results of several studies are compared.

need not occur at times of crisis or to avert failure. Some take-overs will, however, count as rescues. Rescue by being taken over, as already stated, could be a way in which inefficient management is replaced. This is the basis of the theoretical explanation of take-overs called the market for corporate control.[64] This theory suggests that the market value of a company, in an efficient capital market, will reflect its true value, including the value of its current management team. If the company's assets could be managed more efficiently, the value of the company could be increased by changing the management. If the company's assets are being managed so badly that it is in distress and facing failure, a take-over followed by better management could rescue the company. Empirical evaluations of take-overs have been of two types.[65] Studies based on share prices have shown that in general the shareholders of target companies receive a significant positive abnormal return over the period from the bid announcement. The evidence on returns to the acquiring companies is more mixed and often the abnormal returns which are detected, whether positive or negative, are not significantly different from zero.[66] The other type of take-over evaluation is based on reported accounting profits. Evidence on profitability following merger is mostly negative. Studies have usually found that profitability declines following merger.[67]

The second way in which a take-over can be at least part of a rescue attempt is for the distressed company to be the acquirer. Slatter lists growth via acquisition as one of ten generic corporate recovery strategies.[68] An acquisition will need to gain financial support and will therefore be available to only a few firms in a crisis situation, but Slatter claims that "once survival is assured acquisition may be part of the strategy to achieve sustainable recovery."[69] The advantages of becoming an acquirer include permitting the acquirer to implement a product-market reorientation and improving compet-

---

[64] Manne, "Mergers and the Market for Corporate Control," (1965) 73 *Journal of Political Economy* 110.

[65] Taken together the evidence of the two types of study makes take-over activity hard to explain, at least from the point of view of the acquiring company.

[66] There are a number of U.S. studies reporting these results. The most recent and comprehensive U.K. one is R.J. Limmack, "Corporate Mergers and Shareholder Wealth Effects 1977–1986," (1992) 21 *Accounting and Business Research* 184.

[67] The most famous U.K. study is Meeks, *Disappointing Marriage: A Study of the Gains from Merger* (1977).

[68] Slatter, *op. cit.*, p. 78.

[69] *ibid.* p. 96.

itive advantage or reducing competitive disadvantage by providing access to new distribution channels, access to new technology or the opportunity of scale economies by combining operations.[70] The problem with these claims is that the evidence of the empirical studies already outlined does not reveal any advantages to acquiring companies following an acquisition.[71] A take-over or acquisition involves one company acquiring another. If two or more companies combine on an equal footing this may be described as a merger. In the United Kingdom there are different methods of accounting for acquisitions and mergers. The key element in the definition of a merger for accounting purposes is that the parties come together to share in the future risks and benefits of the combined entity.[72] An example of a merger that was also a rescue is the merger in 1978 of three Swedish steel factories as a response to over capacity in the industry. This merger can be seen as a successful rescue when compared to the prospects for the three factories: one would have been closed due to bankruptcy of the parent company; the second would have closed down a major part of its steel production; the third would have operated at a deficit propped up by the government. Overall, the loss of employment would have been far greater than under the merger arrangement.[73]

The third way in which rescues are linked to take-overs is through the failure of an acquisition. Acquisitions are often large projects to the acquiring company. The failure of any project that is large in relation to the size of the company can precipitate financial distress and failure. Slatter identified both big projects and the acquisition of "losers" in a list of frequently occurring factors which are the principal causes of corporate decline.[74] He states:

"The worst of all possible worlds is the acquisition of unrelated firms with no competitive advantage in their marketplace. Such acquisitions are to be avoided at all costs but, unfortunately, they are very common. Typically, when a firm with a weak competitive position is acquired, the

---

[70] *ibid.*

[71] Empirical evaluations of take-overs usually focus on returns. Organization theory sometimes sees merger activity as risk-reducing rather than return-increasing, see Goldberg, *Mergers: Motives, Modes, Methods* (1983), p. 53. Finance theorists would argue that in an efficient capital market there is no need for the company to diversify away risk, as the shareholders can do this by holding an appropriate portfolio.

[72] Financial Reporting Standard (FRS) 6, *Acquisitions and Mergers.*

[73] This merger is described in detail in Goldberg, *op. cit.*, pp. 239–268.

[74] Slatter, *op. cit.*, p. 25.

new subsidiary becomes a cash drain on the parent company . . . management throws 'good money after bad' in the hope of justifying their acquisition decision."[75]

The failure of the new subsidiary could precipitate the failure of the whole group. If, however, problems are recognised soon enough, a rescue may be attempted involving a restructuring including the closing down of activities that are a financial drain. Alternatively, the ailing subsidiary may be sold off. Ravenscraft and Scherer conducted a detailed study of U.S. mergers and sell-offs which reveals that the pattern of divestures follows that of merger activity with a short lag.[76] This suggests that many sell-offs are the result of disappointing take-overs. Table 2.2 gives some indication of the scale of take-over activity involving U.K. companies.

Table 2.2—Acquisitions Involving U.K. Companies

Year	Acquisitions of U.K. Companies by U.K. Companies	Acquisitions of U.K. Companies by Overseas Companies	Acquisitions Overseas by U.K. Companies
1987	1527	61	431
1988	1499	99	648
1989	1330	168	681
1990	779	143	586
1991	506	146	550
1992	432	210	679
1993	526	267	521
1994	674	202	422
1995	482	113	310

Sources:
1988–95: Office for National Statistics, *Acquisitions and Mergers Involving U.K. Companies.* 1987: HMSO, *Financial Statistics*; and Central Statistical Office, *Cross Border Acquisitions and Mergers.*

RESCUES UNDER A LEGAL RESCUE REGIME

Table 2.3 presents the numbers of attempted rescues and liquidations following the introduction of administration orders in the 1986 Act.

[75] *ibid.* p. 49.
[76] Ravenscraft and Scherer, *Mergers, Sell-offs and Economic Efficiency* (1997).

The Act gave an opportunity to holders of floating charges over the company's assets to appoint an administrative receiver rather than an administrator. The available figures on administrative receiverships from 1987 to 1995 show that advantage has usually been taken of this opportunity. Many of the Company Voluntary Arrangements (CVAs) have been coupled with an administration order and so are double counted in Table 2.3. The number of liquidations is also shown in Table 2.3 and this gives an indication of just how few rescues are being attempted. If the figures in Tables 2.2 and 2.3 are looked at together it can be seen that liquidation increases while take-over activity declines. These are symptoms of economic recession.

Table 2.3—Numbers of Attempted Rescues and Liquidations

Year	Administration Orders	Receiverships Including Administrative Receiverships	CVAs	Liquidations (England and Wales)	Administrative Receivership Appointments and Administration Orders
	(1)	(2)	(3)	(4)	(5)
1987	131	1265	21	11439	n/c
1988	198	1094	47	9427	n/c
1989	135	1706	43	10456	1507
1990	211	4318	58	15051	3988
1991	206	7815	137	21827	5734
1992	120	8334	116	24425	5104
1993	112	5362	134	20708	3226
1994	164	3877	264	16728	2107
1995	163	3226	372		2013

Sources:
Columns (1) to (3) Department of Trade and Industry.
Column (4) *Annual Abstract of Statistics* (CSO 1996 ed.).
Column (5) Deloitte Touche figures based on Appointments advertised in the London and Edinburgh Gazette; 1989 and 1990 figures are for England and Wales only.
n/c = numbers not collected.

When new procedures are made available, as under the 1986 Act, there is a period of learning for the "experts" involved, in this case the insolvency practitioners. Initially there can also be a period of uncertainty about how the courts will interpret new legislation. Uncertainty coupled with a lack of experience in the use of the new procedures on the part of insolvency practitioners could be part of the explanation of the small numbers of rescue attempts in the early years. In 1992, as part of a wider review of company law and in view of the low numbers of companies making use of the company rescue provisions, the Insolvency Service set up a working party to investigate the low take-up and the case for change. This has resulted in two consultative documents dated October 1993 and April 1995 and an announcement in November 1995 by the then Minister for Company Affairs of his intention to introduce legislation. During the period of investigation and consultation the numbers of CVAs has increased dramatically. The current CVA procedure, its problems and the plans for change are discussed in Chapter 7.

Numbers of administrative receiverships as a separate category have not been collected. The Department of Trade and Industry figures combine administrative receiverships and other receiverships. The figures collected by Deloitte Touche combine administration orders and administrative receiverships, and from 1991 these figures include Scotland. However, it is clear that the numbers of attempted rescues is far lower than the number of liquidations in any year.

6. Conclusion

In this chapter the concept of corporate rescue has been discussed and a working definition has been offered. Corporate rescue is to be defined as a major intervention necessary to avert eventual failure of the company. The problems in assessing the success of a rescue attempt were also discussed. An assessment of success or failure could depend on when it is being evaluated and by whom.

In the final section of this chapter some other forms of restructuring which sometimes constitute rescue were discussed. Sell-offs, management buy-outs and take-overs could all occur outside legal rescue regimes and may be the right strategy for avoiding the need to enter a rescue regime. For some companies they could be part of the exit from a rescue regime. This chapter has also presented some evidence of the level of different types of rescue activity. The numbers of companies that are using the rescue procedures introduced by the 1986 Act are small. It may be that the opportunities for rescue created by the 1986 Act are adequate, that the practitioners are getting it right and that there are only a few companies where an attempted rescue makes any sense. However, moves at the Department of Trade and Industry indicate that there is a desire to increase the uptake of both CVAs and administration orders.[77]

---

[77] In November 1995 the then Minister for Company Affairs announced his intention to introduce legislation revising CVAs and at the same time announced that he would be seeking views on facilitating administrations and encouraging debt/equity swaps. A paper on these topics was issued in February 1996 with comments to be submitted by May, 10, 1996. Legislation had not been drafted at the time of the Conservative defeat in May 1997.

Chapter 3

The Concept of Distress

1. Introduction

Corporate rescue has been defined as a major intervention necessary to avert eventual failure of the company and has been summarised as drastic action at a time of crisis. In Chapter 2 various types of rescue activity were discussed, but the nature of the crisis was not considered. The definition of rescue means that the crisis must be one which threatens the survival of the company. Companies experiencing such crises are usually described as troubled or distressed and financial distress is usually the prelude to failure. In this chapter the concept of distress is explored in more detail.

2. Distress Based on Default

Many writers refer to distressed or financially distressed companies without giving any definition of these terms. "Distressed" is a convenient word because, like the word "troubled", it acknowledges a problem without having to indicate the source of that problem. One usage of "financially distressed" is in relation to companies which need to renegotiate a debt contract, *i.e.* companies in default.[1] Sometimes default proper is distinguished from technical default.[2]

---

[1] Gilson, John and Lang, "Troubled Debt Restructurings: An Empirical Study of Private Reorganization of Firms in Default," (1990) 27 *Journal of Financial Economics* 315; Gilson, "Bankruptcy, Boards, Banks and Blockholders," (1990) 27 *Journal of Financial Economics* 355; and Tashjian Lease and McConnell, "Prepacks: An Empirical Analysis of Prepackaged Bankruptcies" (1996) 40 *Journal of Financial Economics* 135 all use "financially distressed" in this way.

[2] See Wruck, "Financial Distress, Reorganization, and Organizational Efficiency," (1990) 27 *Journal of Financial Economics* 419; and Gilson (1990) *op. cit.*

Default proper involves a missed payment of either principal or interest. Technical default is the violation of a debt covenant other than one specifying principal and interest payments, for instance a term requiring the company to maintain a minimum level of net worth. Both sorts of default will have consequences, but a default proper will, generally, be much more serious than a technical default. Default proper means that a debt which is due remains unpaid; as proof of the company's insolvency this can lead directly to failure through a petition for a winding up. The consequences of a technical default will depend on the contents of the debt contract. Gilson, John and Lang suggest that in the United States many technical defaults involve "financially healthy firms" and are renegotiated with little trouble.[3] However, management take a great deal of care not to be in technical default.

3. Distress Based on Financial Ratios

Another way of defining a distressed company is by reference to the contents of its published financial statements. Financial statement analysis includes an array of techniques and is employed for a variety of purposes.[4] Ratio analysis is the most frequently used technique. A large number of ratios can be calculated from any given set of accounts; however, they are usually grouped under three headings: profitability ratios; liquidity ratios; and ratios reflecting longer-term solvency.

Profitability—Profitability ratios can be used to assess how effectively an organisation has used its available resources. It is hoped that an evaluation of past performance will assist in the prediction of likely future performance.

Liquidity—Liquidity is concerned with the company's current financial position and, in particular, its capacity to pay its debts as they arise in the short term.

Longer-term solvency—The company's ability to meet its longer-term financial commitments may be captured by ratios that measure the composition of its capital structure.

Distress can be defined in relation to financial ratios. A definition can be in terms of a single ratio or a combination of ratios. For

---

[3] Gilson, John and Lang (1990), *op. cit.*, at 326.
[4] For general treatments of the subject, see Foster, *Financial Statement Analysis* (2nd ed., 1986); and Lev, *Financial Statement Analysis: A New Approach* (1974).

instance, the following is found in the rules of the Reserve Bank of India:

> "1. It [the company] shows a cash loss for the previous year and this situation is likely to continue in the current and next following year and/or
>
> 2. There is an imbalance in its financial structure such as the current assets/current liabilities ratio being less than unity and the debt/equity ratio rising."[5]

Foster defines financial distress more generally as "severe liquidity problems that cannot be resolved without a sizable rescaling of the entity's operations or structure."[6] If distress is defined by reference to the contents of the company's published accounts, insolvency (or bankruptcy) and distress will not be the same thing. Companies can fall into any of the four categories illustrated by the matrix in Table 3.1.

Table 3.1

	Nonfinancially Distressed	Financially Distressed
Nonbankrupt	I	II
Bankrupt	III	IV

Bankrupt companies are those which have filed for formal legal bankruptcy (or insolvency).

Source: G. Foster, *Financial Statement Analysis* (2nd ed. C, 1986), p. 535.

This matrix will be a snapshot. Companies may be moving towards failure or may, via corporate rescue, move out of the problem areas of the matrix. Several points arise from the matrix.

---

[5] Kharbanda and Stallworthy, *Corporate Failure: Prediction, Panacea and Prevention* (1985), p. 61.
[6] Foster, *op. cit.*, p. 61.

First, the distinction that is made in the matrix between bankrupt and nonbankrupt companies is a distinction based on entry into a legal regime. In the United States the bankrupt companies are those which have filed for Chapter 7 or Chapter 11 bankruptcy. In the United Kingdom the bankrupt companies are those which are either in liquidation or have entered a formal legal rescue regime. Bankruptcy in this matrix does not equate with either insolvency or financial distress. Secondly, in the matrix companies can be bankrupt without being financially distressed: category III. This category applies most obviously to the United States, where a Chapter 11 filing does not require proof of insolvency. One way in which a Chapter 11 filing can be used by a solvent company is as protection. Because Chapter 11 establishes a moratorium in which actions against the company are automatically stayed, a solvent company faced with, for example, a large number of product liability suits will find a Chapter 11 filing attractive. In the United Kingdom there may be some companies in category III; these will be companies in voluntary liquidation. They will be bankrupt in that they have entered a formal bankruptcy regime, but the reason for entry need not be financial distress. Companies that are formed for a particular purpose are often voluntarily liquidated once the purpose has been achieved. Thirdly, companies can be financially distressed without having entered a formal legal procedure: category II. These companies are potential rescue candidates. Finally, companies that are both financially distressed and bankrupt are not necessarily beyond rescue; indeed some of them may be in the process of being rescued. The matrix in Table 3.1 serves to illustrate how financial distress does not imply (although it may predict) failure, or even bankruptcy. In the rest of the chapter it is argued that the concept of financial distress can be used in various ways: as a warning signal; as a hurdle; and as a trigger. The relationship between the concept of distress and the concept of insolvency is also discussed.

4. Distress as a Warning Signal

As indicated above, distress can be defined simply in terms of ratios calculated from the company's published accounts. Distress can be a warning signal in that information in a company's current financial results can be used to predict the future. When the accounts are published, information about the company's financial position becomes available to the financial market.[7] Investors, creditors and, in particular, financial analysts are then able to assess whether the company is experiencing financial distress (by reference to financial ratios) *and* to use more sophisticated techniques to make predictions based on the company's current situation. Market prices can drop not only in line with reported bad results but also as a result of analysts forecasting worse to follow. The chances of effecting a successful rescue may be shaped by the publication of a set of bad results and the resulting loss in confidence embodied in a fall in share price.

Market-based accounting research has demonstrated that the market does respond to information released in the annual accounts. First, studies have shown that the market responds to a company's profits or "earnings."[8] Secondly, studies have shown that the market also responds to the information contained in the components of earnings,[9] *i.e.* it is not only the "bottom line" that matters. The ratios used to define distress are usually ratios of components of the balance sheet and/or the profit and loss account. Empirical work also suggests that if the published accounts reveal unexpectedly that the company is distressed, the stock market will respond to this information and there will be negative share price returns. The response to the publication of a company's accounts will, of course, be a response to *all* the price-sensitive information which they convey and what is conveyed by a particular set of results will depend on how they are interpreted. Some of the models which financial analysts can use to predict the failure or survival of a company using current financial results are described in the following chapter. The main point to be made here is that the revelation of a company's distressed situation by the publication of the accounts will act as a warning signal which will produce responses from the market which may, in turn, change the course of a rescue attempt.

---

[7] This applies to quoted companies.

[8] Various statistical methodologies have been employed in these studies, some of which are explained in Belcher, "Techniques for Evaluating Regulatory Change" (1995) 2 *European Journal of Law and Economics* 211.

[9] Lipe, "The information Contained in the Components of Earnings," (1986) *Journal of Accounting Research* (Supplement) 37; Bublitz and Ettredge, "The Information in Discretionary Outlays: Advertising, Research and Development," (1989) 64 *Accounting Review*, 108; Belcher, "Company Reporting of Research and Development Expenditure: A Study of the Decision to Disclose and the Market's Reaction to Disclosure" (1994), Ph.D. thesis University of Manchester.

5. Distress as a Hurdle

A legal rescue regime may be designed specifically for insolvent companies or may be open to all companies as a matter of right. The U.K. and U.S. regimes, as outlined in Chapter 2, differ in this respect. Under the U.S. regime companies enter Chapter 11 as a matter of right. In the United Kingdom an administration order can only be made if the company is insolvent in the sense that it "is or is likely to become unable to pay its debts."[10]

A regime that sets up the hurdle of insolvency before the entrance to a rescue regime must then define both the term insolvency and the ways in which insolvency can be proved. Two of the three types of financial ratio are said to reflect different aspects of solvency. The liquidity ratios are measures of capacity to pay debts in the short-term, and the longer-term solvency ratios are measures of ability to meet longer-term financial commitments. Some connection between distress (defined in terms of financial ratios) and the availability of an insolvency regime (defined in terms of insolvency) might therefore be expected. In fact, the proof required for the granting of an administration order in the United Kingdom is not based on poor liquidity and longer-term solvency ratios, but is instead based on the concept of inability to pay debts:[11] Despite the claims made for financial ratios as measures of short- and long-term solvency they have several limitations which are worth noting:[12] The working capital or current ratio and the liquidity or quick ratio are both used as indicators of a company's ability to meet its short-term cash obligations out of its current assets and will be used here to illustrate some of the problems of financial ratios. These ratios are defined as follows:

$$working\ capital\ (current)\ ratio = \frac{(current\ assets)}{(current\ liabilities)}$$

$$liquidity\ (quick)\ ratio = \frac{(liquid\ assets)}{(current\ liabilities)}$$

$$where\ liquid\ assets = current\ assets\ exlcuding\ stock$$

---

[10] s.8(1) of the Insolvency Act 1986.

[11] Tests of inability to pay debts are discussed in the next section.

[12] On the one hand these limitations may explain why financial distress has not been adopted as the official hurdle in U.K. insolvency law; on the other hand they make the increasing use of accounting-based contracts difficult to explain. Accounting-based contracts are discussed in section 6 below.

In a set of accounts, current assets will be stated at their historical cost. The basic components of current assets are usually cash, debtors and stock. Whilst the cash and debtors figures may be a realistic estimate of the cash available to the company in the near future from these sources, the valuation of stock will not be; the stock will not be sold at its historical cost.[13] The quick ratio is designed to overcome this valuation problem by the exclusion of the stock figure. However, both ratios suffer from a timing problem as they are based on the idea that liabilities which mature in the near future must be covered by existing liquid assets. Lev states: "The major deficiency of the working-capital approach is its sole emphasis on *stocks* of assets and liabilities and the disregard of the *fund flows* aspect. Specifically, in the normal course of operations, current liabilities are discharged by the net cash flows emanating from sales rather than by the liquid assets at hand at the beginning of the period."[14] This suggests that, although financial distress as reflected in financial ratios *can* be used as a hurdle, it may not be the most appropriate hurdle to put in place.

Wruck adopts a definition that appears to overcome the stock/flow problem; she defines financial distress as "a situation where cash flow is insufficient to cover current obligations. These obligations can include unpaid debts to suppliers and employees, actual or potential damages from litigation and missed principal or interest payments under borrowing agreements."[15] This is a definition which encompasses default and prospective default and is closer to the U.K. definition of insolvency than the definitions of financial distress based on financial ratios which have been discussed.

As stated at the beginning of this section, the U.K. rescue regime of administration requires proof that the company "is or is likely to become unable to pay its debts." The Insolvency Act 1986 provides two types of test for proving inability to pay debts.[16] First, there are three "commercial or cash flow" tests of inability to pay debts.[17] Secondly, there is a "balance sheet" test of inability to pay debts.[18]

---

[13] A more thorough treatment of the limitations of ratio analysis with numerical examples is provided by Arnold, Hope, Southworth and Kirkham, *Financial Accounting* (2nd ed., 1994), pp. 297–322.

[14] Lev, *op. cit.*, p. 137.

[15] Wruck, *op. cit.* at 421.

[16] A comparison of definitions of insolvency in other jurisdictions shows that an inability to pay debts is the main definition and this can usually be evidenced by an unpaid judgment debt, see generally Fletcher (ed.) *Cross-Border Insolvency: Comparative Dimensions* (1990).

[17] s.123(1) of the Insolvency Act 1986.

[18] s.123(2) of the Insolvency Act 1986.

The three commercial or cash flow tests are all based on the idea of demonstrating that a particular debt which is due has not been paid. The company is deemed unable to pay its debts: (i) if a creditor who is owed more than £750[19] has served on the company a written demand for payment[20] and has not been paid within three weeks;[21] (ii) if there is evidence that a judgment debt is unpaid;[22] or (iii) "if it is proved to the satisfaction of the court that the company is unable to pay its debts as they fall due."[23]

In *Cornhill Insurance plc v. Improvement Services Ltd*[24] it was held that the failure to pay a debt which was due and undisputed was of itself evidence of inability to pay debts as they fall due for the purposes of section 123(1)(e), that is test (iii).[25] The balance sheet test of inability to pay debts is a form of negative equity. Section 123(2) of the Insolvency Act 1986 states: "A company is also deemed unable to pay its debts if it is proved to the satisfaction of the court that the value of the company's assets is less than the amount of its liabilities, taking into account its contingent and prospective liabilities." This is an alternative test, not an additional hurdle, to proving inability to pay debts. Assets minus all liabilities equals shareholders' funds; this is how a balance sheet balances. If liabilities exceed assets, shareholders' funds are negative.

There are several major problems with section 123(2) which arise mainly because, although it is a sort of balance sheet test, published accounts may not provide all the information necessary for performing this particular test of solvency. The first difficulty is that there is no statutory definition of prospective liabilities and the term is not used in any accounting standards. The second difficulty is that standard accounting practice demands a more nuanced treatment of contingent liabilities than is indicated by the section 123(2) test. The standard accounting practice is that

---

[19] This sum can be increased or reduced under s.416 of the Act.

[20] The formalities of serving written notice can be found in Pennington, *Pennington's Corporate Insolvency Law* (1991), p. 38/9.

[21] s.123(1)(a).

[22] This is a simplification of the separate tests for England and Wales, Scotland and Northern Ireland set out in ss.123(1)(b), (c) and (d) respectively.

[23] s.123(1)(e).

[24] [1986] 1 W.L.R. 114.

[25] It has been suggested that a creditor who has lent the company money which is repayable at some date in the future, but fears that it will not be paid, may be able to rely on section 123(1)(e); the difficulty would be in finding proof which would satisfy the court. See Farrar *et al.*, *Farrar's Company Law* (3rd ed., 1991), p. 684.

"a material contingent loss should be accrued in financial statements where it is probable that a future event will confirm a loss which can be estimated with reasonable accuracy at the date on which the financial statements are approved by the board of directors.

A material contingent loss not accrued under [the above paragraph] should be disclosed except where the possibility of loss is remote.

Contingent gains should not be accrued in financial statements. A material contingent gain should be disclosed in financial statements only if it is probable that the gain will be realised."[26]

Some contingent liabilities will, therefore, be included in the published balance sheet. Others may only be referred to in the notes to the accounts. Those which are remote will not appear in the financial statements at all. Which of these contingent liabilities are to be taken into account for the purpose of the balance sheet test of insolvency is not clear. However, the asymmetric accounting treatment of contingent gains which flows from the fundamental accounting concept of prudence *is* a part of the balance sheet test of insolvency. In *Byblos Bank SAL v. Al Khudairy*[27] it was held that "contingent and prospective liabilities" does not imply that contingent and prospective assets should also be taken into account.

A third difficulty is that published accounts are usually drawn up on the basis that the company is a going concern. The alternative is that the accounts are drawn up on the forced sale or "distress value" basis. The balance sheet test as formulated in section 123(2) does not indicate any particular basis for the measuring of assets and liabilities and there has been no U.K. case in which the basis of accounts for the purposes of the balance sheet test has been at issue. The U.S. case of *Re Taxman Clothing Co. Inc.*[28] is, however, persuasive and may be of some assistance. Under section 547(b) of the United States Bankruptcy Code, certain payments to creditors can be set aside as preferences if made: (1) within the 90 days preceding the bankruptcy; and (2) at a time when the debtor was insolvent. For this purpose a debtor is insolvent if his liabilities exceed his assets. In *Re Taxman Clothing* the company ran a clothes shop. It was made bankrupt and the trustee applied for various payments made to creditors within the

[26] Statement of Standard Accounting Practice (SSAP) *Accounting for Contingencies*. paras 15–17.
[27] *Financial Times*, November 7, 1986.
[28] (1990) 73 C.C.H. Bankr. Dec. 509.

previous 90 days to be set aside as preferences. The creditors concerned argued that the company had been solvent at the time. Shortly before the payments had been made, stock in trade had been valued at $215,000 on a going concern basis. Using this figure, the company's assets had exceeded its liabilities. The trustee argued that the company had been insolvent. The stock held at the date of bankruptcy (which was about the same level as the stock which had been valued earlier) had been sold at auction for $110,000. If this figure was taken as the correct valuation, the liabilities had exceeded the assets. The court held that the going concern value should be used, since at the time there had been no reason to believe that the company would not sell the stock in the ordinary course of its business. The payments were therefore not voidable as preferences as they had not been made at a time when the company was insolvent.[29] This suggests that a going concern balance sheet should be used for the purpose of section 123(2) of the Insolvency Act 1986 unless it seems likely that the company will cease trading in the near future, a formulation which may itself cause problems. Also, there are accounting rules and guidelines which help determine the appropriateness of the going concern basis for the drawing up of accounts and these interact with the concept of insolvency. This problem will be explored in more detail in Chapter 5.

6. Distress as a Trigger

Financial distress can be a trigger for organisational change because it represents a crisis. The nature and management of change are currently issues that are high on the agenda of organisational theorists.[30] Handy has put forward the argument that the very nature of change is changing and that management of *discontinuous* as opposed to continuous change is now the key to success.[31] Financial distress is a point of discontinuous change for a company. Writing about "crisis and renewal", Hurst argues against the conventional wisdom of good organisational strategy as a rational linear process. He states that "Despite the conventional wisdom, there is evidence

---

[29] This case summary is taken from *Clork Gully on Insolvency Judgments 1980–1990* (1991).

[30] Hurst, *Crisis and Renewal: Meeting the Challenge of Organizational Change* (1995).

[31] Handy, *The Age of Unreason* (1990).

that crisis plays an important role in organisational innovation."[32] Wruck, in her examination of recent empirical work on U.S. corporate restructuring and bankruptcy, explicitly argues that financial distress can bring benefits by triggering various responses.[33] First, she argues that incumbent managers and directors can inhibit a firm's ability to recover if new or special skills are required to turn the firm's performance around. She claims that recent empirical results show that "poor stock-price performance is not enough to remove incumbent managers, but financial distress provides a mechanism to initiate top-management changes."[34] Secondly, she draws attention to the fact that firms in financial distress undergo dramatic organisational changes as part of their recovery, refocusing their strategy and undertaking restructuring:

> "Such reorganizations illustrate how financial structure interacts with investment decisions; financial distress forces a change in the firm's economic activities and the way these activities are organized. These restructurings often create value for the firm's claimholders. The same reorganizations probably would have created value before the financial distress, but the impetus for change provided by distress was absent. Financial distress can, therefore, force managers to undertake value-increasing organizational changes they would not have otherwise undertaken."[35]

Financial distress can also trigger technical default. Debt contracts increasingly incorporate conditions expressed in terms of financial ratios. The publication of an adverse set of annual accounts can mean that a company is technically in default even if there has been no failure to pay the interest or capital demanded by the loan agreement. Contracts which make reference to accounting figures in their conditions have been termed accounting-based contracts (ABCs). ABCs have been the subject of investigations in the accounting literature for more than a decade. It has been argued that conditions based on published accounting information are valuable as a means of measuring and monitoring the activities of the contracting parties in order to restrain or motivate their behaviour.[36] This gives financial

---

[32] Hurst, *op. cit.*, at 119.
[33] Wruck, *op. cit.*
[34] *ibid.* at 433.
[35] *ibid.* p. 434.
[36] Watts and Zimmerman, *Positive Accounting Theory* (1986) is the seminal work in this area.

reporting a contracting role as well as the informational role it plays in corporate accountability. Ormrod and Cleaver argue that while the contracting and informational roles are not mutually exclusive, neither are they entirely compatible.[37] Accounting standards often allow director discretion over accounting policy choice and, so long as the effects of policy choices are clearly disclosed, the informational role of financial reporting is not thereby undermined. For the contracting role it is different; director discretion over accounting policy can amount to director manipulation.

The possibility of having to publish a set of accounts that breach a debt contract could, quite conceivably, trigger an exercise in creative accounting as management try to avoid the default. Positive accounting theory predicts that firms approaching a debt covenant violation will make income-increasing accounting choices to loosen their debt constraints.[38] The empirical evidence on this point is equivocal.[39] DeAngelo, DeAngelo and Skinner find no evidence of "systematic attempts to inflate earnings to avoid debt covenant violations or to otherwise portray the firm as less troubled."[40] DeFond and Jiambalvo, however, find that there is "substantial evidence that is consistent with positive manipulation [of the accounts]."[41] If a technical default actually occurs, this can also trigger a response from the loan creditors. Wruck states that "Financial distress gives the creditors the right to demand restructuring because their contract with the firm has been breached."[42] She also claims that this mechanism is value-maximising because it triggers action sooner rather than later; however, the argument put forward in support of *this* hypothesis is not a strong one and she concedes that it only works when the company's value is being steadily eroded.[43]

Financial distress can also trigger entry to a rescue regime. The pressure to enter a regime can come from at least two sources. First, if there is a default in a debt contract the creditors may refuse to renegotiate the terms of the contact in a private workout and instead

---

[37] Ormrod and Cleaver, "Financial Reporting and Corporate Accountability," (1993) 23 *Accounting and Business Research*, No. 91A, 432.

[38] DeFond and Jiambalvo, "Debt Covenant Violation and Manipulation of Accruals" (1994) 17 *Journal of Accounting and Economics* 145; and Watts and Zimmerman, *op. cit.*

[39] This evidence comes from studies that use U.S. data.

[40] DeAngelo, DeAngelo and Skinner, "Accounting Choice in Troubled Companies" (1994) 17 *Journal of Accounting and Economics* 140.

[41] DeFond and Jiambalvo, *op. cit.*, 174.

[42] Wruck, *op. cit.*, at 431.

[43] *ibid.* at 431–432.

demand financial restructuring within a legal rescue regime. Secondly, management may elect to put the company into a rescue procedure. The design of the rescue regime will certainly affect the balance of power as between the management and the creditors. The U.S. regime can be employed by the company's management as a threat.[44] Under the U.K. regime it is more likely to be the secured creditors threatening to "send in the receiver" or unsecured creditors who have supplied goods subject to a retention of title clause seeking to retrieve their goods or prevent the company dealing with them via an injunction. The contrast of creditor and debtor-based regimes is explained in Chapter 2 and the design of rescue regimes more generally is discussed in Chapter 6.

There is a further feature of the U.K. regime which gives management an incentive to apply for an administration order if an adverse set of accounts is produced, and that is the wrongful trading provision, which is a relatively new provision[45] under which civil personal liability can arise. It was introduced because of the difficulties in proving fraudulent trading which under long-established provisions is both a criminal offence[46] and ground for imposing personal liability.[47] The standards of proof demanded for fraudulent trading are therefore those of criminal proceedings. The basic idea of the wrongful trading provision is that if directors keep a company going and deplete its assets when they should have recognised its problems and stopped, they become personally liable. Applications under the wrongful trading provision may only be made by a liquidator, and, if successful, the court may declare the person concerned liable to make a contribution to the company's assets.[48] This will only apply to a person if:

"(a) the company has gone into insolvent liquidation,

(b) at some time before the commencement of the winding up of the company, that person knew or ought to have concluded that there was no reasonable prospect that the company would avoid going into insolvent liquidation, and

---

[44] Franks and Torous, "An Empirical Investigation of U.S. Firms in Reorganization," (1989) 44 *Journal of Finance* 750.
[45] First appearing as s.15 of the Insolvency Act 1985 following a recommendation of the Cork Committee, Cmnd. 8558.
[46] s.458 of the Companies Act 1985.
[47] s.213 of the Insolvency Act 1986.
[48] s.214(1) of the Insolvency Act 1986.

(c) that person was a director of the company at that time."[49]

The first thing that is required in proving wrongful trading is identification of a time when a director of the company knew or ought to have concluded that there was no reasonable prospect of avoiding insolvent liquidation. It is clear that both audited and draft accounts can be examined by the court in order to establish this point.[50] If wrongful trading is proved, the amount of the contribution to be made is then usually calculated by reference to the damage done in the period from that date to the commencement of the winding up. In *Re Produce Marketing Consortium Ltd*[51] Knox J. said: "In my judgment the jurisdiction under sec. 214 is primarily compensatory rather the penal. Prima facie the appropriate amount that a director is declared to be liable to contribute is the amount by which the company's assets have been depleted by the director's conduct which caused the discretion under sec. 214 to arise."

The company's assets are usually depleted in this period because the company continues to trade. The term "wrongful trading" suggests that the provision is concerned with directors who allow companies to continue to *trade* when it is wrong to do so. However, the assets of a company may be depleted in other ways, such as the payment of excessive directors' fees, and it is clear that *trading* beyond the critical date is not required by section 214. All that is required is that the company's assets are depleted at some time after the critical date.[52] The test to be applied in judging a director's behaviour combines both subjective and objective elements, the standard being:

". . . a reasonably diligent person having both—

(a) the general knowledge, skill and experience that may reasonably be expected of a person carrying out the same functions as are carried out by that director in relation to the company, and

(b) the general knowledge, skill and experience that that director has."[53]

The director is thus to be judged "by the standards of the "reasonable" director, even though he himself is lacking or below

---

[49] s.214(2) of the Insolvency Act 1986.
[50] *Re Produce Marketing Consortium Ltd* (1989) 5 B.C.C. 569.
[51] *ibid.* at 597.
[52] It has been pointed out that the title wrongful trading "has no particularly close connection with the subject matter it is supposed to cover"; see Milman and Durrant, *Corporate Insolvency: Law and Practice* (2nd ed., 1994), p. 225.
[53] s.214(4) of the Insolvency Act 1986.

average in knowledge, skill or experience, but by his own higher standards if these are above average."[54] Liability measured in tens of thousands of pounds is common,[55] so there is a real incentive for directors to avoid wrongful trading. However, more than ten years after the introduction of the wrongful trading provisions many directors of small companies remain ignorant of their potential effects. If financial distress is indicated in the accounts and the directors fear liability under section 214, they may want to liquidate the company, but they can petition for an administration order. In *Re Cavco Floors Limited*[56] a company was in severe difficulties and it was essential to continue trading to protect the value of the assets, but the directors were not prepared to continue trading themselves because of the danger that they would be held liable for fraudulent or wrongful trading. There was a bank in a position to appoint an administrative receiver but the amount it was owed was so low that it was not prepared to do so. The directors, fearing a winding-up petition from a creditor who had served a statutory demand, sought an administration order themselves and therefore asked an insolvency practitioner to prepare an independent report pursuant to rule 2.2 of the Insolvency Rules 1986 to accompany the affidavit supporting the petition. This case is an exceptional one; the administration order was made before the petition was presented on the basis of the investigating accountants' report, but it demonstrates how the directors' fear of the wrongful trading provision added to the urgency of an application for an administration order. A set of accounts that reveal financial distress may be good evidence in a case of wrongful trading. Such accounts could therefore trigger an urgent application to enter a rescue regime.

There may be a difference between the degree of financial distress which is actually triggering directors into taking steps to protect themselves from the wrongful trading provisions and the standards which the courts might adopt when called upon to apply section 214 to particular circumstances. Cooke and Hicks discuss the possible standards for judging the prediction of insolvency.[57] They mention two points in time: a time when "warning signs of financial difficulty

---

[54] Sealy and Milman, *op. cit.*, at 256.
[55] In *Re Produce Marketing Consortium Ltd* two directors were held to be jointly and severally liable to pay £75,000.
[56] [1996] B.C.C. 589.
[57] Cooke and Hicks, "Wrongful Trading—Predicting Insolvency" [1993] *Journal of Business Law* 338.

are apparent", and an earlier time when "financial difficulty was less immediate and warning signs less obvious."[58] Cooke and Hicks do not offer a formal definition of either of these points; however, they seem to be contrasting the later time when "professional advice would have predicted insolvency"[59] with the earlier time when "theories"[60] would have predicted insolvency. The "theories" they refer to are the statistical models for predicting failure, which are explained in the next chapter. The courts will expect directors to obtain appropriate professional advice and this is a good point. However, Cooke and Hicks distinguish the advice of professionals who would predict insolvency from "apparent" financial difficulty (maybe financial distress as defined by some simple financial ratios) from the advice of professionals who would predict insolvency from "more general theories" that are "not so well-known" (the more sophisticated statistical techniques). This distinction is spurious. Prediction of failure models *are* relatively sophisticated and for this reason Chapter 4 is devoted to a more detailed description and criticism of the various statistical techniques which can be employed. However, results from several standard models are now routinely calculated using readily available computer programmes.[61] Professional advisers are increasingly likely to have access to such results (at least for quoted companies), and good professional advice will take into account all relevant information. The best professional advice will take account of the results of prediction of failure models, but will also treat such results with proper caution for the reasons explained in the next chapter.

7. Conclusion

In this chapter the concept of distress has been discussed. Distress has an important part to play within the definition of corporate rescue, as it is often financial distress which threatens the company's survival. Financial distress is a crisis which usually demands drastic action.

---

[58] *ibid*. at 340/1.
[59] *ibid*. at 341.
[60] *ibid*. at 342.
[61] The formulae for some of the latest models are closely guarded secrets because of their commercial value.

Distressed companies have been distinguished from "bankrupt" companies, where bankrupt companies are defined as companies that have entered a legal bankruptcy (U.S.) or insolvency (U.K.) regime. It has been argued that financial distress can act as a warning signal, as a hurdle, and as a trigger. As a warning signal, financial distress will affect the market value of the company and may thus shape the course of a rescue attempt. As a hurdle, financial distress could be required for entry to a legal regime. In the United States entry is a matter of right. In the United Kingdom entry is based on "inability to pay debts" rather than financial distress defined in terms of accounting ratios.

As a general rule, the earlier a rescue is mounted the greater its chances of success. If financial distress can trigger rescues to be attempted sooner rather than later, it could be seen as a beneficial influence. Although financial distress requires that attention be paid to company finance first and foremost, it can also trigger other forms of beneficial organisational restructuring, including a change in top management.

Distress can also trigger entry into a legal rescue regime. Debt covenants can be in the form of constraints framed in terms of financial ratios appearing in the published accounts of the company. The directors may seek to manipulate the contents of the accounts in order to avoid default through the violation of such a covenant. If there is a default, there may be a private renegotiation of the debt contract, or the company may enter a legal rescue regime.[62] In the United Kingdom fear of falling foul of the wrongful trading provisions may also mean that distress triggers entry to a legal rescue regime applied for by the directors.

Financial distress can be defined in various ways, two of which are given in this chapter as examples. Simple definitions can be based on one or two financial ratios. The prediction of failure models which are described in the next chapter offer other (more complicated) approaches to assessing the position of a company.

---

[62] In the United Kingdom the creditors are likely to use administrative receivership as a threat. In the United States it is more likely to be the management who would make use of Chapter 11 as a threat.

Chapter 4

The Prediction of Failure

1. Introduction

The appeal of any model or formula that can predict the failure of a company one or two years in advance of its final demise is obvious. The very earliest models began with the simple financial ratios described in Chapter 3. The reasoning behind them was also very simple: If a company is financially distressed *now*, it is predicted to fail. However, not all financially distressed companies do fail, so later models became much more sophisticated. It is not surprising that such models are available commercially and that banks and other financial institutions conduct their own research into new and better techniques for predicting failure and credit scoring in general. The main body of academic work on the prediction of failure has come from departments of accounting and has mostly been published in accounting journals. Even though the level of technical sophistication has increased over the years, the basic idea remains that accounting data in the form of financial ratios can be used to discriminate between failures and non-failures. Ratios rather than absolute values are used in an attempt to control for size. This chapter describes the two main types of techniques *currently* being used in prediction of failure models. These are logit regression and multiple discriminant analysis. The chapter assesses their effectiveness and reveals their limitations.

When creditors, particularly banks, are considering the continued provision of finance or the extending of further finance to a company, one of the tools employed is likely to be a prediction of failure model. The results of such models may influence lending decisions both about *whether* to lend and about the *terms* of the loan. They could, therefore, have a part to play in the construction of a rescue package (discussed in Chapter 7); the decisions of secured creditors (described in Chapter 8); and the decisions of unsecured loan creditors (described in Chapter 9). Prediction of failure models have a part to play in relation to the tests of insolvency, described in Chapter 3. There has also been a suggestion that the results of one of the oldest established prediction of failure tests, Altman's Z-score,[1] should be employed as part of the going concern testing procedure.[2-3] These are all *practical* applications of the prediction of failure tests described in this chapter.

Before going into more detail about the tests themselves, it may be useful to consider the claims made for prediction of failure models. When they were first devised it was undoubtedly hoped that they would eventually be able to "predict" failure. A negative result for a company could be read as "this company will fail within one year." The early hopes for the models have, however, been somewhat tempered by experience. Even Taffler, who has developed several prediction of failure models for the United Kingdom and is a leading exponent of them has stated: "A negative Z-score is *not* a prediction of bankruptcy and the Z-score model should not be treated in practical usage as a prediction device. . . . What a Z-score below the solvency threshold is pointing out is that this particular company has financial difficulties."[4]

The statement "this company has financial difficulties" is much weaker than the statement "this company will fail." If these models indicate distress rather than predict failure, perhaps the best way of viewing them is as pointers to the need for a rescue to be attempted. This chapter first gives an account of the early techniques employed in the prediction of failure; secondly it considers the later developments; thirdly it explains the limitations of such models; and finally it discusses the prediction of the need for rescue in the context of a model that deliberately sets out to distinguish different levels of distress rather than focussing on the failure/non-failure dichotomy.

This chapter describes statistical techniques and problems arising out of statistical methodology. This is done in a fairly gentle way and

---

[1] This is described in more detail below.

[2-3] The going concern concept is discussed in more detail in Chap. 5. This particular suggestion is reported in Pratten, *Company Failure* (1991), paper prepared for the Financial Reporting and Auditing Group of the Institute of Chartered Accountants in England and Wales, p. 57.

[4] Taffler, *Applications of the Z-score Approach in Financial Analysis* (1992), paper read to the British Accounting Association.

is not intended only for the statistically competent. However, for readers who wish to avoid all contact with statistics, the main conceptual points of the chapter appear in its introduction and concluding section. It is hoped that readers who take the option of moving directly on to the chapter's concluding remarks will not be unduly disadvantaged.

2. Early Prediction of Failure Techniques

The most widely used technique in the prediction of failure is multiple discriminant analysis (MDA). This was first used for the prediction of failure of U.S. companies by Altman in 1968,[5] and Altman's Z-score is still used in many financial institutions. The Z-score is a weighted sum of financial ratios for the individual company, and the prediction of failure or non-failure depends on whether the particular company's score is higher or lower than a critical value. For example:

$$Z = a \cdot x_1 + b \cdot x_2 \ldots + k \cdot x_n$$

where the x's are various financial ratios and a to k are weights. If we consider a Z-score comprising only two ratios, companies can be positioned on a diagram on the basis of these two ratios and MDA can then be thought of as a way of drawing a line that best separates failures from non-failures. This partitioning will not be perfect, and one measure of performance for this technique is the percentage of companies accurately categorised. Diagram 1 illustrates this intuitive, two-dimensional, explanation of MDA. The model would classify companies northeast of the dividing line as non-failures and companies with combinations of ratios falling to the southwest of the line as failures. The model would, therefore, predict three failures as non-failures and two non-failures as failures in this diagram. The weights a to k in the Z-score formula are calculated using a particular sample of companies and will change depending on the sample used in their estimation. Altman's Z-score formula has a particular set of weights

---

[5] Altman, "Financial Ratios, Discriminant Analysis and the Prediction of Corporate Failure" (1968) 23 *Journal of Finance* 589.

to be applied to a particular set of financial ratios. The formula for this model is available, but it must be remembered that it was constructed more than 25 years ago. The particular ratios and weights for models constructed more recently are often kept a secret, as they may have commercial value.[6]

Diagram 1

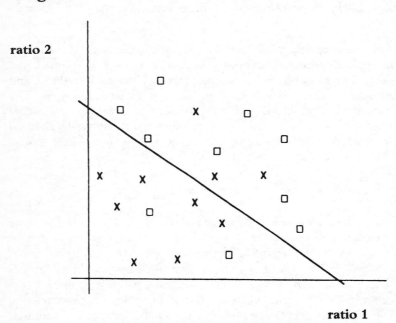

x = failures
□ = non-failures

Companies plotted according to values of two financial ratios showing how a linear discriminant function would partition the sample.

---

[6] Altman was involved in the development of the later "Zeta" model for which he claims greater predictive accuracy than the original Z-score. Details of the later model are not available to the outside user. See Altman, Haldeman and Narayanan, "Zeta Analysis, A New Model to Identify Bankruptcy Risk Corporations" [1997] 1 *Journal of Banking and Finance* 29.

In MDA the ratios used are selected simply because they produce good predictive accuracy for the particular sample of companies under investigation. The links between poor profitability or liquidity, for example, and failure are in a "black box" and explanations of why particular variables work usually follow the statistical analysis. There are some economists who would argue in favour of this type of approach, an approach which says "so long as the predictions are good, underlying theory is superfluous." However, most work in economics begins with a story, a theory of how economic agents behave or how variables interact, and the techniques used in economics reflect this. Some of the more recent work on the prediction of failure has been performed by economists and draws on their techniques. In the next section the main technique that has been used by economists for modelling the failure of companies is explained.

3. Later Developments

Logit is a form of regression analysis which has been employed by economists to model the failure of companies. Regression analysis is a favourite tool of economists and is usually explained in terms of one economic variable being caused by a combination of other economic variables; for instance, the number of insolvencies may depend on or be caused by changes in interest rates, labour costs and GDP. In this example[7] the number of insolvencies is called the dependent variable and can take any positive value. Logit analysis is a form of regression which copes with situations where there are a limited number of outcomes, for instance failure and non-failure. These outcomes (dependent variables) are assigned the values 1 and 0. The financial ratios are the independent variables causing the outcome. Diagram 2 shows how a sample of companies could be plotted on a diagram. The gearing ratio is chosen as a convenient example of one ratio which may be seen as causing failure. It is argued that the higher the debt : equity (or gearing) ratio, the higher the probability of failure. This is because the interest on debt *must* be paid regularly, but dividends need not be paid to holders of equity.

---

[7] Taken from Hudson and Cuthbertson, "A Rising Tide of Bankruptcies" (1991) 7 *Insolvency Law and Practice* 138.

Diagram 2

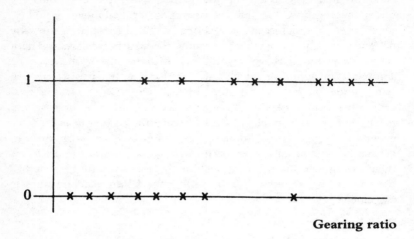

Gearing ratio

1 = failure
2 = non-failure

Companies plotted according to values of gearing ratio and classification as failure or non-failure

As profits fall, companies with large amounts of debt relative to equity are likely to encounter problems in meeting their obligations to pay interest earlier than companies with lower gearing ratios. As a failure to make interest payments usually gives the creditor the right to appoint a receiver, companies with high gearing ratios are more likely to fail than companies with lower gearing ratios, other things being equal. The failures appear on the line y=1 and the non-failures on the line y=0. Logit analysis fits a curve to the plotted points and the better the "fit" of this curve the better the performance of the model in terms of explaining failure and non-failure. In practice models have many independent variables, but again a two-dimensional representation serves to indicate the basic idea of the technique. Diagram 3 shows the fitting of a curve. "Logit" comes from the type of curve fitted and "probit" is a similar technique using a different form of curve. For a particular company a logit model will give the probability of failure; companies can be classified using these probabilities and the accuracy of this classification reported as for MDA.

Diagram 3

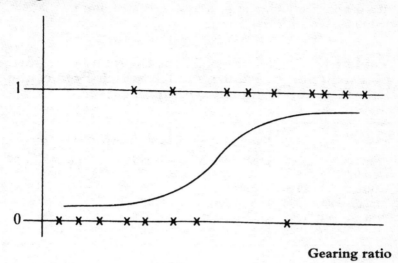

1 = failure
2 = non-failure

A curve fitted to the points in Diagram 2

4. The Limitations of Prediction of Failure Models

Table 4.1 shows a small selection of results which have been reported in studies that have employed either MDA or logit/probit analysis. A full review of work in this area is beyond the scope of this short chapter. The results that are summarised in Table 4.1 have been selected to illustrate various points, but the general levels of predictive accuracy appearing in the table are representative. Some explanation of Table 4.1 might be useful at this stage. The original sample comprises the companies used in the initial modelling process; the holdout sample is a separate set of companies used to test the performance of the best model generated from this process. On first inspection it appears that the more recent studies cannot improve on the early work. However, research in this area is continuing, with published work being of two types: research that is seeking to improve the models, either by refining the earlier methods or by taking newer approaches, and research that is seeking to demonstrate that the problems inherent in such models mean that they do not, and cannot be expected to, work.

Table 4.1—Percentage of Firms Correctly Classified by Prediction of Failure Models which Predict the Failure of the Company within One Year

Study	Year	Data	Method	Original Sample	Holdout Sample
Altman[a]	1968	U.S.	MDA	95%	84%
Deakin[b]	1972	U.K.	MDA	97%	79%
Ohlson[c]	1980	U.S.	Logit	96%	N/A
Zmijewski[d]	1984	U.S.	Probit	97%	96%
Platt & Platt[e]	1990	U.S.	Logit	90%	90%
Lau[f]	1986	U.S.	Logit	96%	80%

Sources:

[a] Altman, "Financial Ratios, Discriminant Analysis and the Prediction of Corporate Failure" (1968) 23 *Journal of Finance* 589.

[b] Deakin, "A Discriminant Analysis of Predictors of Business Failure" (1972) 10 *Journal of Accounting Research* 167.

[c] Ohlson, "Financial Ratios and the Probabilistic Prediction of Bankruptcy" (1980) 18 *Journal of Accounting Research* 109.

[d] Zmijewski, "Methodological Issues Related to the Estimation of Financial Distress Models" (1984) *Journal of Accounting Research* 22, supplement.

[e] H.D. Platt and M.B. Platt, "Development of a Class of Stable Predictive Variables: The Case of Bankruptcy Prediction" (1980) 17 *Journal of Business Finance and Accounting* 31.

[f] Lau, "A Five-state Financial Distress Prediction Model" (1987) *Journal of Accounting Research* 127, spring.

The main problem with the early models is that they do not perform well when applied to different samples of companies and at different times. In Table 4.1 the percentage accuracy for the holdout sample is significantly lower than for the original sample for the studies by Altman and Deakin. This may be because the models are not stable over time, meaning that the particular combination of variables which works well when the model is estimated fails to perform well at other times. The Altman and Deakin studies estimate using a sample in one period and perform validation tests on a holdout sample from a different period. Zmijewski, however, takes a holdout sample from the estimation period and his validation test therefore looks much better. This is just one illustration of the problems involved in interpreting the results of this type of work. The Platt and Platt study addresses the problem of bad performance in holdout samples; they argue that this is due to insufficient attention to industry effects rather than instability over time. If the best model for predicting failure is different depending on industry (what constitutes high gearing may differ between industries, for instance), this could explain why a general model based on an original sample comprised of a particular mix of industries does not perform well on other samples with other mixes of industries. Platt and Platt control for these industry effects and do achieve similar results in the original sample and the holdout sample from a different period.

In research it is possible that ratios based on financial statements released after the date of failure are used to "predict" that failure. In a live situation the set of accounts that would be most appropriate for the proper operation of the model may not have been drawn up. In fact, delay in the production of the company' s accounts is sometimes used in itself as an indicator of financial distress. This is one reason why the levels of predictive ability achieved in the research work may not be achievable in practice. Another more technical reason for the overstatement of predictive power arises from the use of matched samples where the number of failures and non-failures are equal. A matched sample will not be random, as a failed company will have a better chance of selection than a surviving one, but some studies using matched samples proceed as if the sample were random, causing performance to look better than it really is. There is some disagreement about the effects of oversampling failed companies and companies with complete data; Zmijewski claims that the resulting biases do not materially affect the models' predictive validity.

The suggestion that the formula for any one model, for instance Altman's Z-score, could be universally applied to all companies and for all time seems somewhat dubious. A study by Piesse and Wood demonstrates just how poorly such "universal" models perform when applied to a random sample of companies.[8] This study tested Altman's Z-score, a model devised by Taffler which is based on U.K.

---

[8] Piesse and Wood, "Issues in Assessing MDA Models of Corporate Failure: A Research Note" (1992) 24 *British Accounting Review* 33.

data[9] and a model now offered commercially by Datastream.[10] The results revealed a very high incidence of error in predictions coming from all three models. The authors claim that the "matched sample, known outcome methodology" used in "conventional" studies has resulted in a major understatement of classification errors.[11] They maintain that a model can only claim to produce valuable (predictive) information if it performs with a high level of accuracy within a framework of a truly *ex ante* decision environment.[12] There is no indication that MDA models which are currently available come up to this standard, and Taffler has admitted that in the early 1980s 60 per cent of companies with negative Z-scores survived.[13]

The Ohlson study appears in Table 4.1 because this was the first application of logit analysis in this context. Ohlson also used a genuinely random sample and thus avoided the problems of matched samples referred to above. MDA is only valid under the assumption that the discriminating variables (ratios) are distributed multivariate normal and there is plenty of evidence that this is not the case. This is a major technical problem with the use of MDA. A second associated problem is that recent work has suggested some non-financial variables which could improve models, but again MDA is not a valid technique unless these extra variables have the assumed distributional properties. In particular, an independent variable which can only take the values 1 and 0 (for yes and no), for instance a variable for qualification of the audit report, cannot validly be used in MDA. Despite many demonstrable technical weaknesses, however, MDA is a technique which remains in use.

5. Prediction of the Need for a Rescue Attempt

The general term "failure" has been employed in this chapter; however, each study has its own definition of what constitutes

---

[9] Details of this model have not been released by Taffler. Piesse and Wood had to effectively recreate the model from information available in two of Taffler's published articles: Taffler, "The Z-score Approach to Measuring Company Solvency" (1983) 87 *The Accountant's Magazine* 91; and Taffler, "Empirical Models for the Monitoring of U.K. Corporates," [1984] *Journal of Banking and Finance* 199.

[10] Datastream is an on-line database of company accounting and share price information.

[11] Piesse and Wood, *op. cit.*, at 41.

[12] *ibid.* at 40.

[13] Taffler (1992), *op. cit.*, at 19.

failure. Some only count liquidation as failure; others include financial distress of other kinds within the definition. Most of the studies referred to in Table 4.1 are of U.S. data. This is because most of the advances seem to happen in the United States first, with replication on U.K. data coming later. U.S. terminology therefore appears in many of the important studies. The final study referred to in Table 4.1 is of particular interest in the context of a book about corporate rescue because it attempts to predict not simply failure and non-failure but also various degrees of financial distress. Five states are defined in this study, ranging from financial stability through reduced or omitted dividend payments, default on loan payments (interest and/or principal) and protection under Chapter 10 or 11 of the U.S. Bankruptcy Code, to bankruptcy and liquidation. A multinomial logit is employed in the estimation of the model which allows for more than two outcomes; this is not possible in MDA. The overall results of Lau's study look quite good, but accuracy falls for prediction of the individual states. This is to be expected, as the five-state model demands more from the data.

As already stated, Lau's study is of particular interest in the context of corporate rescue. If the model is really capable of distinguishing entry into bankruptcy and liquidation from other, lesser, forms of financial distress, it has the potential of distinguishing companies heading for a rescue attempt from those heading directly into liquidation. Some caution is, however, necessary. Even if this model works it should be noted that what it is doing is distinguishing the sorts of companies that currently go into a rescue regime from those that currently go straight into liquidation. The question of whether the right companies are entering these legal procedures is not addressed at all. All the other problems associated with the application of a research model to a live situation will also continue to apply.

By explicitly including the early stages of financial distress, what Lau's model may be doing is giving an earlier warning of the problem. It may be that it is in this way that the need for a rescue attempt can be predicted. All the results shown in Table 4.1 are from one-year models; in other words, they are predictions of failure next year. Separate models would be needed to predict failure in two or three years time. These have been constructed by some researchers. As time to failure increases the predictive accuracy of the models usually declines, as would be expected. One piece of work on prediction well in advance of failure is Goudie's 1987 paper.[14] This is a complicated piece of work which links changes in the economy to the prediction of failure for individual companies. It has been argued that prediction of failure models may be time, industry, country and size specific.[15] Over time the prevailing economic climate changes. Research in the field of macroeconomics indicates that changes in interest rates and Gross Domestic Product (GDP) influence the number of insolvencies. The prediction of failure models described so far suggest that the probability of failure next year depends on ratios calculated from this year's accounts and maybe some previous accounts and some company specific non-financial variables. In these models, if a bank overdraft is bad news it is bad news at all times, irrespective of whether interest rates are high and rising or low and falling.[16] Goudie's study is unique in its attempt to feed economy-wide change into the prediction of the outcome for individual companies. It incorporates a model of company behaviour which is itself integrated within the Cambridge Growth Project's multisectoral dynamic model of the U.K. economy. The model of company behaviour is used to project the variables available at n periods prior to failure for n-1 years ahead. This gives the forecasts of the financial ratios one year before failure and an ordinary one-year model can then be applied to these forecast values. This paper is important because it shows that researchers in the United Kingdom can produce interesting, innovative and useful work in this area and British researchers are capable of rising above the simple replication of U.S. ideas on British data.

6. Conclusion

This chapter has provided a brief introduction to prediction of failure models and put these models into the context of corporate rescue

---

[14] Goudie, "Forecasting Corporate Failure: The Use of Discriminant Analysis within a Disaggregated Model of the Corporate Sector," (1987) 150 *Journal of the Royal Statistical Society* 150.

[15] On the questions of size and country it seems that some non-financial variables matter more in small companies and that models estimated for large quoted U.S. companies perform badly when applied to small unquoted U.K. companies. On the question of industry, see Platt and Platt, *op. cit.*

[16] The amount of bank interest paid will, however, fluctuate with the interest rate and this will be reflected in the accounts.

attempts. It can be seen that such models throw up at least as many problems as they do answers. Researchers are well aware of the many pitfalls involved in the estimation, interpretation and application of the models. The difficulties are such that an uncritical application of one "universal" model is very dangerous. The mood of researchers is currently one of being cautious not to overstate the claims that can be made for prediction of failure models.[17] At the same time, the formulae for various prediction of failure models are increasingly being applied to large quantities of company accounting information which is being made available on an array of electronic databases. It is because the Z-score and other formulae are very simple to calculate that their routine use in, say, the going concern test can be suggested. It is to be hoped that, if the results of such calculations are ever produced in court as evidence of a company's financial health or evidence of what the directors ought to have known about the company's financial health,[18] they are treated with proper caution.

Despite the problems discussed in this chapter, prediction of failure models are still being researched into and employed by major providers of finance such as high street banks. These institutions tend to be secretive about this sort of work. However, it is fairly clear that the result of a prediction of failure model would only be one element feeding into a lending decision.

---

[17] This applies to the researchers who are trying to improve the models. There are also those who see no merit in the models at all, for example Piesse and Wood, *op. cit.*

[18] This would be in the context of the wrongful trading provisions discussed in Chap. 3.

Chapter 5

The Going Concern Concept

1. Introduction

In this chapter the concept of the company as a going concern is explored, at first in a non-technical way (section 2). The bulk of the chapter, however, is concerned with the technical use of the going concern concept as employed by accountants. Accounts are usually drawn up on the basis that the company is a "going concern" in the technical sense. Each time a set of annual financial accounts is drawn up, the dirctors of the company should satisfy themselves that the use of the going concern basis is appropriate. If it is not, the reporting of going concern problems can become a self-fulfilling prophesy. Section 3 of the chapter explains four ways in which a company's reporting of going concern problems can impact on the course of a rescue attempt. First, the publication of difficulties may precipitate actual failure if the company's stakeholders lose confidence in it and try to withdraw. Secondly, the disclosure of going concern problems could mean the breach of a debt covenant. Thirdly, a going concern problem could make the company legally insolvent. Finally, the directors of a company with going concern problems will need to consider their position with respect to the wrongful trading provisions very carefully.

Section 3 of the chapter establishes that the decision as to whether a set of accounts can legitimately be prepared on the going concern basis can be crucial to the course of a rescue attempt. In section 4 the technicalities of the going concern concept are investigated: the concept is defined and its legal and regulatory status explained, the responsibilities of the company's directors and auditors are considered, and the official guidance on the matter which has been produced by the accountancy bodies is described and critically assessed. Section 5 explores the links between the going concern concept and the legal definition of wrongful trading, and section 6 provides some concluding comments.

2. The Going Concern as the Result of Corporate Rescue

One definition of a successful rescue is the survival of the company as a going concern. Another definition is the preservation of the commercial enterprise.[1] These definitions parallel stated aims of the bankruptcy and insolvency laws in the United States and the United Kingdom respectively. The motive for introducing Chapter 11 procedures in the United States was to increase the possibilities of firms emerging from reorganisation as going concerns. Even in the United Kingdom where the insolvency regime is heavily creditor-based, one of the aims of insolvency law is "to provide means for the preservation of viable commercial enterprises capable of making a useful contribution to the economic life of the country."[2] Common to both regimes is the idea that the emergence of a firm that is a *going concern*, or is *viable*, is a worthy aim. Looking back to the discussion in Chapter 2, it should also be noted that the success of a rescue attempt could be seen in the emergence of a going concern.

In order to come out of a rescue as a going concern, keeping going during the rescue is crucial. This applies whether the rescue attempt is made informally or using a formal rescue procedure. In an informal rescue the key to keeping going is the maintenance of sufficient trust and confidence. If a large scale financial restructuring of the company is being attempted informally, secrecy may also be a key factory.[3] In a formal rescue the moratorium on actions by creditors may allow the company to continue trading. However, keeping going may require the cooperation of key suppliers. Suppliers are under no obligation to continue to supply and can refuse to do so as a means of extracting payment.[4] This is discussed in more detail in Chapter 9.

---

[1] A phrase taken from the Cork Report; K. Cork, "Insolvency Law and Practice: Report of the Review Committee," Cmnd. 8558 (1982), 53.

[2] *ibid*. at 55.

[3] These elements are highlighted in Flood, Abbey, Skordaki and Aber, *The Professional Restructuring of Corporate Rescue: Company Voluntary Arrangements and the London Approach* (1995), ACCA Research Report No. 45.

[4] *Leyland DAF Ltd v. Automotive Products plc* [1993] B.C.C. 398.

3. Financial Statements and the Course of Corporate Rescue

The main proposition of this chapter is that the application of the going concern concept can have an impact on the course of a corporate rescue. A company's directors and auditors must both review the appropriateness of the going concern basis. However, the technical definition of a "going concern" does not lend itself to clearcut decisions regarding its appropriateness. There is now some official guidance from the accountancy profession for both directors and auditors, but much is still left to the exercise of judgment. Technicalities are discussed in more detail in the next section of the chapter. For the present purposes it is sufficient to state that if a company cannot, without qualification, be considered a going concern, the problem must be recognised in the company's annual accounts. It is, therefore, through the drawing up of the accounts that technical going concern problems can have an impact on a rescue attempt. The contents of a company's financial statements may influence the course of a rescue in four ways:

(1) STAKEHOLDER CONFIDENCE

If the information that is contained in a company's annual financial statements includes surprisingly bad news about its financial health, its stakeholders may lose confidence in it and try to withdraw; Under the efficient market hypothesis a company's share price properly reflects the present value of its expected future cashflows. Surprising, adverse information disclosed in a set of accounts can change the expected value of furture cashflows and therefore cause the company's share price to fall. Shareholders who lose confidence in the company's ability to survive may seek to sell their shares at this point and may thereby cause a further fall in share price. A sudden and dramatic fall in a company' s share price can change the course of a rescue attempt by disturbing arrangements which may be progressing for further financial support. If shares are being sold below their nominal value, the raising of further capital from the equity market will be ruled out. The raising of loan capital may also be jeopardised. A fall in share price may also open the way for a takeover bid which could change the shape of the company's future, but may facilitate its rescue in some form.

Although the proposition that the release of accounting information can shape the company's future by shaking stakeholder confidence can be supported by reference to an efficient market and the price mechanism, faith in this particular hypothesis is not required to make the necessary link. Indeed, the view that a loss of confidence can only operate to shape a company's future via movements in its share price is a restricted one, as it excludes the possibility of more direct responses by other stakeholders to the bad accounting news.[5] Direct responses by suppliers of goods, suppliers of finance and employees must be recognised as possibilities. Suppliers of goods who receive the news that a company has going concern problems may immediately refuse to supply the company or may require cash on delivery. On receipt of such news the company's suppliers of finance are likely to review their outstanding loans and be less inclined to continue support for the company. Employees may begin actively to seek alternative employment and, if they possess particular skills or firm-specific know-how, departures may affect the company's ability to continue its operations. The claim being made here is that a loss of confidence can be reflected in a fall in the company's share price or in a more direct change in the company's relationships with its stakeholders in the form of a threat to withdraw or actual withdrawal. Any of these responses to the release of the news of going concern problems will affect the company's ability to deal with those problems and thus affect its ability to stage a rescue.

(2) ACTIONS BY SECURED CREDITORS

The news of a company's going concern problems will undoubtedly reach its major suppliers of finance. Under (1) above the news is seen as generally making lenders less willing to support the company. The publication of problem accounts may have the more drastic result of disclosing the breach of a debt covenant and thus allowing secured creditors to appoint a receiver. This is because secured creditors may have tests written into their loan agreements (debt covenants) which enable them to enforce their securities on the occurrence of an event determined by reference to the financial statements, and, although the appropriate financial statements for this type of test will be a

---

[5] It also fails to explain how a loss of confidence could operate in unquoted companies.

74

contractual matter, the published audited accounts are the normal point of reference. The appointment of a receiver will undoubtedly change the company's position regarding its possible rescued.[6]

(3) Tests of Insolvency

If the publication of the company's accounts disclose that it not only has a going concern problem but is also technically insolvent under one of the statutory tests, its creditors have the option of petitioning for its winding up and its directors or creditors may be able to petition for an administration order. In section 4 below the relationship between the going concern concept and statutory insolvency is explained more fully. One way of disclosing going concern problems in the accounts is to note that they exist but to continue to apply the going concern concept to arrive at the reported accounting figures. A company with this (lesser) type of going concern problem may not be insolvent if the balance sheet test of insolvency set out in section 123(2) of the Insolvency Act 1986 is applied to its accounts.[7] A company with a more severe going concern problem may have to draw up its accounts on a forced sale basis. This would change the reported figures for the worse and such a company would be much more likely to be insolvent under the section 123(2) balance sheet test. The proposition here is that a going concern problem can affect a company's balance sheet figures and thus its balance sheet solvency or insolvency. Balance sheet insolvency can have an impact on the course of a corporate rescue by precipitating or permitting a petition for a winding up or an administration order.

(4) Tests for Wrongful Trading

To prove wrongful trading it must be shown that the director "knew or ought to have concluded that there was no reasonable prospect

---

[6] Receivership is discussed in more detail in Chap. 8.
[7] The ways in which the statutory balance sheet test under s.123(2) of the Insolvency Act 1986 differs from a balance sheet prepared as part of the company's annual accouts are explained in Chap. 3, the main definitional problem areas being "contingent and prospective" liabilities.

that the company would avoid going into insolvent liquidation."[8] The Cork Report on Insolvency Law and Practice describes the situation as one of striking the balance between two courses: the right to go on and the obligation to stop.[9] It has been suggested in Chapter 3 that a company's financial statements may indicate that the directors have reached the point where they have the obligation to stop trading. The evidence may be obvious from the face of the accounts or come from an analysis of the accounts which may be a simple construction of financial ratios or a more complicated model for the prediction of failure. In assessing what the company directors "knew or ought to have concluded", the courts will not confine themselves to looking at the company's financial statements issued to shareholders; information drawn up for internal, management purposes and the company's accounting records can also be scrutinised. However, a set of financial statements which explicitly acknowledges a going concern problem should cause the directors to at least address the question of whether the company has a real prospect of avoiding insolvent liquidation. Thus a going concern problem may change the course of a rescue attempt by forcing the directors to assess their position. They will effectively have to second-guess what a court might decide at a later date: Do these accounts disclose a right to go on (trading) or an obligation to stop? If the directors believe that, given the accounting information, they have an obligation to stop, a rescue attempt may be aborted. Thus, the prospect of the directors' personal liability being dated from the preparation of the problem accounts may shape the course of a rescue attempt by halting it.

4. The Going Concern Concept

It has already been stated that the company's directors and auditors both have responsibilities with regard to the application of the going

---

[8] s.214(2)(b) of the Insolvency Act 1986. Wrongful trading also requires the company to have gone into insolvent liquidation; s.214(2)(a) of the Insolvency Act 1986. Section 214(6) states: "For the purposes of this section a company goes into insolvent liquidation if it goes into liquidation at a time when its assets are insufficient for the payment of its debts and other liabilities and the expenses of the winding up." This is another, differently worded, balance sheet test, but it requires an assessment of the position at the time the company goes into liquidation and an insolvency practitioner's statement of affairs is therefore the most likely source of evidence.

[9] Cork, "Insolvency Law and Practice: Report of the Review Committee," Cmnd. 8558 (1982), 58.

concern concept. The directors' responsibilities in this area have recently been reappraised as part of a more general move to encourage good corporate governance practices.

DIRECTORS' RESPONSIBILITIES FOR THE COMPANY'S ACCOUNTS

The first responsibility of the directors regarding company accounts is to keep proper accounting records. Under section 221 of the Companies Act 1985 the company is under a statutory obligation to keep accounting records which are sufficient to show and explain the company's transactions and are such as to disclose with reasonable accuracy, at any time, the financial position of the company and a company officer's default under this provision is an offence.[10] The Cork Report identifies the state of the books of account as the principal determining factor in striking the balance between the right to go on and the obligation to stop trading.[11]

The second responsibility of the directors is to prepare (or have prepared) a balance sheet and a profit and loss account for each financial year.[12] This part of the directors' duties has been further emphasised by the Cadbury Code of Best Practice, which recommends that a brief statement of directors' responsibility for preparing the accounts should appear in the report and accounts. The purpose of such a statement is to make it clear that responsibility for preparing the accounts rests with the board of directors, and to remove any misconception that the auditors are responsible for the accounts. This means that the directors of listed companies should be reminded of their responsibilities each time the annual accounts are prepared.[13] Both standard accounting practice and the Companies Act 1985 presume that accounts are to be prepared on the basis that the company is a going concern. The going concern concept is one of the four fundamental accounting concepts set out in Statement of Standard Accounting Practice (SSAP) 2, "Disclosure of Accounting Policies." Standard accounting practice is that in the absence of a clear statement to the contrary, there is a presumption that the four

---

[10] s.221 of the Companies Act 1985.
[11] Cork, *op. cit.*, at 58.
[12] s.226 of the Companies Act 1985.
[13] Compliance with the Cadbury Code of Best Practice is voluntary, but Stock Exchange listing obligations require listed companies to report as to whether they comply or not.

fundamental concepts have been observed. SSAP 2 defines the going concern concept in the following terms: "[T]he enterprise will continue in operational existence for the foreseeable future. This means in particular that the profit and loss account and balance sheet assume no intention or necessity to liquidate or curtail significantly the scale of operation."[14]

Schedule 4 of the Companies Act 1985 sets out the required form and content of company accounts and states that "the company shall be presumed to be carrying on business as a going concern."[15] There is no statutory definition of "going concern" and the definition in SSAP 2 is, therefore, the best indication of its statutory meaning.[16] If the going concern presumption is incorrect, this must be revealed in the accounts. Paragraph 15 of Schedule 4 of the Companies Act 1985 states: "If it appears to the directors of a company that there are special reasons for departing from any of the principles stated above in preparing the company's accounts in respect of any financial year they may do so, but particulars of the departure, the reasons for it and its effects shall be given in a note to the accounts."

If directors are to discharge their responsibilities properly, each time a set of accounts is prepared they should consider whether the going concern presumption can be sustained. The statutory requirements alone mean that if the accounts are silent on this issue the directors can be assumed to have decided that the company *is* a going concern.

The view that existing law requires the directors to consider the appropriateness of the going concern concept is not, however, universal. The going concern concept was included in the deliberations and pronouncements of the Committee on the Financial Aspects of Corporate Governance (The Cadbury Committee), which reported in December 1992. It stated that "in view of the understandable public criticism of the audit process when companies collapse without apparent warning, there are strong arguments for amending company law to place an explicit requirement on directors to satisfy themselves that the going concern basis is appropriate, and

---

[14] SSAP 2, para. 14.
[15] Sched. 4, para. 10 of the Companies Act 1985.
[16] Accounting standards now have statutory recognition: para. 36A, Sched. 4 of the Companies Act 1985 requires the accounts to state whether they have been prepared in accordance with applicable accounting standards and "particulars of any material departure from those standards and the reasons for it shall be given." Small and medium-sized companies are, however, exempt from this requirement.

to report accordingly to shareholders."[17] The Code of Best Practice drawn up by the Cadbury Committee therefore recommends that the directors should state in their report and accounts that the business is a going concern, with supporting assumptions or qualifications as necessary.[18] To help directors who now have to make a going concern statement in their company's accounts, the Cadbury Committee set up a Working Group on Going Concern which issued its own statement in November 1994 entitled "Going Concern and Financial Reporting: Guidance for Directors of Listed Companies Registered in the U.K."[19] This semi-official pronouncement on the going concern concept will subsequently be referred to as the Guidance. It is of interest, as it provides a checklist of relevant factors for directors to take into account when considering whether the company is a going concern. It also briefly mentions some problems arising out of the interplay of the going concern concept and the legal definition of insolvency.

Although the Guidance provides a list of appropriate procedures which directors should perform before making a going concern statement, it does not offer an easy formula for deciding whether the company is a going concern or not. It states: "When directors have undertaken all the individual procedures they consider appropriate, they should consider the range of potential outcomes in the context of the probability of occurrence to determine the likely commercial outcomes. They should also be aware of the implications arising from interaction between the various factors."[20]

This part of the Guidance is particularly unhelpful. "The range of potential outcomes" could be innumerable. The assignment of a probability of occurrence to these outcomes would be guess-work. Determining the likely commercial outcomes suggests a narrowing of the range, but no method is offered for doing this. The directors have three options: to decide that the company is a going concern; to decide that the going concern basis is appropriate but that there are going concern problems that must be disclosed to the shareholders; to decide that the company is not a going concern. If, after careful consideration of all the "likely commercial outcomes," the directors decide that the going concern concept is inappropriate, the accounts

---

[17] *The Cadbury Report*, para. 5.19.

[18] *Cadbury Code of Best Practice*, para. 4.6.

[19] The reference to listed companies is because the Cadbury Code of Best Practice is designed primarily for listed companies.

[20] *The Guidance*, para. 41.

may be drawn up on the basis of a forced sale. The Guidance states that: "The generally recognised alternative to the going concern basis is to assume that the company will be broken up. This may significantly diminish the value of assets previously reported in the balance sheet since it assumes that the assets will be subject to a forced sale and not realised in the normal course of business."[21]

AUDITORS' RESPONSIBILITIES REGARDING THE GOING CONCERN CONCEPT

The auditors have to form an opinion as to whether the accounts prepared by the directors show a true and fair view of the company's state of affairs. In order to do this they have to consider the appropriateness of the basis on which the accounts are drawn up and the adequacy of the going concern disclosures included by the directors.[22] If the accounts are prepared on the going concern basis and the auditors consider this to be inappropriate, they can issue a qualified audit report.[23] There are various ways in which auditors can qualify their report depending on the exact circumstances. Serious and lesser forms of qualification can be distinguished by knowledgable readers. Auditors clearly believe that a qualification can have a serious effect. The literature on the effect of audit qualifications is equivocal.[24] On the one hand, it appears to show auditors as reluctant to qualify their reports because qualification may in itself precipitate the collapse of the company. On the other hand, many companies whose accounts are qualified do not fail. In one study only three out of 51 companies whose accounts were qualified actually failed.[25]

---

[21] *The Guidance*, para. 15.

[22] It is submitted that this would be part of the auditor's general remit to form an opinion as to whether the accounts show a true and fair view; it is now required formally under Statement of Auditing Standards (SAS) 130 "The Going Concern Basis in Financial Statements." Guidance for auditors in connection with any statement made by the directors in compliance with the Cadbury Code of Best Practice has been issued separately in Audit Bulletin 1994/1 "Disclosures relating to corporate governance (revised)."

[23] Where the basis is appropriate, but the disclosures relating to the situation inadequate, the auditors can issue an unqualified opinion with an explanatory paragraph. For more detail see SAS 130 "The Going Concern Basis in Financial Statements."

[24] This is discussed in Pratten, *op. cit.*

[25] Barnes and Hooi, "The Strange Case of the Qualified Success" [1987] *Accountancy*, November, 32.

THE GOING CONCERN CONCEPT IN RESCUE SITUATIONS

In section 3 it was suggested that going concern problems revealed in a company's accounts could make for practical difficulties in carrying through a rescue attempt. The causality can also run the other way; the fact that a rescue is being mounted or is contemplated must be considered by the directors when they are deciding on the appropriateness of the going concern basis. Three types of rescue scenario can be distinguished. First, a rescue operation employing one of the legal rescue regimes may be contemplated; second, the company may need to renegotiate the terms of its borrowing (outside legal rescue regimes) in order to survive; and third, corporate rescue may take the form of a major restructuring. The Guidance deals with each of these possibilities. On legal rescue regimes it states that because "going concern" means operational existence for the foreseeable future,

> "[t]he going concern concept is unlikely to be compatible with the intention or necessity to:
>
>> enter into a scheme of arrangement with the company's creditors;
>> make an application for an administration order;
>> place the company into administrative receivership or liquidation."[26]

The intention to make an administration order, for whatever purpose, makes the going concern basis inappropriate according to the Guidance. Thus, taking the most favourable situation, the intention to make an application for an administration order on the basis that the company is merely *"likely to become* unable to pay its debts"[27] (even though it is presently financially solvent) and for the purpose of achieving "the survival of the company, and the whole or any part of its undertaking, as a going concern"[28] would, under the Guidance, be incompatible with the use of the going concern basis in accounts currently under preparation. This is a strange, if not perverse, result. Directors who see the need for a legal rescue regime in advance of the crisis itself may find themselves advised that accounts should not be prepared on a going concern basis or that, if they are so prepared, the audit report may include a going concern qualification. It is clear that an ailing, but financially solvent, company that is attempting to

---

[26] *The Guidance*, para. 13.
[27] s.8(1)(a) of the Insolvency Act 1986.
[28] s.8(3)(a) of the Insolvency Act 1986.

continue as a going concern could fail the going concern test as formulated in the Guidance.

It is submitted that the forced sale basis would also be inappropriate when an administration is intended because a petition for an administration order is usually accompanied by a financial statement[29] specifically designed to demonstrate how the outcome under administration would be different from, and preferable to, the alternative scenario, which is a break-up of the company. The guidance does not recognise this problem and offers forced sale as the only alternative to the going concern basis.[30] Directors may be discouraged from considering a rescue under an administration order if such an intention could have a drastic, even suicidal effect on a set of accounts currently under preparation.

The Guidance uses the case of a company that needs to renegotiate the terms of its borrowing in order to survive as an example of a situation where the going concern basis can legitimately be adopted despite doubts about the going concern presumption, but appropriate disclosure of the circumstances is required. The example of disclosure given in the Guidance reads:

> "The company is in breach of certain loan covenants at its balance sheet date and so the company's bankers could recall their loans at any time. The directors continue to be involved in negotiations with the company's bankers and as yet no demands for repayments have been received. The negotiations are at an early stage and, although the directors are optimistic about the outcome, it is as yet too early to make predictions with any certainty. In the light of the actions described elsewhere in the Operating and Financial Review, the directors consider it appropriate to adopt the going concern basis in preparing the accounts."

This allows a company attempting an informal workout to escape the most drastic effects of having to report figures on a forced sale basis, but it means that total secrecy cannot be maintained. If there is

---

[29] The financial statement could be part of a report by an independent person (usually an accountant or insolvency practitioner) pursuant to r. 2.2 of the Insolvency Rules 1986. A r. 2.2 report is described as "desirable but not compulsory" when making an application for an administration order. However, excessive detail in such reports has now been criticised in a practice note.

[30] Forced sale is the only alternative basis offered by the Guidance; however, the use of the going concern basis with the expression of reservations is suggested as being appropriate in some circumstances at paras 50/51.

a breach of a loan covenant that has the effect of making the debt "due immediately", then the company may already be insolvent on the statutory test of being unable to pay its debts as they fall due.[31] Thus, under the Guidance it may be possible for a technically insolvent company to adopt the going concern basis. Conversely, the Guidance states in two separate paragraphs that "[d]oubts on the ability of a company to remain a going concern do not necessarily mean that the company is or is likely to become insolvent"[32] and "[w]here a company is not a going concern, the company is not necessarily insolvent."[33]

A rescue which can be described as a major restructuring may not present a going concern problem.[34] The Guidance states:

> "In recent years it has become commonplace for companies to be restructured. Some companies regard this as an ongoing process since they need to adapt to changing markets if they are to continue to be successful. It is generally accepted that such major restructuring does not adversely affect the suitability of the going concern basis for drawing up the financial statements."

However, appropriate procedures and an overall assessment of the situation by the directors would still be expected. A major restructuring which includes an intention to significantly curtail the scale of the company's operations would present the most difficulty regarding the going concern concept.

5. The Going Concern Concept and Wrongful Trading

In section 3 it was suggested that going concern problems revealed in a company's accounts could cause the directors to recognise that they also have a wrongful trading problem. The Guidance offers very little help to directors in this regard. It says only that if the going concern basis is not appropriate for the annual accounts the directors should consider "whether section 214 of the Insolvency Act 1986 applies"[35]

---

[31] Although it is being argued that the company is already technically insolvent, the bank is unlikely to petition for a winding up without issuing a formal demand for payment.

[32] The Guidance, para. 23.

[33] *ibid*. para. 54.

[34] If it does not require the use of a legal rescue regime.

[35] The Guidance, para. 54.

and "consider taking professional advice".[36] It appears that there is no formal connection between making the right decision about the firm's going concern status as reported in the accounts and making the right decision about keeping going or ceasing to trade for reasons of wrongful trading. However, information collected for a proper going concern decision under the Guidance may be good evidence that the directors ought to stop trading or risk liability under section 214.

The thrust of the argument as presented in section 3 was that directors making an assessment of the company's going concern status should also consider the wrongful trading position. The reverse may also apply, so that directors who wish to monitor their position regarding wrongful trading properly may not be able to continue to apply the going concern concept. There has been a hint in one reported case that the wording of the wrongful trading provision may require directors to have a non-going concern balance sheet prepared in certain circumstances if they are to monitor the company's financial position properly. Liability for wrongful trading arises from the time the directors "knew or ought to have concluded" that insolvent liquidation was unavoidable. The court, therefore, has to establish a "start date". In *Re Purpoint Limited*[37] no accounts had been drawn up and in these circumstances the court was willing to impose its own "start date" on a basis which seemed reasonable. In his judgment Vinelott J. said:

> "It was impossible, given Mr Meredith's total failure to ensure that proper records were kept and that proper cash flow calculations and net worth calculations were made, to ascertain the precise extent of the company's net liabilities at the end of 1986, or the extent to which [they] were increased by the continuance of the company's trading after the end of 1986."

The reference to "net worth calculations" has been interpreted by one author as implying that a non-going concern balance sheet should have been prepared.[38] As already stated, this is only a hint of what the courts might demand of directors. The *basis* of the accounts was not the main problem in *Re Purpoint Limited*; it was the lack of *any* accounts which was the difficulty.

---

[36] *ibid.* para. 23.
[37] [1991] B.C.C. 121.
[38] Jones, "Insolvency and the Balance Sheet," (1993) 9 *Insolvency Law and Practice* 136.

6. Conclusion

Corporate rescue always involves a significant risk of failure. In most cases, a rescue attempt can only succeed if the company can continue trading and can emerge from the process as a going concern. The rescue process itself is, therefore, a very practical test of the company's going concern status. In the field of accounting the going concern concept takes on a technical meaning. It is a concept which is fundamental to both the normal keeping of accounting records and the routine drawing up of financial accounting statements. However, there is an overriding requirement that a company's accounts should show a "true and fair view," which means that accounts should not be prepared on the going concern basis if it is inappropriate.

In this chapter the points at which financial statements can impinge on a rescue attempt have been outlined. The directors' responsibilities for keeping accounting records and having accounts prepared have been emphasised. The going concern concept and the official Guidance on its applicability have been explained. It has been noted that directors contemplating the use of an official rescue regime may find that they should not be preparing accounts on a going concern basis. But, directors performing informal restructuring or attempting an informal renegotiation of a debt contract (a workout) may be able legitimately to continue to use the going concern basis. Possible interactions between the going concern concept and the wrongful trading provisions have also been pointed out.

Chapter 6

The Design of Legal Rescue Regimes

1. Introduction

The concept of rescue includes the formal and informal; it includes activities relating to marketing and production as well as financial arrangements. The concept of corporate rescue and the scope of rescue activities are discussed in Chapter 2. The concept of rescue also involves a crisis which usually takes the form of financial distress even if the underlying problem comes from the external environment or poor decisions in other areas of the firm's operations. Financial distress can be a warning signal, a hurdle to be overcome in entering insolvency proceedings and/or a trigger. These ideas are presented in Chapter 3. If the warning signals can be read, including perhaps the results of more sophisticated prediction of failure models as described in Chapter 4, a rescue may be mounted sooner rather than later. The idea of distress as a helpful catalyst depends on the company reaping the benefits of the shock to the organisation. As noted above, many changes which are required to rescue a company may be strategic and organisational, but it is *financial* distress which usually provides the crisis point. Financial distress can manifest itself in a poor set of accounts, in the inability to pay debts as they fall due (which means insolvency), or in an accounting crisis regarding the going concern concept. Interactions between these three problems are discussed in Chapter 5.

This chapter is about the design of legal rescue regimes. The best design for a regime will depend on the objective of the legislation. There could be a general aim of maximising the country's level of economic activity, measured in terms of production or employment. One way of approaching this would be to encourage investment by giving creditors maximum security through an assurance that the contracts they make will be upheld, *i.e.* the courts will enforce priorities strictly. This would be a creditor-based rescue regime with few actual rescues, but (maybe) increased overall economic activity. Another approach would be actively to promote the rescue process by offering easy access to a moratorium on creditor actions. This may increase rescue activity (it has done so in the United States), but may also disturb the pattern of investment via the financial markets. Lenders may be less willing to make loans in the ordinary way because they will have no assurance that their priority will be upheld. They may also begin deliberately to seek out as customers companies undergoing a rescue, especially if loans to such companies are given a statutory super priority. In Chapter 2 it was suggested that judging the success or failure of an individual rescue attempt was not a simple task. Judging the success or failure of an individual rescue regime is similarly complicated and far from clear-cut.[1]

In this chapter various types of rescue regime are compared. The first way in which a comparison can be made is on grounds of economic efficiency (section 2). Another way of considering the effectiveness of the various regimes is to examine how the various decision-makers are likely to respond to a given regime in a situation of adversity (section 3). A final element that should be taken into account in the design of a rescue regime is the uncertainty which surrounds the whole process of attempting to rescue a company (section 4).

2. A Taxonomy of Rescue Regimes

In this section it is assumed that the criterion for a good rescue regime is economic efficiency. Economic theory suggests that the process of insolvency or bankruptcy should serve as a screening process designed to eliminate only those firms that are economically inefficient and whose resources could be better used in some other activity.[2] At a general level the design of an insolvency regime should

---

[1] Franks and Torous suggest five criteria for judging the comparative efficiency of bankruptcy codes: premature liquidation, adherence to the terms of the debt contract, costs of insolvency, the effect on investment and the effects on other stakeholders' interests. These criteria do not all work in the same direction. A code which adheres closely to the terms of debt contracts is likely to encourage premature liquidation. See Franks and Torous, "Lessons from a Comparision of U.S. and U.K. Insolvency Codes" (1992) 8 *Oxford Review of Economic Policy* 70.

[2] White, "The Corporate Bankruptcy Decision" (1989) 3 *Journal of Economic Perspectives* 129.

address the question of how to ensure that the company's assets are put to the best use in the context of the economy. At a more specific level there are two issues which an *insolvency* regime must tackle: how to value the company and how to allocate that value to the shareholders and creditors, that is how to judge the relative merits of claims on the assets of the company. A *rescue* regime may also need to consider the ways in which new finance can be attracted.

Before embarking on a discussion about the best way to design a rescue regime, it should be noted that the whole idea of design as an exogenous activity may be flawed. Easterbrook argues that legal rules endure because they are efficient or because they transfer wealth.[3] As wealth transfers are an implausible explanation of the current U.S. bankruptcy regime, he argues that efficiency is the better explanation. Thus, for Easterbrook it is not good design which produces economic efficiency, but economic efficiency which explains changes in the law.[4] Whichever way the causality flows, it is true to say that design activity occurs and views on good design are expressed by theorists and practitioners.

In designing an insolvency regime various choices can be made and some of the key alternatives are set out in Table 6.1 below. In most countries the introduction of new proposals are in fact re-design rather than design. Proposals may look like a new package but usually they leave at least one of the elements in Table 6.1 untouched. For example, contracting out of the ultimate legal procedure (liquidation) is usually impossible, and proposals for new rescue regimes usually retain liquidation as the ultimate threat. On the other hand, proposals to allow contracting out to occur usually leave the other elements of Table 6.1 intact. An exception to the norm of design as re-design is the situation in Eastern Europe where recently countries have had to grapple with the question of what kind of market economy is best suited to their future needs, and this has included the choice of a bankruptcy law.[5]

---

[3] Easterbrook, "Is Corporate Bankruptcy Efficient?" (1990) 27 *Journal of Financial Economics* 411.

[4] *ibid*. at 417.

[5] Aghion, Hart, and Moore, "The Economics of Bankruptcy Reform" (1992) 8 *Journal of Law, Economics and Organization* 523.

Table 6.1—Some Choices in the Design of an Insolvency Regime

Area	Choice	
Trading:	Cease trading	Keep the company running
Creditors' actions:	Moratorium on all actions	No moratorium
Time for procedure:	Short time limit	Open ended, no time limits
Priority of creditors:	Preserve absolute priority, the creditors' bargain	Allow renegotiation of the creditors' bargain
Control:	Leave control with the management	Give control to an insolvency practitioner
Legal procedure:	Mandatory if certain criteria are met	Voluntary (a) if certain criteria are met OR (b) with no criteria to be met
Contracting out of the legal procedure:	Possible	Impossible

The taxonomy of regimes below includes regimes that exist in some form in either the United Kingdom or the United States and regimes that are merely proposals. The purpose of the taxonomy is to highlight the essential characteristics of actual and proposed regimes and to assess their economic efficiency in a general way.

LIQUIDATION

The essential characteristic of liquidation is that the company will be wound up. Liquidators can only keep the company's business going insofar as it is *necessary* for the beneficial winding up of the business.[6]

---

[6] Sched. 4, para. 5 of the Insolvency Act 1986.

In practice liquidation means an immediate, or almost immediate, selling off of the company's assets, usually piecemeal. Liquidation under current U.K. law is not a rescue procedure. Premature liquidation is economically inefficient.

RECEIVERSHIPS

The essential characteristic of a receivership is that the interests of the secured creditors dominate other interests. Analysing receivership in terms of economic efficiency, Webb finds that:

> "if debenture-holders have claims on a common pool of assets, the receivership system may lead to an equilibrium in which the company is prematurely and inefficiently liquidated. The problem stems from the feature of this system which allows creditors to act in individualistic self-interest. They have the right to recover the value of their claim without considering the overall value of the pool of assets upon which they draw. This may force the company to liquidate its assets even though on efficiency grounds it should continue business."[7]

On the other hand, if there are some more junior creditors: "A debenture-holder who is fully secured is not going to worry too much if the company is making losses provided his own security is not in jeopardy."[8] It is the unsecured creditors who take the first losses, but this is, after all, the creditors bargain. A receivership *may* result in a rescue, and administrative receivership was designed with a view to converting more receiverships into rescues. However, the essential feature of a receivership was not abandoned and the secured creditors' interests continue to predominate even in an administrative receivership.

REORGANISATION

The essential features of reorganisation are an automatic moratorium on actions against the company and the drawing up of a plan for the financial reorganisation of the company. A regime of this sort is

---

[7] Webb, "An Economic Evaluation of Insolvency Procedures in the United Kingdom: Does the 1986 Insolvency Act Satisfy the Creditors' Bargain?" [1991] *Oxford Economic Papers* 144.

[8] *ibid.* at 145.

available under Chapter 11 of the U.S. Bankruptcy Code. In the United Kingdom administration was introduced as a rescue regime, and it too has the essential features of reorganisation. The differences between Chapter 11 and administration have already been noted in Chapter 2. Reorganisation is thought to be beneficial to the economy, as it preserves as going concerns companies that would otherwise have been prematurely liquidated. Unfortunately, it can also preserve companies that, in the interests of economic efficiency, ought to be liquidated. Reorganisation can have a short time limit or be almost indefinite. The latest proposal for a new CVA procedure with a moratorium has the features of a reorganisation and has a time limit of 28 days, which can be extended for an additional period which is not to exceed two months. In contrast one U.S. railroad spent 13.3 years in Chapter 11.[9] Reorganisation regimes can leave the company's management in control or replace them with an insolvency practitioner. The advantages of a rescue regime based on reorganisation are that it allows an appraisal of the whole situation and the constructing of a whole package, including the raising of new finance if necessary, and it can prevent premature liquidation. In the United Kingdom the fact that administrative receivership takes precedence over administration dampens this effect.[10] The proposed CVA procedure would take precedence over administrative receivership and may, therefore, be more economically efficient. The proposals which are made for the financial reorganisation of the company often involve deviations from the terms of debt contracts, and the regime may allow the raising of new finance with a statutory super priority. These features count against economic efficiency on the criterion of fulfilling the creditors' bargain.

WORKOUTS "IN THE SHADOW" OF A FORMAL REGIME

The essential features of workouts "in the shadow" of a formal regime are that there is a renegotiation of the terms of at least one creditor's bargain; that there is no compulsory moratorium during the renegotiation; and that failure to renegotiate will most probably

---

[9] Franks and Torous, "An Empirical Investigation of U.S. Firms in Reorganization" (1989) 44 *Journal of Finance* 753.

[10] Assessing the effects of individual procedures is difficult; more difficulties arise when assessing the economic efficicency of a regime with several procedures in place.

mean entry into a formal insolvency regime. Workouts, by their very nature, must take place without a moratorium on creditor actions. Individual creditors can therefore pursue their own claims and effectively prevent a workout. Alternatively, one creditor could attempt a "holdout". This supposes that most creditors will compare the result of agreeing to a workout (less than 100 per cent of their claim) with the result of entering into a formal insolvency regime (even less). This will make a workout seem attractive. However, 100 per cent agreement is required for a workout to go ahead. One creditor holding out for their full 100 per cent could disrupt the plan for all the other creditors and may therefore be given 100 per cent. This is called the holdout problem. If all the creditors holdout for 100 per cent there can be no agreement and no workout.

It has been argued that private workouts must be cheaper than reorganisations because they avoid the costs of court supervision. If this is so, workouts that rescue companies which would otherwise have had to go through a formal rescue regime are economically efficient. However, all workouts will require legal advice and the drafting of legal documents, so the cost advantages are an empirical matter. The financial restructuring that takes place in a private workout can include debt/equity swaps. In the United Kingdom these have mostly occurred in the restructuring of very large distressed companies. In February 1996 the Insolvency Service issued a paper on encouraging debt/equity swaps "as a rescue mechanism," suggesting that model schemes might be devised which could increase creditor familiarity and reduce the cost of advice.

AUCTIONS

The essential characteristics of an auction regime are an automatic moratorium and the sale of the business as a going concern to the highest bidder. The stay on creditor actions prevents dismemberment of the assets of the business. In terms of economic efficiency, auctions have the benefit of moving assets to their best uses; the auction yields the highest value available from any future user.[11] They also preserve the creditors' bargain, as they provide a pot of money which can be distributed according to the priority rights existing at the time the company enters the insolvency procedure. In

---

[11] See Easterbrook, *op. cit.*, at 412.

theory, immediate auction of the company as a going concern is economically efficient.

There are, however, some problems with auctions in practice. The theory assumes that there are well-informed buyers bidding for the company. In practice finding even one prospective buyer may be a time-consuming and expensive task. Auctions can therefore be a costly procedure. The decision to sell is also glossed over in the simplest theories of auctions. Secured creditors may be willing to accept an early offer which may undervalue the company but covers their debt. Junior creditors will be willing to wait longer in the hope of a higher offer, as they have nothing to lose by a delay. Only the "residual claimants" who bear the costs of the auction and collect the marginal receipts from the sale have the incentives to make the right decisions about timing and minimum price.[12] However, it is only possible to identify the residual claimants if the value of the company is known.

An automatic auction may be a rescue regime because the aim is to sell the company as a going concern. The regime would permit bids from existing shareholders, creditors or employees and in theory all bidders have free access to the capital market. In practice, finding financial backing for a bid is likely to be a major problem.

CONTRACTING OUT

The essential feature of contracting out is that it allows creditors to agree *ex ante* to avoid formal procedures. If a legal rescue procedure is expensive and time-consuming, private workouts may be used as a cheaper alternative. In both the United Kingdom and the United States private workouts are feasible, but they must be negotiated "in the shadow" of the formal rescue regime. As noted above, the shadow of the formal regime can lead to a holdout problem. It has been argued by at least one theorist that it would be more efficient to allow the company and its creditors to contract out of the formal legal procedure completely.

One suggestion which has been made is that such a contact would have two elements; a term requiring the company to make a successful workout offer, and a term under which a workout plan could be approved by a majority of creditors (unanimity would not

---

[12] *ibid.* at 415.

be required). Contracting out is not permitted under U.K. or U.S. law. The suggestion referred to above was made by Schwartz in 1993 and was made with particular reference to the U.S. position. Under U.S. law both types of terms are at present illegal. Majority rule clauses are banned under the Trust Indenture Act and bankruptcy waivers are banned whether made by individuals or firms.[13] A contract term requiring a firm to make a successful workout offer would commit the parties to reorganise privately according to the rule of distribution that the parties have adopted and so would entail a waiver of the parties' rights to use the legal bankruptcy process. Contracting out would undoubtedly involve large transactions costs, and it is submitted that these costs would outweigh any other efficiency gains.

3. Decision-making in Adversity

The design of a legal rescue regime can take into account two types of decision: decisions of individual agents and court decisions.

INDIVIDUAL DECISION MAKING

The search for an economically efficient bankruptcy procedure, which has been outlined above in the taxonomy of regimes, implicitly assumes that economic agents act rationally. The most general formulation of the rationality axiom postulates a complete preordering of alternatives (by the agent) and a choice which is not dominated (in preference) by another available one. This general axiom implies that all possible choices are known to and investigated by the decision-maker; this is objective rationality. The set of available choices can be narrowed to that perceived by the agent; this is subjective rationality. For Hahn rationality means that the superior advantage of an action serves as its explanation.[14] Langlois states: "The criterion for economic rationality is . . . the logical consistency of the agent's actions with his or her knowledge and preferences. And since . . . that knowledge and those preferences logically imply a best

---

[13] *In re Tru Block Concrete Products Inc.* (1983) 27 Bank Rep. 486.
[14] See Hahn, *Equilibrium and Macroeconomics* (1984), pp. 2–3 for a brief discussion of the problems of the rationality axiom.

course of action, the agent is rational only when he or she selects that particular best course."[15]

At the level of the individual agent, objective rationality means maximisation. In economics this can be utility maximisation, where utility can embrace more than wealth; for instance managers can have preferences for prestige (large, plush offices) and wealth (directors' remuneration). The narrower concept of wealth maximisation is, however, widely used.

When modelling the behaviour of the firm, there is the problem of how individual, rational, maximising decisions translate into corporate decisions. Profit maximising models of the firm can be contrasted with behavioural models. In profit maximising models, managers ensure that corporate decision-making maximises profit and the wealth of the owners of the firm.[16] Behavioural models emphasise the divorce of ownership from control and postulate that those in control organise the company for their own ends, which need not coincide with profit maximisation. In times of plenty, behavioural models assert that managers have some degree of discretion and can "get away with" less than maximum profits. In times of adversity the demands of shareholders become more urgent so that in the limit, *i.e.* insolvency, managers are forced to become profit maximisers. In adversity, both the profit maximising and behavioural models of the firm assert that profit-maximising decisions will be taken by managers.

The theory of the market for corporate control[17] suggests that the operation of the capital market will ensure that inefficient management teams will be replaced by more efficient ones through the mechanism of a take-over. If the market value of a company accurately reflects the value of its assets as currently managed, better management would increase the company's value and so a bid at above the current market price could be justified. Under this theory, the threat of a take-over is also supposed to act as a spur to existing

---

[15] Langlois (ed.), *Economics as a Process* (1986) p. 226.

[16] Profit maximisation is itself an ambiguous concept in that decisions that maximise short-term profits may not maximise profits in the long run. There is some argument in the literature as to whether it is possible for firms to make apparently rational decisions which lock them into ultimately inferior situations; this is called path dependence. Without path dependence, maximisation of the expected present value of future income (long-term profit maximisation) will maximise owners' wealth.

[17] Manne, "Mergers and the Market for Corporate Control" [1965] *Journal of Political Economy*, 73.

management teams encouraging them to maximise the wealth of the shareholders in order to avoid being subject to take-over bids. Under this theory management have no room to manoeuvre; even in times of plenty they must maximise profit or risk being replaced.

To summarise: The design of a legal rescue regime can be based on arguments of economic efficiency. Such arguments involve models of decision making which assume that agents act rationally. Economic rationality is usually translated into maximisation. At the level of the firm there are two competing types of model, but in situations of severe adversity both types predict that managers will take profit-maximising decisions.

If the argument in favour of a particular rescue regime is that it is economically efficient and this argument assumes that companies maximise profit, it is important to know whether the management decisions which are actually being made in situations of adversity are profit-maximising ones. Empirical work in this area is scarce and powerful empirical tests are difficult to construct. One approach to assessing whether or not management decisions taken in times of adversity are good for shareholders is to look at the stock market response to such decisions. This has been done by Khanna and Poulsen[18] using an event study methodology.[19] The events they studied were publicly announced management decisions concerning, for instance, changes in top management, plant closures or down-sizing, loan and credit agreement extensions and new debt. They discovered no significantly negative stock market responses to such announcements and tentatively concluded that management decisions for distressed companies were not perceived as value-reducing. The methodology employed for this study meant that the authors included several caveats to their results:

> "First, while we measure managerial behaviour through reported news stories of actions by successful[20] and unsuccessful managers this is only a crude measure of managerial decision making. For example, we do not measure market response to bad strategy implemented over time or

---

[18] Khanna and Poulsen, "Managers of Financially Distressed Firms: Villains or Scapegoats?" (1995) 50 *Journal of Finance* 919.

[19] See Bowman, "Understanding and Conducting Event Studies" (1983) 10 *Journal of Business Finance and Accounting* 561 or Strong "Modelling Abnormal Returns: A Review Article" (1992) 19 *Journal of Business Finance and Accounting* 533 for descriptions of this methodology.

[20] The study was a sample of distressed firms and a control sample of more successful firms.

poor execution of an announced project. Second, event study analysis only determines the value of the unanticipated portion of any announcement. If it is widely known that the firm is in financial distress and it is expected that managers will make poor decisions, the observed decisions may simply be no worse than the expectations."

Khanna and Poulsen imply that shareholder approval (or at least the lack of shareholder disapproval) of management decisions means that the decisions made were good ones. No distinction is made between the interests of the company and the interests of the shareholders, and no other interests are taken into account. It has already been indicated that an assessment of the success of a rescue attempt may depend on who is asked for an opinion. In practice there will be several, if not many, individuals and groups who have a stake in the outcome of a rescue attempt. Even a profit-maximising management decision may not be in the best interests of all the different types of stakeholders. Some of the interested parties have both a stake in the outcome and the power to make decisions that will affect the outcome, while others have a stake in the outcome but no decision-making power.

A different type of study was conducted by Nelson, whose methodology was to perform case study post-mortems on a small sample (13) of U.S. companies under Chapter 11.[21] He adopted a model of three tiers of response to adversity and claimed that "the most surprising aspect of the responses to severe adversity is the tendency of firms to select inappropriate responses."[22] He stated that "[m]any sample firms concentrated on avoiding bankruptcy and/or liquidation with such tenacity that it was doubtful that profit maximization remained a goal."[23] This is out of line with theoretical models of both the profit maximising and the behavioural types, but may nevertheless be a true reflection of managerial decision making under severe adversity. Another finding of Nelson's case study was that, under severe adversity, a divergence of interests contributed importantly to the inability of the company as a whole to cope effectively with its problems.[24]

---

[21] Nelson, *Corporations in Crisis* (1981).
[22] *ibid*. 76.
[23] *ibid*. 42.
[24] *ibid*.

COURT DECISIONS

One answer to the problem of a divergence of interests could be to design a rescue regime in which the court decides whether or not to allow a rescue attempt to be made. The legislation must then set out the grounds for granting access to the rescue regime. If the court is to make economically efficient decisions, the grounds for permitting a rescue could be that it is a wealth- or utility-maximising course of action (compared with the alternative of immediate liquidation). The difficulty in this approach is in converting the chosen concept of maximisation into a concrete decision rule which can be applied by the courts. One decision rule which could be adopted is to ask the courts to approve the course of action that maximises expected gains (or minimises expected losses). To calculate expected gains the probability of various outcomes must be multiplied by the payoff is that outcome actually occurs, for example a rescue attempt could either succeed and result in a company worth £1 million or fail and result in a company worth nothing. If these two outcomes are equally likely, the expected gain is 0.5 × £1 million plus 0.5 × £0, which equals £0.5m. The court could compare this with the expected gain from an immediate liquidation; for example the assets could be sold immediately for £400,000. The decision rule which tells the court to take the option that maximises expected gains ensures that, if the "game" is repeated many times actual gains will be maximised. This is a good way of proceeding in the context of the economy as a whole, where the game is repeated over many distressed companies.

There are two points to be made about this decision rule; first, for the particular company the game can only be played once; secondly, for any one company there will only be one outcome and this will not be the "expected gain," as this number represents a sort of average gain over many plays of the same game. In the example the expected gain is £500,000, but there can only be three outcomes:

(1) Rescue is attempted and is successful: £1 million gain.

(2) Rescue is attempted and is unsuccessful: no gain.

(3) Liquidation of the company: £400,000 gain.

Other decision rules may be more appropriate to a one-shot game, for instance the rule that says, "take the option that minimises the maximum amount of regret which could be experienced." In the example, if rescue is attempted and fails the company will regret the £400,000 which could have been obtained by immediate liquidation. If the company is liquidated the company will regret the extra £600,000 which could have been gained from a successful rescue. It should be noted that both the decision rules outlined above focus on overall gains to "the company" and express outcomes in terms of the value of the company. The gains are all assumed to be calculated net of the costs of the relevant rescue procedure.

The Insolvency Act 1986 provides an example of a rescue regime where the court must decide whether to allow the rescue attempt to proceed or not. Under section 8(1)(b) of the 1986 Act, an administration order may only be made by the court if it is "likely to achieve" one or more of the four purposes set out in section 8(3), which states:

> "The purposes for whose achievement an administration order may be made are—
>
> (a) the survival of the company, and the whole or any part of its undertaking as a going concern;
>
> (b) the approval of a voluntary arrangement under Part 1 [of the Act];
>
> (c) the sanctioning under section 425 of the Companies Act of a compromise or arrangement between the company and any such persons as are mentioned in that section; and
>
> (d) a more advantageous realisation of the company's assets than would be effected by a winding up;
>
> and the order shall specify the purpose for which it is made."

There has been some trouble over the interpretation of the word "likely." In *Re Consumer & Industrial Press Ltd*[25] "likely to be achieved" was interpreted as likely on a balance of probabilities, which means more likely than not, and this view was accepted in *Re Manlon Trading Ltd.*[26] A judge would have to rate the probability of achieving the purpose as greater than 0.5 per cent for this test to be passed. However, in *Re Harris Simons Construction Ltd*[27] this formula was rejected by Hoffmann J., who took the view that an order could be

---

[25] (1988) 1 B.C.C. 68.
[26] (1988) 4 B.C.C. 455.
[27] [1989] 1 W.L.R. 368; (1989) 5 B.C.C. 11.

made if there was "a real prospect" that one of the four purposes might be achieved. The real prospect test was then followed in *Re Primlaks (U.K.) Ltd*,[28] *Re SCL Building Services Ltd*[29] and *Re Rowbotham Baxter Ltd*.[30] In a discussion of the first four cases on this issue Hill suggests that, for the present, "likely" means there is "a real prospect" and this translates into a probability of 0.5 or more of success.[31] This, of course, takes no account whatsoever of the payoffs involved in success or failure. A rule that seeks to maximise expected returns could allow an attempt at rescue where the probability of success was very slight if the gains from a successful attempt were high enough. This illustrates just one place where the construction of the 1986 Act does not accord with the most obvious statistical solution to the problem. However, it is extremely difficult in practice to estimate either the expected returns from the various alternative courses of action or the probability of success for any chosen strategy. The cost of lengthy court cases where experts debate these numbers could be the worst of all possible worlds.

4. Uncertainty

The models of economic efficiency discussed so far either assume that individuals make decisions in which they maximise wealth or utility given known alternatives, or ask the court to choose between known alternatives, again in terms of maximisation. There are an increasing number of economists who argue that "the agent of economic theory is not best conceived as rational in the narrow sense of maximising within a framework of known alternatives."[32] This is basically an argument that says uncertainty is important; however, uncertainty can take several forms.

In the three-outcome example used in the previous section, the form that the future can take is known in advance. The range of outcomes that can occur "tomorrow" is known "today." The processes designed to cope with this form of uncertainty are calculations of expected gains and the revision of probability estimates. The

---

[28] (1989) 5 B.C.C. 710.
[29] (1989) 5 B.C.C. 746.
[30] [1990] B.C.C. 113.
[31] Hill, "Company Voluntary Arrangements" (1990) 6 *Insolvency Law and Practice*, 47.
[32] Langlois, *op. cit.*, p. 5.

agent's task is to *estimate*. In practice it is a feature of the decision-making process that it is sequential. Each company in need of rescue has an array of options open to it, but the set of options available at any particular time depends on a series of decisions made in the past. Timing of decisions may be absolutely vital and the probability of a rescue being successful may be changing rapidly for a company facing a crisis.

Another form of uncertainty is where the agent knows some components of the future and knows that there will be other components, but not what they will be. This form of uncertainty is characterised by ignorance about some future possibilities which already exist but are yet to be discovered. This sort of uncertainty could be reduced by the agent's alertness to hitherto unperceived opportunities. The agent's task is to *discover*.

A final form of uncertainty has been associated with economists who have been labelled "radical subjectivists." Littlechild states:

> "They [the radical subjectivists] emphasize the imagination needed to create alternatives between which decisions are made, and hence the inevitable uncertainty associated with the outcomes of decisions. In this view, the future is not so much unknown as non-existent or indeterminate at the time of the decision. The agent's task is not to *estimate* or to *discover*, but to *create*."[33]

This type of uncertainty has been called structural uncertainty.[34] Whereas risk and maximising rationality give rise to mathematically tractable economic models, structural uncertainty and imagination are difficult to model formally. One theoretical model of company behaviour in which the company in adversity is faced with structural uncertainty is that of Nelson and Winter.[35] They see the firm as continually searching; at any time it knows and operates one set of "routines" and is searching for new routines in an imaginative way. In Littlechild's terminology, the searching process involves creation rather than estimation or discovery. Expansion is seen as an optional response to success, but response to failure is mandatory. Under pressure the firm has to search for a new routine that would be viable

---

[33] Littlechild, "Three Types of Market Process" in Langlois, *op. cit.*, p. 29. The characteristics of the three types of uncertainty are also taken from Littlechild, *op. cit.*, pp. 28–30.

[34] Langlois, *op. cit.*, p. 228.

[35] Nelson and S.G. Winter, *An Evolutionary Theory of Economic Change* (1982).

in the prevailing environment. "[T]he initiation of the search under conditions of adversity has implications for the quantity and quality of the resources that may be devoted to it" and "if the search is successful in the limited sense that the firm begins to attempt to carry out a new routine" then "the firm itself may live on, at least temporarily."[36] The process which Nelson and Winter describe in their model has something of the feel of a rescue procedure, although their model does not deal with rescues explicitly.[37]

5. Conclusion

In this chapter problems in the design of legal rescue procedures have been examined from three angles. First, a taxonomy of rescue regimes has been used to assess economic efficiency in a general way. Secondly, it has been argued that assumptions about how decisions are made in times of adversity have an impact on the design of rescue regimes. Most economic models assume rationality and, in particular, profit maximisation. Thirdly, the impact of uncertainty has been considered. Decisions concerning a distressed company will almost certainly be made in the presence of "structural uncertainty," which is especially difficult to model.

---

[36] *ibid*. p. 122.

[37] Nelson and Winter's model is an evolutionary one. In the context of corporate rescue the selection mechanism of the evolutionary model may become a tautology so that survival becomes its own explanation. What is needed to save the model from this tautology is an independent criterion of survival value; a problem for which survival is the answer. For future discussion on this point see Gould, *Ever Since Darwin* (1977).

PART II

CURRENT UNITED KINGDOM LAW

Chapter 7

Arrangements with Creditors

1. Introduction

The Company Voluntary Arrangement (CVA) was introduced in 1985 as a new way for companies to make arrangements with their creditors. A scheme under what is now section 425 of the Companies Act 1985 had been available since 1907, but was seen as expensive and cumbersome, and was little used. Very poor uptake of the CVA especially in its early years was a cause of concern[1] and in 1993 the DTI's Insolvency Service began a consultation process with a view to the introduction of new additional procedures designed to give companies of all types and sizes readier access to a rescue procedure appropriate to them. The consultation process led eventually to a statement by the Minister for Company Affairs of his intention to introduce legislation for a new scheme, which in this chapter is referred to as the 28-day moratorium scheme Other schemes will remain in place and the new scheme, if it ever reaches the statute books, is to be available only for small companies as defined by section 247 of the Companies Act 1985.

In this chapter the existing schemes are presented first. The 28-day moratorium scheme is then discussed. The chapter concludes with a section on informal ways of making arrangements with creditors. In relation to large U.K. companies, the London Approach is explained. The features of informal arrangements made by large U.S. companies are then discussed. Finally, informal financing possibilities for U.K. small companies are explored.

2. Creditors' Schemes of Arrangement under Section 425 of the Companies Act 1985

For a long time Companies Acts have included a power of the company to compromise with its creditors and members. This

---

[1] *See* Chap. 2.

provision remains an option and can now be found in section 425 of the Companies Act 1985. Lingard claims that before 1939 creditors often accepted some form of composition.[2] Writing shortly after the major reform of Insolvency Law, Lingard also suggested that schemes of arrangement might become more fashionable again due to the introduction of the wrongful trading provision which gives directors the incentive to take advice at an earlier stage than before.[3] Schemes of arrangement under section 425 require the consent of a majority in number representing 75 per cent in value of the creditors, or class of creditors, present and voting either in person or by proxy. Unanimous consent is not required and, if the compromise or arrangement is sanctioned by the court, it is binding on all the creditors, or class of creditors, and the company. However, the procedure involved in a section 425 scheme is "cumbersome and expensive."[4] Writing in 1995, Milman and Chittenden describe section 425 as "largely under-utilised in practice"[5] and state:

> "The reasons for this are the cost and delay in securing the necessary consents of interested parties and then obtaining the formal sanction of the court. The protracted nature of this procedure was even more debilitating when one considers that the law provided no formal moratorium facility to protect the company's assets whilst the reconstructive arrangement was being worked out, though the courts in the exercise of their discretion might refuse to lend their assistance to a creditor seeking to enforce a judgement against the company's assets while such a scheme was being put together. Another problem was the inflexibility of any scheme arrived at; any necessary changes would require further meetings to be called and fresh sanction from the court. Furthermore, where such schemes were employed it would almost invariably be in the context of a larger company having a sophisticated profile of creditor/shareholder groups. Small companies had little recourse to them."[6]

The number of visits to court can also increase due to lack of court direction. Section 425(1) states that, where an arrangement is proposed, class meetings of the creditors are to be summoned "in such

---

[2] Lingard, *Corporate Rescues and Insolvences* (2nd, ed. 1989), p. 53.
[3] *ibid*. p. 54.
[4] *ibid*.
[5] Milman and Chittenden, *Corporate Rescue: CVAs and the Challenge of Small Companies*, ACCA Research Report No. 44 (1995), p. 1.
[6] *ibid*. pp. 1–2.

manner as the court directs." However, the court will not decide which classes are appropriate on the initial hearing of the summons. This means that a whole scheme can have been negotiated, voted on and come to a final hearing before the court expresses its dissatisfaction with the classification of creditors. A reclassification involves the calling of more meetings and another court hearing. It may have been possible to remedy the faults in the section 425 scheme, but the approach to reform in 1985 was to leave section 425 in place and add a new procedure: the company voluntary arrangement (CVA). The 1995 proposals for a further reform leave both section 425 and the CVA in place, simply adding a further rescue mechanism in the form of the 28-day moratorium scheme. There is nothing to suggest that section 425 will be anything but rarely used.

3. Company Voluntary Arrangements under Sections 1 to 7 of the Insolvency Act 1986

The CVA procedure which now constitutes Part I of the Insolvency Act 1986 is available to a company in financial distress. The company does not have to prove that it is insolvent, or even that it is likely to become insolvent. The directors of the company can initiate a CVA proposal so long as the company has not entered administration or liquidation.[7] If the company is in administration the administrator[8] can propose a CVA, and similarly if the company is in liquidation a proposal can be made by the liquidator.[9]

The proposal for a CVA must provide for some person who is qualified to act as an insolvency practitioner in relation to the company to be "the nominee" who is "to act in relation to the voluntary arrangement whether as trustee or otherwise for the supervising of its implementation."[10] Where there is already an administrator or liquidator in office, they will usually act as nominee themselves, and a separate, and slightly abbreviated, procedure is laid down for cases where the nominee is the liquidator or administrator. Where the directors are making the proposal, they will need an insolvency practitioner to act as nominee. The procedure, as laid

---

[7] s.1(1) of the Insolvency Act 1986.
[8] And, by the wording of s.1, no one else.
[9] And (again), by the wording of s.1, by no one else.
[10] s.1(2) of the Insolvency Act 1986.

down, is for the directors to prepare the proposal for the intended nominee. The nominee then has 28 days[11] to make a report to the court. However, in practice the directors will, in most cases, begin by consulting an insolvency practitioner, who will assist them in drawing up the proposal. The required contents of the proposal are set out in rule 1.3 of the Insolvency Rules 1986.[12] An examination of rule 1.3 reveals that the directors are more likely than not to need expert help in drawing up a proposal. Whilst some of the accounting items can be stated "so far as within the directors' immediate knowledge," thus lessening the need for expert advise, other items may require an expert' s experience and judgment, for instance the requirement to state the proposed duration of the voluntary arrangement. Directors are extremely unlikely to have had previous experience in proposing a CVA.[13] At this point it should be noted that only a very small number of insolvency practitioners have actually conducted a CVA. In the consultative document issued in 1993 the Insolvency Service reported that "[s]ome 49 per cent of all CVAs launched to date have been supervised by just four insolvency practices"—there are about 2,000 insolvency practitioners (IPs).[14] Flood *et al.* state:

> "In our research [into CVAs] we found that three individuals' names arose time and time again. They were the key CVA players. Each had done around 30 to 40 CVAs, constituting between 30 and 40 per cent of the total number. This made them experts in the field. Other IPs generally had done up to a handful of CVAs. . . Without doubt, those engaged in the work have a missionary zeal about it. One such practitioner, Mark Goldstein, has set up his own firm to do only company rescue: he will not undertake normal insolvency work."[15]

Milman and Chittenden report that "[m]any insolvency practitioners have little knowledge of the ins and outs of CVAs, let alone practical experience of their potential."[16] Their survey work produced some

---

[11] Or such longer period as the court may allow; s.2(2) of the Insolvency Act 1986.

[12] r. 1.3 is stated in full as Appendix 1 to this volume.

[13] The Insolvency Service state that: "There is plentiful anecdotal evidence that the CVA procedure is little known or understood by directors," Insolvency Service, *Company Voluntary Arrangements and Administration Orders: A Consultative Document* (1993), para. 2.45.

[14] *ibid.*

[15] Flood, Abbey, Skordaki and Aber, *The Professional Restructuring of Corporate Rescue: Company Voluntary Arrangements and the London Approach*, ACCA Research Report No. 45 (1995), p. 18.

[16] Milman and Chittenden, *op. cit.* p. 4.

200 licensed insolvency practitioners who conceded that they had no CVA experience.[17] These findings suggest that discussion of the CVA procedure as a possible method for rescuing the company will depend on the directors' choice of professional advisers.

If the directors successfully contact or are put in contact with an appropriate insolvency practitioner, they may decide to proceed with a CVA. As stated above, it is likely that the IP will assist the directors in drafting a proposal. The next steps, as set out in section 2 of the Insolvency Act 1986, are for the directors to formally give notice of the proposal to the nominee and for the nominee to make a report to the court. Section 2(3) sets out the documents which must be submitted to the nominee. They are:

"(a) a document setting out the terms of the proposed voluntary arrangement, and

(b) a statement of the company's affairs."

The contents of the proposal document are specified by rule 1.3 and, according to rule 1.4, formal notice to the nominee will start to run from the time when the proposal document is received. The statement of the company's affairs can be delivered to the nominee up to seven days later (rule 1.5). The nominee must submit a report to the court within 28 days (or longer if the court permits) after being given notice stating:

"(a) whether, in his opinion, meetings of the company and of its creditors should be summoned to consider the proposal, and

(b) if in his opinion such meetings should be summoned, the date on which, and time and place at which, he proposes the meetings should be held."[18]

The nominee can submit a negative report to the court and withdraw from further contact with the company. However, there is nothing to prevent the company from pursuing the same proposal with another nominee. When the nominee reports positively to the court, the date, place and times of the meetings of the company and the creditors must be specified and, under section 3(1), it is then the nominee's duty to summon the meetings accordingly. The

---

[17] *ibid*. p. 10.
[18] s.2(2) of the Insolvency Act 1986.

Insolvency Act 1986 gives no guidance about the summoning and conduct of the meeting; however, the Insolvency Rules make up for this. They lay down strict rules about the date of the meeting (not less than 14 or more than 28 days from the date of the report to the court); notice of meetings (at least 14 days); and the contents of the notice. Rule 1.13 contains rules about the convenience of the venue; the convenience of the time of the meetings; the availability of proxy forms; and the holding of the creditors meeting in advance of the company meeting, but on the same day and in the same place.[19] Meetings must be conducted in accordance with the rules.[20]

The meetings must decide whether to approve the proposed voluntary arrangement, with or without modifications.[21] If the proposal is modified, both meetings must approve the same modifications.[22] The requisite majorities for approval of the proposal are as follows: for the creditors' meeting, a majority *in excess* of three-quarters in value of the creditors present in person or by proxy and voting on the resolution,[23] for the members meeting, more than one-half in value of the members present in person or by proxy and voting on the resolution.[24] The same person will chair both meetings, and it is the duty of the chairman to report the result of each meeting to the court.[25] These reports must be filed within four days of the meetings being held.[26] The date of filing can be important because challenges of the decisions of the meetings must be made within 28 days of the time when the relevant report is filed.[27] Challenges can be made on two grounds: first, that the voluntary arrangement is unfairly prejudicial to the interests of a creditor, member or contributory of the company, and second, that there has been some material irregularity at or in relation to either of the meetings.[28] If the voluntary arrangement is approved, section 5(2) of the Insolvency Act 1986 states that it takes effect "as if made by the company at the

---

[19] r. 1.21 covers adjournments.
[20] s.4(5) of the Insolvency Act 1986.
[21] s.4(1) of the Insolvency Act 1986.
[22] s.5(1) of the Insolvency Act 1986.
[23] r. 1.19(1) of the Insolvency Rules 1986.
[24] r. 1.20(1) of the Insolvency Rules 1986. Rule 1.18(2) entitles members with no voting rights in the normal way to record a vote for or against the proposal; however, r. 1.20(2) states that such votes are to be left out of account when determining if the necessary majority has been obtained.
[25] s.4(5) of the Insolvency Act 1986.
[26] r. 1.24(3) of the Insolvency Rules 1986.
[27] s.6(3) of the Insolvency Act 1986.
[28] s.6(1) of the Insolvency Act 1986.

creditors' meeting" and it binds all creditors who were entitled to vote at the meeting and had notice of it, including absentees and dissentients. Once the arrangement has taken effect it must be implemented. This is usually done by the person who was the nominee; however, at the implementation stage that person is known as "the supervisor."[29]

The major advantages of the CVA over a scheme of arrangement under section 425 of the Companies Act 1985 are that court involvement can be minimal and that modifications to the original proposal can be made more easily. The major disadvantage of the CVA is that there is no stay on creditors' actions during the process. The only way out of this difficulty is for the company to obtain an administration order and for the administrator to propose a CVA. This immediately incurs more costs and involves the directors giving over most of their powers to the administrator. One solution to this problem would be to offer distressed companies a regime with the cost advantages and flexibility of the CVA but coupled with a moratorium on creditor actions. The proposed 28-day moratorium scheme aims to do just this.

4. 28-day Moratorium Scheme

Some of the main barriers to the use of the Insolvency Act 1986 CVA provisions were identified in a consultative document issued by the Insolvency Service in October 1993 as:

> "Lack of a moratorium on creditors' rights;
> Lack of funding;
> Secured creditors' rights to appoint a receiver;
> Directors' lack of knowledge and IPs' lack of experience of the provisions;
> Rescue attempted too late."[30]

A new CVA procedure incorporating a 28-day moratorium on creditors' rights and a pre-emption on the secured creditors' right to appoint a receiver was seen as the main solution to these problems.

---

[29] s.7(2) of the Insolvency Act 1986.
[30] *Company Voluntary Arrangements and Administration Orders: A Consultative Document* (1993), para. 2.1.

After receiving the responses to the initial proposal for a new CVA procedure, the Insolvency Service issued a second consultative document in April 1995 and in November 1995 the then Minister for Company Affairs announced his intention to introduce legislation "to effect a scheme broadly as described in the [second] consultative document when Parliamentary time allows."[31] The consultation process had originally aimed to give "companies of *all types and sizes*" readier access to a rescue procedure appropriate to them.[32] With the issue of the second consultative document the aim had become "to make company rescues simpler, cheaper and more accessible, particularly for the *smaller company*."[33] The intention to legislate stated that "usage [of the new procedure] will be restricted to *small companies* as defined in section 247 of the Companies Act 1985."[34]

The key elements of the new scheme are explained in the consultative document as follows:

> "An initial 28 day moratorium during which creditors will not be able to take action against the company (unless the court gives leave). This will provide a necessary breathing space for companies to assess rescue prospects and, if appropriate, come to a binding arrangement with creditors. The management will remain in control but will be subject to supervision and a restriction on the disposal of assets. There will be other safeguards to prevent abuse. The moratorium will be binding on all creditors, including secured creditors.
>
> Floating charge holders will be required to give the company five working days notice of their intention to appoint an administrative receiver. This will give the company a short time to see whether a CVA is appropriate. The notice can be abridged where the company consents or where the court gives leave. There will be provisions to prevent disposal of assets during that period and penalties for abuse."[35]

If approved, the new scheme is to be binding on all creditors, including unknown creditors, except creditors whose existence is deliberately concealed by the directors. It is also to be binding on all

---

[31] DTI press release P/95/839.

[32] *Company Voluntary Arrangements and Administration Orders: A Consultative Document* (1993), p. 10, para. 3.

[33] *Revised Proposals for a New Company Voluntary Arrangement Procedure: A Consultative Document* (April 1995), p. 10, para. 3.

[34] DTI press release P/95/839; italics added.

[35] *Revised Proposals for a New Company Voluntary Arrangement Procedure: A Consultative Document* (April 1995), p. 3.

shareholders.[36] Existing holders of floating charges (mostly banks) were strongly opposed to the new scheme. The Law Society's Insolvency Law Sub-Committee also expressed their concern, stating:

> "The two-fold alteration of the rights of a secured creditor—the requirement for such a creditor to give five days' notice before appointing an administrative receiver and the binding of such a creditor by the moratorium—involves a new and substantial erosion of secured creditors' rights and we do not consider that the supposed benefits justify this change. Indeed, we consider the changes may damage the rescue culture more than they help."[37]

By making the 28-day moratorium scheme available to only the smallest companies, the erosion of secured creditors' rights will only occur in relation to small loans and so may be more palatable to the providers of finance. Under the current legislation secured creditors have control over most rescue/liquidation decisions. This power is explored in more detail in the next chapter. Any new legal rescue scheme in the United Kingdom is likely to lessen the power of secured creditors and so face resistance. One of the arguments against change is that distressed companies very often need both a breathing space *and* additional funding if a rescue attempt is to succeed. The raising of extra funding often depends on the maintenance of a good relationship with the company's existing bankers, and the use of a rescue procedure which works against the interests of banks (such as the 28-day moratorium scheme) may damage that relationship and so precipitate disaster rather than further the rescue attempt. This argument is weak; banks currently have the power to appoint an administrative receiver, and given the choice between rescue and receivership they usually choose to appoint. A scheme that suspends the right for a short time cannot, it is submitted, make this situation any worse and may make it better by giving companies time for more interaction with their bankers. A stronger argument against a change in the rights of secured creditors is that creditors may become generally less willing to finance businesses. If the overall effect is for a few more companies to be rescued, but for many others to fail to raise sufficient finance to be launched, the economy as a whole will

---

[36] *ibid*. para. 22.
[37] *The Insolvency Act 1986 Revised Proposals for a New Company Voluntary Arrangement Procedure Consultative Document: Response by the Insolvency Law Sub-Committee, Law Society* (July 1995).

not be helped. Resistance from the financial community and a different political agenda under the new Labour Government are currently combining to make the prospects of the 28-day moratorium scheme reaching the statute books in the near future appear slim.

5. Informal Arrangements

This chapter is concerned with the ways in which distressed companies can make arrangements with creditors and so avert failure. Informal arrangements are those that are made outside legal insolvency or bankruptcy and without the benefit of a legally imposed moratorium on creditor actions. By definition informal arrangements are not bound to follow set schemes and are not restricted by time limits and other aspects of court supervision. However, informality, in the sense of the absence of court supervision, does not imply a total lack of structure.

A very important feature of informal arrangements is that they require the unanimous consent of the affected creditors.[38] In situations where there are substantial amounts owing to trade creditors informal agreements may be difficult to achieve for several reasons. Firstly, the claims of trade creditors tend to be heterogeneous which makes overall exchange offers difficult. Secondly, trade creditors are perceived as being acrimonious and unsophisticated and, therefore, less amenable to making such arrangements than banks.[39] In contrast banks are seen as having more homogeneous claims and being more amenable to making rescue arrangements. Thus, informal arrangements are made mostly in situations where banks are the main creditors concerned. Informal arrangements are perceived as successful in this type of setting and there is a general acknowledgment that the role of banks in company rescues can be crucial:

> "How banks respond to appeals for assistance from companies in financial difficulty is crucial not just for their own profitability but also, at a national level, for future levels of productive capacity. It is in everyone's interest that businesses which offer a reasonable prospect of

---

[38] This is the situation in both the United Kingdom and the United States.

[39] Gilson, John and Lang, "Troubled Debt Restructurings: An Empirical Study of Private Reorganization of Firms in Default" (1990) 27 *Journal of Financial Economics* 323.

viability survive and that only those which by general consent are hopeless causes are put into the hands of liquidators."[40]

The mention of liquidators is a reminder that informal arrangements are made "in the shadow" of formal legal procedures. Whilst it is fairly clear that an informal arrangement is preferable to a liquidation, it is less clear that an informal arrangement is preferable to a plan agreed under a formal *rescue* regime. There are two main arguments in favour of informal arrangements. First, informal arrangements may be less costly. This is a view put forward in the United States, where the direct costs of Chapter 11 as a rescue regime are particularly high.[41] Second, informal arrangements can be made secretly at a time when adverse publicity could damage confidence in the company, especially the confidence of the company's suppliers. This is a view put forward in the United Kingdom where adverse publicity is seen as one problem with administration as a rescue regime.[42] Three types of informal arrangement are discussed in this section: Large-scale workouts for U.K. companies under the London Approach; large-scale workouts in the United States; and small-scale informal financing arrangements for U.K. companies. In the United States a form of reorganisation that is a hybrid of the informal and formal has been developed over the last ten years and this approach is discussed as part of the review of U.S. trends.

THE LONDON APPROACH

The London Approach, as its name suggests, was developed in London and early forms of the approach always involved the Bank of England as broker and commercial banks as the creditors. It is an approach which is only appropriate for very large companies that have borrowed vast sums of money.[43] A typical setting for the London Approach would be a company with banking facilities from a large number of banks; a figure of 30 banks has been mentioned as normal,[44] and arrangements involving between six and 106 banks

---

[40] Kent, "The London Approach" (1993) 33 *Bank of England Quarterly Bulletin* 110.
[41] Gilson, John and Lang, *op. cit.*; Wruck, "Financial Distress, Reorganization and Organizational Efficiency" (1990) 27 *Journal of Financial Economics* 419.
[42] Flood, Abbey, Skordaki and Aber, *The Professional Restructuring of Corporate Rescue: Company Voluntary Arrangements and the London Approach,* ACCA Research Report No. 45 (1995), p. 83.
[43] Flood *et al., op. cit.*, p. ii.
[44] Kent, *op. cit.*, at 110.

have been observed.[45] If such a company breaches one loan covenant, for instance an interest cover covenant, cross-default clauses in other financial facilities will usually mean that the single breach of covenant puts the company into a position where its entire borrowing is repayable on demand. The directors of the company then face the possibility that further trading will breach the wrongful trading provisions and make them personally liable.[46] What the company needs is immediate help, but no publicity.

The London Approach has four main tenets:

(1) Banks are initially supportive and don't rush to appoint receivers.

(2) Decisions about a company's future are made on the basis of reliable information which is shared among all parties to a workout.

(3) Banks and, where appropriate, other creditors work together to reach a collective view on whether and how a company should be given financial support.

(4) Pain is shared on an equitable basis.[47]

It has been described as "a set of principles aiming to provide a flexible frarnework."[48] Flood *et al.* also claim that "to the bankers involved in the London Approach its genius lies in the informality and infinite flexibility with which it can be moulded and shaped."[49] Within its "infinite flexibility," however, the approach usually operates in four phases.[50]

(1) A voluntary "standstill" covering all debt owed.

(2) An investigation of the company's affairs by investigating accountants.

(3) Negotiation orchestrated by the "lead bank."

(4) If the negotiation is successful, a new financing agreement for the company which must then be monitored.

---

[45] Flood *et al.*, *op. cit.*, p. 28.
[46] s.214 of the Insolvency Act 1986.
[47] Kent, "The London Approach: Distressed Debt Trading", (1994) 34 *Bank of England Quarterly Bulletin* 172.
[48] Flood *et al.*, *op. cit.*, p. ii.
[49] *ibid.*, 32.
[50] *ibid.*, 28.

In the first phase lenders agree amongst themselves a moratorium. What is usually required in the very short term is a freezing of lenders' exposure at its existing level or within agreed limits, a preserving of the status quo as regards security and the provision of short-term finance.[51] A standstill allows information to be gathered and a plan to be formulated. Unanimity of lenders is needed for the first stage, and it is at that stage, that a "lead bank" must be identified.

The second phase is the commissioning of an independent accountant's report. The lead bank commissions the report and briefs the accountants; this prevents a proliferation of instructions and requests from individual lenders and allows an effective report to be drawn up quickly. The investigating accountant has the difficult task of producing a report, with urgency, which is concise but full enough to prevent any delay being caused by lack of information. The position of each class of lender must be set out clearly in the report.

The third phase is the formulation and negotiation of a plan. The lead bank's role at this stage has been described as "a delicate balancing act."[52] It is crucial that the lead bank commands respect and is a "consolidating force."[53] In practical terms a good lead bank is one which provides the fullest information possible to all lending banks.[54] The role of the lead bank having been emphasised, it should be pointed out that a successful workout also depends on the attitudes of other lenders. All the lending banks need to recognise their responsibilities to attend meetings and to be constructive. There are two main ways in which a creditor can fail to be fully cooperative during a workout. First, as any plan requires the unanimous support of the affected creditors, a creditor can simply refuse to agree to the proposed arrangement. This problem has led the Bank of England to consider whether it would be possible to replace unanimity with qualified majority voting.[55] There is, however, a significant degree of market pressure, which means that "[a]bank which frustrates an orderly workout for a company may find that other banks are less likely to be constructive next time round when their roles are reversed."[56] Second, the recent development of a secondary market in

---

[51] Floyd, "Corporate Recovery: The London Approach" (1995) 11 *Insolvency Law and Practice* 82.

[52] Kent, *op. cit.*, at 113.

[53] Floyd, *op. cit.*, at 83.

[54] Kent, *op. cit.*, at 113.

[55] *ibid*. at 115.

[56] *ibid*. at 112.

distressed corporate debt within the United Kingdom means that individual lenders can now sell their debt and escape further involvement with the troubled company. Debt sales are a two-edged sword; they can be a solution to fundamental disagreements between lenders but they may also spoil efforts to preserve value in viable businesses by damaging confidence.[57] The Bank of England is monitoring developments in the secondary market in distressed corporate debt. It has an interest in the efficiency and reputation of London as a financial centre and so wants the market to be responsible and professional. More specifically, the Bank of England now sees the London Approach as the "established culture in the United Kingdom for dealing with companies in financial difficulty"[58] and is anxious to see the secondary market in debt develop under the umbrella of the London Approach, not in opposition to it. It is hoped that the spirit of the London Approach can be extended to encompass secondary trading in distressed debt and, as the volume of debt trading continues to grow, that market practices will evolve which uphold that spirit.[59]

The details of workout plans will depend on individual circumstances. The tenet of the London Approach, which states that pain is shared on an equitable basis, indicates that any plan is likely to involve some pain for all lenders. Although it is difficult to generalise about the contents of workout plans, debt/equity swaps have been increasingly employed in London Approach workouts, and in 1996 the Insolvency Service's policy unit produced a consultation paper on "Encouraging debt/equity swaps."[60] In a debt/equity swap lenders agree to exchange some or all of their debt for equity shares. A special category of preference shares is usually created for the purpose of the swap. Holders of these shares will have priority as to dividends and repayment; sometimes there will be an option to convert to ordinary shares. The main thrust of the DTI consultation paper is that, as it is evident that debt/equity swaps can provide an important means for a financially troubled company to reorganise its affairs, more should be done to encourage them to be employed in appropriate cases. The DTI consider it inappropriate to legislate to require creditors to participate in a compulsory debt/equity swap.

---

[57] Kent, *op. cit.*, at 173.

[58] *ibid.* at 173.

[59] *ibid.* at 174. The idea of a code of practice for debt trading has been considered and rejected as too likely to induce a response to the letter rather than the spirit.

[60] DTI, February 1996; response to be received by May 10, 1996.

Increased usage is to be promoted by making both creditors and their professional advisers more aware of debt/equity swap possibilities. This may be achieved by the development of best practice and a pooling of knowledge and experience. The development of model debt/equity swap schemes, workable as they stand or adaptable to suit particular circumstances is suggested as potentially helpful. This would mean that each individual debt/equity swap no longer had to be tailor-made and costs may fall. In the United Kingdom debt/equity swaps have been used predominantly to restructure large distressed companies and most have been effected through the London Approach. The DTI consultation paper aims to raise the profile of debt/equity swaps as a rescue mechanism so that directors and advisers are generally more familiar with them.

One of the reasons that the London Approach has so far been restricted to very large rescue attempts is that a successful workout can be very costly; a figure of £6 million has been suggested.[61] The costs associated with a workout have caused some concern. Both the Insolvency Service and the Bank of England would like to see a reduction in costs which have been described as excessive. The DTI see the solution to the problem in familiarity with the development of best practice. Kent, however, sees the problem of high costs as resulting from a proliferation of lawyers, accountants and other advisers. He states that "fees and costs are never too low; they are always too high."[62] The legal, administrative and advisory fees associated with a workout are termed the *direct* costs. A rescue attempt also incurs *indirect* costs, which have been defined as "opportunity costs imposed on the firm because financial distress affects its ability to conduct business as usual."[63] Three types of indirect costs have been identified by Wruck.[64] First, if a legal rescue procedure is used, the firm usually loses the right to make some decisions without legal approval; this is a "cost" that does not arise in an informal workout. Second, financial distress can reduce demand for the firm's product and increase its production costs. Demand may fall if custom depends on expectations of the firm's survival; for instance sophisticated machinery may only be purchased if the expectation is that the manufacturer will survive to service and repair

---

[61] Flood *et. al.*, p. ii.
[62] Kent, *op. cit.*, at 113.
[63] Wruck, *op. cit.*, at 437.
[64] *ibid*.

it. Production costs may rise if financial distress affects the firm's ability to negotiate input prices and credit terms with suppliers. This is where a *private* workout is thought to be less costly. The third area of indirect costs is management time spent resolving financial distress. However, the definition of indirect costs as "opportunity costs" needs to be remembered in this context. Management time spent on a productive restructuring of the firm's debt, perhaps accompanied by appropriate strategic changes, may be time well spent. The value of management time should only be considered to be an indirect cost to the extent that it could have been spent more productively elsewhere. In the United Kingdom empirical evidence on the size of direct costs is not readily available. Some empirical studies have been carried out in the United States where more information is put "on the record." Estimating the size of the indirect costs of financial distress is difficult because they represent lost opportunities. However, it is believed that indirect costs are generally lower for workouts than for rescues under legal rescue regimes. Lower indirect costs provide one explanation for the occurrence of informal restructuring.

OUT-OF-COURT RESTRUCTURING IN THE UNITED STATES

Empirical studies of the restructuring of distressed companies in the United States contribute to a general understanding of the potential advantages and disadvantages of out-of-court arrangements. These studies are of public companies; this means large companies with publicly traded debt. In the United Kingdom the London Approach may have been appropriate for the informal restructuring of such companies. In the United States there are currently three ways in which a restructuring can be achieved. First the company can make an out-of-court exchange offer which is a private recontracting of the debt. This can be a debt for debt exchange offer or an offer in which a combination of debt and equity is offered for debt. Second, the restructuring can be proposed under Chapter 11. Third, the restructuring can be a "prepackaged" Chapter 11 or "prepack". A prepack is a hybrid of Chapter 11 and private renegotiation in which the company negotiates a reorganisation plan with its creditors and possibly solicits acceptances of the plan prior to filing for bankruptcy under Chapter 11. The company then files for Chapter 11 and simultaneously files a plan of reorganisation. Because of the advance negotiation with creditors, a confirmation hearing can be scheduled quickly, leading to a quick exit from bankruptcy. Betker cites the fastest prepack case as one in which the reorganisation plan was confirmed just 29 days after the Chapter 11 filing.[65]

Table 7.1—Restructuring of Public Firms in the United States

Year	Traditional Chapter 11 Filings by Public Firms	Distressed Exchange Offers for Public Debt	Prepackaged Chapter 11 Filings.
1986	148	10	1
1987	112	15	0
1988	121	17	1
1989	132	15	3
1990	113	25	5
1991	120	25	10
1992	78	16	17
1993	71	12	20

Source: Betker, "An Empirical Examination of Prepackaged Bankruptcy" (1995) 24 *Financial Management* 4.

Table 7.1 shows the numbers of distressed public company restructurings in the three different categories from 1986 to 1993. Over the period there were a total of 135 informal arrangements achieved by exchange offers. Over a similar period a total of 150 London Approach workouts were accomplished in the United Kingdom.[66] The trends in the United States have been for the increasing use of out-of-court restructuring in the late 1980s followed by the increasing use of prepacks in the early 1990s. Several U.S. studies have investigated the costs of the three approaches; however, some caution is required when interpreting the results of this work. Tashjian, Lease and McConnell state:

"On most measures considered, prepacks lie between out-of-court restructurings and traditional Chapter 11 reorganizations. Accordingly, it is tempting to conclude that a prepack is a more efficient mechanism for

---

[65] Betker, "An Empirical Examination of Prepackaged Bankruptcy" (1995) 24 *Financial Management* 3.
[66] Flood *et. al.*, p. ii.

resolving financial distress than a traditional Chapter 11 reorganization, but less efficient than out-of-court restructuring. Unfortunately, because the firms in our sample have *chosen* to reorganize by means of a prepack (presumably because that represents the most efficient form of reorganization for the firm), that conclusion is unwarranted. Thus, our study, like those that precede it, is unable to resolve the question of whether one form of reorganization is more efficient than another."[67]

The problem with the empirical work is that it is not possible to know whether it is the companies whose restructuring costs would be low in any event that chose to restructure via a workout, or the choice of a workout as the restructuring mechanism that reduces the costs. Betker's study of 49 U.S. prepacks suggests that workouts would be chosen by more companies if they were achievable. Many of the prepacks he studied were "pre-voted," that is the creditors voted for the proposals before the (concurrent) filing of the bankruptcy petition and the plan of reorganization. In 11 cases the company asked the creditors to vote on two issues: would they accept an exchange offer, and would they accept the prepackaged reorganisation plan. The first choice for the company would be a workout via an exchange offer, but this is subject to the holdout problem. In these 11 cases the exchange offer failed to gain sufficient support, but the prepack, which is only subject to the majority voting rules of Chapter 11, took place. Prepacks are thought to have two main advantages over workouts: first they avoid the holdout problem, as just described; and second, a reorganisation under Chapter 11 used to have two tax advantages not available in an informal workout. First, if a firm reorganises out of court, forgiven debt counts as taxable income of the company under the tax code. If creditors forgive the same debt in Chapter 11, it does not count as taxable income. This advantage still exists, but Betker calculated that none of the 49 companies he studied would have had to have paid tax on cancellation of indebtedness income had their prepacks been completed as workouts instead. The second tax advantage of a Chapter 11 filing was that it allowed a more flexible use of net operating losses. Betker estimated the present value of future tax savings from the less restrictive use of net operating losses to be relatively large: on average 3 per cent of the company's assets. However, the "stock-for-debt exception," which was the basis for this advantage, was repealed as

---

[67] Tashjian, Lease and McConnell, "Prepacks: An Empirical Analysis of Prepackaged Bankruptices" (1996) 40 *Journal of Financial Economics* 137.

from January 1, 1995.[68] The disadvantages of a Chapter 11 filing are minimised in a prepack first by reducing the time in Chapter 11 to a minimum and, secondly, by reducing the disruptions to normal business during the short period in Chapter 11.

Another factor that could have encouraged the use of prepacks in the early 1990s was the decision in the LVT case, a decision which meant that a workout followed by a Chapter 11 filing would in most cases mean a loss to bondholders. In the LVT case it was decided that once a firm completed a debt-for-debt exchange offer (*i.e.* a workout), in a subsequent bankruptcy (Chapter 11 filing), bondholders had a claim equal to the market value of the new debt, not the face value of the old debt. Since the new debt in most distressed exchanges sells for less than par, bondholders fearing a subsequent Chapter 11 filing would be reluctant to give up their old claims. The decision was overturned in 1992, but in the opinion of bankruptcy specialists there remains some uncertainty on the issue.[69]

The U.S. empirical work also provides evidence about the contents of informal workouts. Gilson, John and Lang report on the use of the following restructuring terms: extension of maturity (used in 48 per cent of restructurings); reduction of interest or principal (used in 73 per cent of restructurings); and distribution of equity securities (used on average in 74 per cent of restructurings). They also distinguish restructurings of publicly traded debt and bank debt. They state:

> "Although 51.4% of bank restructurings resulted in bank lenders receiving equity in the firm, holders of publicly traded debt are given equity securities 86.7% of the time. The latter difference is a likely consequence of various legal and regulatory factors that make it prohibitively costly for banks to hold large amounts of equity in publicly traded companies."[70]

In conclusion, the U.S. experience of informal arrangements with the creditors of large companies indicates that while out-of-court restructurings may be less costly than Chapter 11, the problem of one creditor holding out for a better deal remains significant. Prepacks are one solution to the holdout problem and their use has increased in the United States in the early 1990s. It has been found

---

[68] See Betker, *op. cit.,* for a more detailed explanation of the U.S. tax position.
[69] *ibid.* at 8.
[70] Gilson *et. al.,* (1990) *op. cit.,* at 333. See this reference for details of the various legal and regulatory factors.

that private renegotiation of debt is more likely to succeed when more debt is owed to banks and less likely to succeed when there are more distinct classes of debt outstanding,[71] and these conclusions fit with the experience of the London Approach.

SMALL-SCALE INFORMAL FINANCING ARRANGEMENTS FOR U.K. COMPANIES

Small companies are important to the U.K. economy. They make a significant contribution to the Gross National Product, and they are said to generate jobs and to be important inventors and innovators.[72] At the end of 1993 small firms (including those without employees) accounted for 50 per cent of non-government employment and 40 per cent of U.K. turnover, that is value of sales, work done and services rendered, excluding VAT. Large business (3,000 in number) accounted for 37 per cent of employment and 41 per cent of turnover. These figures are taken from statistics collected on the Inter-Departmental Business Register (IDBR), which is a relatively new register administered by the National Office for Statistics, holding records of all enterprises registered for VAT and all enterprises operating a PAYE scheme. Table 7.2 sets out these statistics. Of course, many of the enterprises on the IDBR are not companies, but the small and medium-sized enterprises included 600,000 companies at the end of 1993. This means that about 18 per cent of the small and medium-sized enterprises, by number, are companies.

Small firms are not only important, they are of growing importance. Dunne and Hughes state: "Economy-wide estimates of the size distribution of businesses by turnover or employment point . . . unambiguously to an expanding role for the smallest businesses in the 1980s."[73] They also state: "Our international comparison shows that the U.K. trends we have described are part of a general upward drift since the 1970s in the share of small enterprises and establishments in the European economies."[74]

---

[71] *ibid.* at 316.

[72] See Storey (ed.), *The Small Firm: An International Survey* (1983), p. 23, for discussion of this point; it is stated that "[s]mall firms have a striking record of innovation."

[73] Dunne and Hughes, "The Changing Structure of Competitive Industry in the 1980s" in Driver and Dunne (eds.), *Structural Change in the U.K. Economy* (1992), p. 113.

[74] *ibid.* p. 114.

Table 7.2—Contribution of Small, Medium and Large Enterprises to the U.K. Economy at the End of 1993

	Small Enterprises	Medium-sized Enterprises	Small and Medium-sized Enterprises	Large Enterprises
Employment:	50%	13%	63%	37%
Turnover:	40%	19%	59%	41%

Small is defined as having 0–99 employees.
Medium-sized is defined as having 100–499 employees.
Large is defined as having 500 employees or more.

Source: Calculated from DTI statistics presented in Dale and Kerr, "Small and Mediuum-sized Enterprises: Their Numbers and Importance to Employment" [1995] *Labour Market Trends* 451.

Assessing the contribution of small companies is not, however, a simple matter. Behind the general conclusions of the economists lie several complications: First, there are over 40 different definitions used by government of a small firm in the United Kingdom alone.[75] Under section 247 of the Companies Act 1985 a company is a small company if it satisfies at least two of the following criteria:

(1) Turnover not more than £2.8million

(2) Balance sheet total not more than £1.4million

(3) Number of employees not more than 50.

Many of the companies that are labelled "small" in the DTI statistics will not qualify as small under section 247 of the Companies Act 1985. Secondly, the statistics showing a substantial growth in the number of small firms in the United Kingdom over the last 25 years need careful interpretation because some of the increase arises through improved data collection.[76] Thirdly, as Dunne and Hughes point out, the longer-run dynamics of the increasing share of smaller

---

[75] Cross, "Small firms in the United Kingdom" in Storey (ed.), *The Small Firm: An International Survey* (1983).

[76] See Dunne and Hughes, "The Changing Structure of Competitive Industry in the 1980s" in Driver and Dunne (eds.), *Structural Change in the U.K. Economy* (1992).

firms have yet to be worked out. We do not yet know the degree to which the small business structures which have been created are dependent upon the strategic behaviour of larger industrial and service sector businesses for their future growth and development.[77] Finally, Brown, Hamilton and Medoff argue that enthusiasm for small firms as the creators of jobs is misplaced because jobs in small firms offer lower wages, less benefits, poorer working conditions and less job security than jobs in large firms.[78] Whilst acknowledging these difficulties, it is submitted that there is sufficient evidence for the claim that small companies play an important role in the economy.

There is also evidence that large numbers of small firms fail. Reid conducted a longitudinal study of small entrepreneurial firms in Scotland and reported that of the 73 firms he started with, 54 were still in business three years later: a staying in business estimate of 74 per cent over a three-year period[79]; a failure rate of 26 per cent. A yardstick for small firm survival over a three-year period which is widely quoted is the rate of 60 per cent established by Storey and Johnson[80]; a failure rate of 40 per cent. It has also been estimated that companies with fewer that 15 employees account for over 80 per cent of company insolvencies.[81] A second characteristic of small companies is that they frequently fail. The poor take-up of the CVA has already been noted. In addition to noting the generally small numbers of CVAs taking place, Milman and Chittenden report that plcs are "slightly over represented in the CVA context" and that "[i]n terms of size of company, it as apparent that for very small businesses, say with a turnover of less than £100,000, even a modestly priced CVA may be too expensive to exploit."[82]

There are, then, three key points which relate specifically to small companies: they are important in the economy; they fail very frequently, and the CVA has not proved successful in rescuing them. For very large companies the London Approach has been developed as an alternative, informal way of rescuing viable businesses. As far as

---

[77] Dunne and Hughes, *op. cit.*, pp. 113–114.

[78] Brown, Hamilton and Medoff, *Employers Large and Small* (1990).

[79] Reid, "Staying in Business" (1991) 9 *International Journal of Industrial Organization* 551.

[80] Storey and Johnson, *Are Small Firms the Answer to Unemployment?* (1987). This yardstick and the results of some other studies are discussed further in Reid, *op. cit.*

[81] Insolvency Service, *Company Voluntary Arrangements and Administration Orders: A Consultative Document* (1993), para. 1.9.

[82] Milman and Chittenden, *op. cit.*, p. 5.

small companies are concerned informal rescues are usually dependent on the rescheduling of an existing debt contract with an individual bank or the raising of extra finance. Rescheduling is discussed briefly below. The raising of extra finance is then considered. Three potential sources of finance are discussed: banks, venture capitalists and business angels. Three major contrasts which are drawn in this discussion are between loans and overdraft facilities; between debt and equity capital; and between larger and smaller capital requirements. The financing of small firms in general is a huge topic and it is only considered here in so far as it can be part of a rescue operation. Storey provides an excellent summary of the theoretical and empirical work on the financing of small firms.[83]

Rescheduling

A technical breach of a loan agreement will usually give the lender the power to appoint a receiver. In the context of U.K. small firms Cressy states:

> "Although, hard empirical data on rescheduling of bank loans to small firms is difficult to come by, banks are often quoted as saying that they prefer, other things [being] equal, not to have to call in the receiver under loan default. Negotiations thus often take place after the firm has technically breached the conditions of the loan in the form of attempts at debt rescheduling."[84]

Debt rescheduling allows the company to survive for the time being by reducing its debt servicing obligations in terms of reduced capital repayments and/or interest charges. There is no direct injection of finance. The crucial point about a rescheduling decision is that the bank as a secured creditor has the power, not only to say "no" to the company's requests for help, but also to precipitate the company's demise. Decision making by a failing company's secured creditors is examined in more detail in the next chapter.

Extra Finance from Banks

Banks can and do rescue small companies by offering extra finance at times of crisis. Rescues by banks are sometimes referred to as "bank

---

[83] Storey, *Understanding the Small Business Sector* (1994), Chap. 7.
[84] Cressy, *Small Firm Insolvency: The Bank's Decision Problem* (Warwick Business School Research Papers, 1991), p. 4.

rescues" and the bank providing the extra finance is usually already a major creditor of the company. Bank lending to small companies rose sharply during the 1980s. At the time of the Bolton Committee report (1971)[85] term loans to small firms were almost unheard of. Since then there has been a fairly continuous growth of importance of term loans to small businesses, and a lower dependence on overdrafts. However, in May 1991 only 30 per cent of National Westminster Bank's total lending to small firms was in the form of term loans,[86] and many small companies are financed by overdrafts.[87] Bank overdrafts are repayable on demand and so an increased overdraft facility may save the company but will also make it more dependent on the bank's willingness to continue to extend the facility. Loans may be made subject to covenants which, if broken, cause the loan to be repayable immediately, but problems with loans are more likely to occur at the end of the fixed term when re-financing may be sought. If new money is offered, a bank *may* be able to obtain additional security at the expense of little additional risk, but this is subject to the provisions of the Insolvency Act 1986 under which transactions at undervalue, preferences and extortionate credit transactions may be set aside.[88]

A rescue attempt will only be worthwhile and attract extra finance if there is a core business which is likely to survive and thrive. The strategic components of rescues are discussed in Chapter 2 where it is suggested that the concept of rescue should include strategic as well as financial restructuring. If a business which is in difficulties can demonstrate that it has a feasible strategy for survival it is more likely to be able to raise the extra finance it needs. However, raising extra finance from a bank will mean increasing the debt/equity ratio. Reid, Jacobsen and Anderson state that good competitive strategy means, among other things "a prudent use of debt finance for proper purposes of growth and development (*e.g.* purchase of new plant) rather than for 'putting out fires' (*e.g.* solving cash-flow crises)."[89] Empirical work on bank lending decisions concentrates on loans

---

[85] Bolton, *Report of the Committee of Inquiry on Small Firms*, Cmnd. 4871 (1971).
[86] Bannock and Doran, *Venture Capital and the Equity Gap* (1991).
[87] Berry, Crum and Waring, *Corporate Performance Evaluation and Bank Lending Decisions* (1993).
[88] s.238–244 of the Insolvency Act 1986.
[89] Reid, Jacobsen and Anderson, *Profiles in Small Business: A Competitive Strategy Approach* (1993), p. 177. This conclusion was reached in the context of in depth case studies of small firms.

requested for specific projects such as the start of a new business, the purchase of a particular piece of equipment or the expansion of an existing business. The factors that generally feed into bank lending decisions have been investigated by several researchers. Innes (1990) reported that, in a postal survey of bankers employed by three Scottish joint-stock banks, 89 per cent of respondents *always* assessed the management of the company when making a corporate lending decision.[90] For a small, financially distressed company to obtain a bank loan it is clearly important to be able to demonstrate management competence. Berry, Crum and Waring found that bank lending officers with authority to make lending decisions, within limits, were often doing so in a relatively unsophisticated way and that the institutional image of the loan evaluation process differed substantially from the reality.[91]

A bank rescue will only be possible if the company's management can demonstrate that they are competent, that they have a core business with some potential, that they have a sound strategy for the future, that the change in gearing ratio will not itself cause problems, and that they will not simply be "putting out fires." It must also be remembered that, although distressed companies may approach their bank[92] looking for a rescue package, it is often the situation that the bank as the secured lender is the creditor threatening to take action.[93]

Venture Capital

Problems of high gearing and the associated high debt servicing obligations can be avoided by raising equity rather than debt capital. Small companies are not able to raise equity on a securities market, but may be able to obtain "informal investment" in the form of either venture capital (larger amounts) or an investment by an individual business angel (smaller amounts).[94] Business angels are

---

[90] Innes, "External Management Auditing of Companies: A Survey of Bankers" (1990) 3 *Accounting, Auditing and Accountability* 18.

[91] Berry, Crum and Waring, *op. cit.*, at 80.

[92] In practice it will be *their* bank: ". . . small business customers . . . do not have a choice of bank. This is because the occasion on which firms most want to move banks is when they have been denied credit facilites. Yet this is precisely the time when the business is in most difficulties and will look least attractive to an alternative banker." Storey (1992), *op. cit.*, p. 236.

[93] See the brief treatment of rescheduling above and Chap. 8 for further discussion of the powers of secured creditors.

[94] Sometimes the term "informal investment" is used to cover investment by venture capitalists and business angels, as here. Sometimes it is used to describe the activities of business angels as opposed to venture capitalists.

discussed in more detail below. The raising of venture capital will only be a possibility for the larger "small companies," as it is equity capital in fairly large amounts (in practice over £400,000). It has been defined as "long-term capital which is invested in high risk ventures, typically new companies and especially new technologies, which offer the possibility of gains to compensate for the risks involved in such investments."[95] Its special features are that it is capital provided for entrepreneurs, it is sometimes accompanied by the provision of business skills,[96] the venture capitalist will usually want a significant equity stake,[97] the venture capitalist will want a seat on the board, and the venture capitalist will be seeking a capital gain rather than income from dividends[98] and so will be looking for a suitable exit route after about five years.[99] In the United Kingdom the amount invested by venture capitalists grew rapidly during the 1980s, fell slightly in 1990 and 1991, but has since increased again. In 1993 total venture capital investment was £1,422 million.[1]

Venture capital is of particular interest in the context of corporate rescue as a source of finance for management buy-outs. Storey reported that in 1991, 55 per cent of the total sum invested by venture capitalists in the United Kingdom was in management buy-outs; in 1989 it was 53 per cent and in 1990 it was 61 per cent.[2] In a sample taken in 1992–1993 Mitchell, Reid and Terry found 40 per cent of venture capital investment to be in buy-outs.[3] Venture capitalist investors accept only about 3 per cent of all proposals made to them each year. Points that have already been made in relation to bank finance will apply to applications for venture capital: the company's management must be able to demonstrate that they are competent, that they have a core business with some potential, that they have a sound strategy for the future. In addition, for venture capital investment the proposal may need something that is specifi-

---

[95] Reid, "Fast Growing Small Entrepreneurial Firms and their Venture Capital Backers: An Applied Principal-Agent Analysis (1994)" University of St Andrews, C.R.I.E.F.F. discussion paper No. 9421, at 3.

[96] Dixon, "Venture Capitalists and the Appraisal of Investments" (1991) 19 *Omega* 333.

[97] Stakes between 6 per cent and 57 per cent have been reported; see Mitchell, Reid and Terry, "Post Investment Demand for Accounting Information by Venture Capitalists" (1994) University of St Andrews C.R.I.E.F.F. discussion paper No. 9424 at 10.

[98] Dixon, *op. cit.*

[99] Mitchell, Reid and Terry, *op. cit.*, at 10.

[1] *ibid.* at 5.

[2] Storey (1992), *op. cit.*, p. 222.

[3] Mitchell, Reid and Terry, *op. cit.*, at 10.

cally attractive; this may be an opportunity to contribute particular business skills or that the nature of the business itself fits well with the interests of venture capital investors, *e.g.* a business based on a new technology. Timing is important in the raising of venture capital, as it takes about 15 weeks from the submission of a proposal to a potential investor to the completion of the investment.[4] In the context of a company rescue, the search for a potential investor will have to be conducted expeditiously and success may depend on obtaining good advice very quickly. The longest-established U.K. body that promotes informal investment is the Venture Capital Report (VCR), which publishes a monthly magazine as well as an annual directory of sources of venture capital.

Business Angels

"Business angels" are another potential source of finance for small businesses. Business angels are private individuals willing to make equity investments in young independent businesses. In the United States business angels invest four times as much as the venture capital industry, support ten times as many businesses and are one of the first options for an entrepreneur seeking external capital. In the United Kingdom business angels are less well established as a source of finance, and there are currently a number of private and quasi-public initiatives which exist to promote informal investment by linking angels with investment opportunities. The biggest initiative in Scotland is LINC, the Local Investment Networking Company, which is a non-profit-making scheme run through local enterprise agencies and sponsored by Scottish Enterprise, the European Commission's European Regional Development Fund and various private sector bodies. LINC operates a database to link angels and potential investors in return for a small subscription fee. Corporate rescue is not the objective of organisations that promote informal investment. Their objective is to link business angels with appropriate investment opportunities, which are usually in new and growing companies. However, accountants specialising in turnaround work sometimes use such agencies, and informal investment may thus be part of a rescue package for a small company or a small part of a larger concern.

---

[4] *ibid*, at 10.

Business angels are individuals who have surplus funds often coupled with a desire to take an active part in a business. LINC's literature on informal investment in Scotland states:

> "Most angels are successful entrepreneurs: a smaller proportion are senior managers from larger companies. They are predominantly male, and aged between 40 and 55. They are not over-wealthy and few are millionaires. They will invest in relatively small amounts . . . the average investment is around £35,000 although a small number of deals are of £250,000 or more . . . Angels tend to invest in industries in which they have direct experience and in companies to which they feel they can add value. Personal empathy with the company owners is vital."

A rescue financed by informal investment will only be a possibility if there is a good match between a business angel's preferred type of investment and the investment opportunity presented by the business seeking to be rescued. As the amount of informal investment increases in the United Kingdom the chances of businesses finding suitable and willing angels should also increase.

6. Conclusion

This chapter has covered a wide range of ways in which arrangements can be made with creditors, including the making of compromises and the raising of extra finance. Creditors' schemes of arrangement under section 425 of the Companies Act 1985 are extremely rare, but a brief explanation of these provisions has been included for completeness. The company voluntary arrangement under sections 1–7 of the Insolvency Act 1986 is more frequently employed but has produced a disappointing number of company rescues. A major barrier to the use of CVAs is the lack of enthusiasm on the part of insolvency practitioners. More than ten years after the introduction of this new rescue mechanism many IPs remain unfamiliar with its operation and only a small proportion of IPs have conducted CVAs. Another problem with the CVA is the lack of a moratorium on creditors' actions. The proposal for a new 28-day moratorium scheme attempts to solve this problem, but the proposal has been opposed by bankers and may never reach fruition.

The chapter includes a lengthy coverage of informal ways of making arrangements with creditors. In the context of very large companies informal arrangements are important because of their increasing use. They can offer secrecy and, possibly, lower costs. In the context of very small companies informal arrangements are important because a CVA may be too expensive to be considered. Discussion of informal arrangements does not, however, mean that the law is unimportant, as all informal arrangements are made in the shadow of insolvency law and are therefore ultimately shaped by it. For a successful rescue to be accomplished the company needs sufficient finance for its future operations and this often means obtaining new finance. Sources of finance have therefore been included as a part of making arrangements with creditors for the future of the company.

The rescue procedures discussed in this chapter can all be initiated by the directors of the company. As indicated in the discussion of CVAs and the proposals for change, the ability of the directors to both initiate and carry through a rescue attempt is limited by the power of secured creditors who often make the crucial decisions concerning a distressed company's future. The power of secured creditors is the subject of the next chapter.

Chapter 8

Decision Making by Secured Creditors

1. Introduction

The way in which secured creditors can influence the path of a rescue attempt is investigated in this chapter. The discussion here focuses on the formal rescue regimes available under U.K. law. Before the reform of insolvency law in 1985 following the Cork Report, receivership was a formal procedure which *may* have been a vehicle for corporate rescue, but rescue activity was very unusual. The reforms were intended to encourage more rescue attempts, but the new procedures left a great deal of power with the secured creditors. The need for further reforms has been acknowledged in the mid 1990s. One proposal is the 28-day moratorium scheme, described in the previous chapter, which shifts the balance of power away from the secured creditors. The arrangements with creditors which have been described in Chapter 7 can be initiated by the directors and accomplished without the directors surrendering their power to run the company (whether they involve compromises with creditors or the refinancing of the company). However, all these arrangements must be made in the shadow of insolvency law, and insolvency law in the United Kingdom is currently heavily creditor-based.

The starting point for the discussion which follows is the scenario of a distressed company with secured creditors. The position of the secured creditors will depend to some extent on the particular creditors' bargain that has been struck. Insolvency law also has an impact on the position of such creditors. Creditor-based insolvency regimes place more emphasis on enforcing the creditors' bargain, whereas debtor-based regimes place greater emphasis on maintaining the company as a going concern by suspending creditors' rights.

Under a debtor-based regime creditors are often forced to accept less than they bargained for. The U.S. regime,[1] by offering entry into Chapter 11 to the company as a right, allows the company to make the crucial decisions regarding insolvency. The U.K. regime,[2] on the other hand, is one in which the secured creditors can make the crucial decisions. In the next section the creditors' bargain is considered. Sections 3, 4, 5 and 7 of the chapter then cover four possibilities which the secured creditors have control over: the decision to reschedule the debt; the decision to appoint a receiver; the decision to appoint an administrative receiver; and the decision to allow an administration order to be made by not exercising the option to appoint an administrative receiver. In section 6 there is a brief explanation of receivership in Scotland.

2. The Creditors' Bargain

When a company raises finance a bargain is struck. The best way of illustrating the sort of bargain that creditors often make is by listing main conditions of a typical debenture trust deed. First it should be noted that risk and return are related; in general, investors will accept lower returns on less risky investments and expect higher returns if they accept more risk.[3] Investing in equity (shares) is riskier than investing in debt (debentures).

The contents of a typical debenture trust deed are as follows.[4]

(1) The security for the debt. This will recite the properties charged in the case of a mortgage or, where the charge is "floating," state what is covered—usually the whole of the undertaking, property and assets of the borrowing company together with those of some or all of its U.K. subsidiaries. Where a business has adopted a group structure, the main assets of the group are often held by the operating subsidiaries, not the parent company. A debenture stock issued by a parent company with a floating charge only on its own

---

[1] A debtor-based regime.
[2] A more creditor-based regime.
[3] For theories linking risk and return, see Brealey and Myers, *Principles of Corporate Finance* (5th ed., 1996), Chap. 8.
[4] For further details on debt securities more generally, see Frost and Hager, *Debt Securities* (1990).

assets would then be unsatisfactory, as the charge would apply to the shares in the subsidiaries and not the assets owned by the subsidiaries. In a modern trust deed the debenture is therefore secured on the assets of a "charging group" of companies. The assets and profits of the charging group can then be employed in the application of all the rules of the trust deed.

(2)   Payment of interest. The deed will state the amount due and the due dates of payment.

(3)   Redemption. The date of repayment will be stated and if there is an option to redeem earlier, possible dates will be given and the notice required will be specified (usually three months).

(4)   Restrictions and requirements. Many types of restriction have been thought of to protect the debenture holder for instance:

- (a) Interest cover—The company's average profits and losses over, say, the past three years must be sufficient to cover the interest on the particular borrowings at least, say, four times.

- (b) Earlier maturity—The company could be prohibited from raising other debt finance, except in the form of bank borrowing, with a maturity date earlier than that specified in this debenture.

- (c) Overborrowing—The company's overall borrowing could be limited to one and a half times the shareholders' capital and reserves.

- (d) Prior ranking debt—There may be a power to raise prior ranking debt but only with the consent of the trustee and only for the purpose of acquiring further assets. Thus the asset and income cover already specified will remain unimpaired.

- (e) Redemption of share capital prohibited—The borrowing company will be forbidden to redeem or pay off any of its share capital. This will also apply to the share capital of subsidiaries in the charging group.

(5)   Power to supervise transactions in the assets of the company. A typical "Tickler" clause would read: "The company may not, except with

139

the consent of the trustee, sell, transfer, lend or otherwise dispose of the whole or any part of its undertaking or, except in the normal course of trading, its assets whether by a single transaction or a series of transactions, nor may the company make any significant alterations in the nature of the business." This clause protects the creditors from changes that may affect the security behind the company's borrowing. It also means that a rescue attempt (being a major intervention) may require the consent of the trustee, although the clause is usually subject to various provisos about not hampering the development of the company's business.

(6) Provision for the debenture stockholders to modify their rights by extraordinary resolution. Lenders cannot make the terms more stringent without the consent of the company. The power to make the terms less stringent, however, permits the rescheduling of the debt.

(7) Provisions for the realisation of the security. Mortgages, charges and debentures under the company's seal or executed so as to take effect as a deed contain statutory powers implied under the Law of Property Act 1925. These are the power to sell the company's property which is subject to the mortgage or charge and the power to appoint a receiver of the income of such property. However, these powers cannot be exercised to enable debenture holders to realise their security in all situations where there is a risk of the security deteriorating or being dissipated.[5] The trust deed will therefore contain express provisions for the realisation of the security which are much wider than the statutory powers. Typical events entitling the debenture holder to appoint a receiver are:

(a) Failure to meet a demand to pay principal or interest which is justified by the terms of the debenture. This covers breaches of (2) and (3) above.

(b) Failure by the company to perform any of its obligations or observe any of the restrictions placed on it by the debenture. This covers breaches of (4) and (5) above.

---

[5] Under the Law of Property Act 1925 the powers to sell company assets or to appoint a receiver can only be exercised if the principal of the debt secured by the mortgage or charge is due and has remained unpaid for three months after a written demand for its payment has been made on the company, or if interest on the debt is in arrears and unpaid for two months, or if the company has broken some other obligation imposed on it by the mortgage on debentures.

(c) The presentation of a petition for administration or the initiation of a CVA.

(d) The presentation of a winding up petition or the passing of a resolution to liquidate the company voluntarily.

(e) The levying of distress or execution against the company's assets.

Events covered by (a) and (b) are breaches of the terms of the particular bargain struck by the creditors. The events specified in (c), (d) and (e) are more general indicators of a company's poor financial health.

Having established the general nature of the creditors' bargain, two main points can be made. First, the law both adds to and influences the bargain. Second, the bargain made when the finance is raised is important in determining the bargaining power of the creditors when a rescue is being attempted.

3. The Decision to Reschedule Debt

In Chapter 7 it is suggested that the directors of a financially distressed company may be able to effect its rescue by negotiating the rescheduling of a loan. In most circumstances where the company seeks a rescheduling there will have been a breach of a loan covenant giving the creditor the right to appoint a receiver. The negotiation of a rescheduling is therefore dependent upon the forbearance of the secured creditors and the decision-making power lies with the creditors, although the directors will obviously seek to influence the decision.

At this point the creditors have various options: they can agree to reschedule their debt; they can appoint a receiver or administrative receiver, whichever is appropriate; they can agree to an initial, voluntary short-term moratorium while an arrangement is agreed with all the company's creditors[6]; if administration is proposed as a method of rescuing the company, they can forbear to appoint an administrative receiver, thus giving their go-ahead for the administration order. There are a few theoretical models that are relevant to the

---

[6] As described more fully in Chap. 7.

creditors' decision. Two types of models can be distinguished: those, that employ a game-theoretic approach to a "bankruptcy" decision which is being made by the firm's creditors and the company itself acting in coalition, and those where the decision is being taken by the firm's major creditor acting alone and with little or no reference to the shareholders. Cressy[7] has argued that a coalition model may be appropriate in the context of very large firms; their premises certainly fit well with the empirical reality of the London Approach. However, a coalition model is not suitable in the context of small firms. Cressy's own model is concerned with the conditions under which a creditor will choose to reschedule the loan rather than to appoint a receiver and thus precipitate "bankruptcy" or "liquidation."[8] In Cressy's model firms with higher asset values and lower bankruptcy costs will receive larger loans in the first place. However, these firms have a smaller chance of having their debt rescheduled " since they are relatively more valuable dead than alive." Another outcome of Cressy's model is that higher expected earnings increase the proba- bility of the debt being rescheduled. This may be the most useful part of the model, as it reveals how the company's directors may by able to influence the creditors' decision. For the directors to be in a position to request a rescheduling of the debt, they need to have a credible plan of the firm's future. A plan with higher expected earnings (which are credible) may influence the decision in favour of a rescheduling of the debt.

4. Receivers

When considering receivers, various distinctions can be made. A receiver can be appointed by the court or under the terms (express or implied) of the mortgage or debenture; and, since 1985, receivers have been designated as "administrative receivers" or plain "receivers." Both these distinctions have implications for the conduct of the receivership. Administrative receivers were first created by the

---

[7] Cressy, *Small Firm Debt Rescheduling Versus Insolvency: The Bank's Decision Problem*, SME Centre, Warwick Business School.

[8] There are some problems relating to the terminology employed in these models. Cressy assumes that appointing a receiver precipitates "bankruptcy" and uses "bankruptcy" as synonymous with "liquidation". U.S. models of the "bankruptcy" decision sometimes use "bankruptcy" to mean Chapter 11, as an alternative to "liquidation."

Insolvency Act 1985 and given new powers and responsibilities with a view to facilitating more corporate rescues. The provisions concerning administrative receivers are now to be found in the Insolvency Act 1986.

The appointment of a receiver by the Court of Chancery was an ancient equitable remedy available to creditors. The power of the court (all divisions of the High Court) to appoint a receiver is now to be found in the Supreme Court Act 1981.[9] The power is given for the purposes of putting property into safe hands until the rights of interested parties are determined, and the remedy is available to all creditors both secured and unsecured. Receivers appointed by the court are extremely rare. If there is a power to appoint without the assistance of the court it will be used. Most situations where the appointment of a receiver would be an appropriate remedy are now covered by express provisions of the sort illustrated in section 2 above or by terms implied under the Law of Property Act 1925, or both. Receivers appointed by the court are under the directions of the court and are appointed to act impartially in the interests of all parties. Receivers appointed under the terms of a debenture are appointed with a primary duty to realise the secured assets in the interests of the debenture holders.

Turning now to the second distinction, that between administrative receivers and ordinary receivers, as the category "administrative receiver" was designed to encourage corporate rescue it is fair to assume that ordinary receiverships were not producing many rescues. Indeed, the assumption made in Cressy's model of the rescheduling decision, that receivership inevitably leads to liquidation, came close to the truth. Pennington describes a corporate recovery whilst in receivership as "exceptional."[10] There were two major problems with receiverships as a vehicle for corporate rescue. First, receivers appointed under a debenture are appointed to act in the interests of the debenture holders, not the company as a whole. Second, receivers appointed under a debenture had, until administrative receivership was invented in 1985, to look to the debenture itself for their powers. If the implied terms of the Law of Property Act 1925 had to be relied upon, the powers of the receiver were limited to the receiving of income from the relevant property and the sale of the property. From the point of view of the secured creditor, these two powers are

---

[9] s.37.
[10] Pennington, *Pennington's Corporate Insolvency Law* (1991), p. 427.

adequate to achieve the return of their capital and accrued interest.[11] From the point of view of a potential rescue, where the eventual emergence of a going concern can depend crucially on keeping going through the crisis, these two powers are inadequate.

Receivers who do not come under the definition of an administrative receiver, that is ordinary receivers, still have to look to the debenture for their powers. Most of these ordinary receivers will be appointed under the terms of a fixed charge only. Their job will be simply to sell the particular security, and if, as is likely, this is the company's land and buildings the continuation of the company's business as a going concern becomes difficult. The situation is complicated only by the fact that it is standard practice for the debenture to provide that the receiver will act as the company's agent. However, "the agency is a legal fiction the purpose of which is to insulate the debenture holder from any contractual liabilities incurred and the consequences of any wrongful acts committed by the receiver."[12] There is no obligation for the receiver to obey the company as principal, but there may be a duty not to injure the principal's interests by failing to tales reasonable care. Cases on this point include *Standard Chartered Bank v. Walker*,[13] where the duty was expressed as "a duty to use reasonable care to obtain the best possible price which the circumstances of the case permit"; *Cuckmere Brick Co. Ltd v. Mutual Finance Ltd*,[14] where the receiver's duty was to take reasonable care to obtain the proper or true market value on the date of the sale of the assets, but the receiver was held to be free to choose when to sell and was not obliged to wait for the market to rise; *Knight v. Lawrence*,[15] where by failing to serve rent review notices the receiver failed, as custodian of the charged property, to take reasonable care that its value was not diminished; *American Express International Banking Corp. v. Hurley*,[16] where the receiver owed a duty of care to the guarantors of the company's debt; and *Lathia v. Dronsfield Bros Ltd*,[17] where it was held that the receiver owed no duty of care to the ordinary creditors of the company. In two fairly recent cases, *China and South Sea Bank Ltd v. Tan Soon Gin*[18] and *Downsview*

---

[11] Providing the assets sold by the receiver command a high enough price.
[12] Milman and Durrant *Corporate Insolvency: Law and Practice* (2nd ed., 1994).
[13] [1982] 3 All E.R. 938; [1982] 1 W.L.R. 1410.
[14] [1971] Ch. 949; [1971] 2 All E.R. 633.
[15] [1991] B.C.C. 41.
[16] [1985] 3 All E.R. 564.
[17] [1987] B.C.L.C. 321.
[18] [1990] 1 A.C. 536.

Nominees Ltd v. First City Corporation Ltd,[19] it has been confirmed that the duties owed by receivers are governed by the principles of equity rather than negligence, the basic equitable obligation being for the receiver to act in good faith. It is not yet clear how the earlier cases cited above which were based on claims of negligence will be treated by the courts in the future. What is clear is the basic principle that the receiver's primary duty is to realise the assets in the interests of the debenture holders.

The situation regarding receivers can now be summarised. Receivers appointed by the court are rare. Receivers appointed without the assistance of the court are of two types: "administrative receivers" and plain "receivers." Administrative receivers are discussed in the next section. Ordinary receivers have a primary duty to realise the assets that comprise the security in the interests of the debenture holders. If an event has occurred which, under the terms of the debenture, entitles the debenture holder to appoint a receiver, the decision to appoint or not lies with the debenture holder. The directors can try to influence that decision, and it was suggested in the previous section that credible plans for the company's future which include favourable expected earnings figures may be of assistance. If an "ordinary" receiver is appointed their powers can be limited to the receiving of income from the relevant property and the sale of the property and will be so limited if the appointment is made by virtue of terms implied under the Law of Property Act 1925. Control of the company does not pass to an ordinary receiver and the company's directors remain in office. However, the effect of entering even an "ordinary" receivership may be to precipitate a liquidation. The asset(s) which the receiver is to sell is (are) usually vital to the running of the company's business and the news of the receivership will affect the company's trading relationships with both customers and suppliers. Receivership is a remedy for the secured creditor; it represents the enforcement of the creditor's bargain. It was not designed as a rescue regime and is not concerned with preserving the company or any part of it as a going concern.

5. Administrative Receivers

Administrative receivership was created with a view to seeing more distressed companies emerge as going concerns. An administrative

---

[19] [1993] 2 W.L.R. 86.

receiver is defined as "a receiver or manager of the whole (or substantially the whole) of a company' s property appointed by or on behalf of the holders of any debentures of the company secured by a charge which, as created, was a floating charge, or by such a charge and one or more other securities."[20]

The critical elements in this definition are the floating charge and the receiving or managing of the whole (or substantially the whole) of the company' s property. An administrative receiver will, by definition, be taking charge of the whole (or substantially the whole) of the business, including the company's stock-in-trade. Before the creation of administrative receivers it was possible to appoint a receiver and manager rather than a simple receiver; the business could then be continued (managed) but always with a view to realising the assets in the interests of the debenture holders. Also, before 1985 receivers and managers had to look to the debenture under which they were appointed for their powers. Administrative receivers have been given 23 statutory powers, which are currently to be found in Schedule I of the Insolvency Act 1986.[21] The contents of the debenture under which the administrative receiver is appointed can still, however, be important, as the debenture can override the statutory powers. Section 42(1) of the Insolvency Act 1986 states that an administrative receiver's powers are deemed to include the powers specified in Schedule 1 except in so far as they are inconsistent with any of the provisions of the debentures. If the statutory powers apply, on entering administrative receivership, although the directors remain in office, effective control of the company passes from the directors to the administrative receiver.[22] The 23 powers have been described by Sealy and Milman as covering almost every eventuality.[23] Third parties are protected by section 42(3), which provides that a person dealing in good faith and for value does not need to enquire about the administrative receiver's powers. Administrative receivers have one further statutory power; section 43 of the 1986 Act allows them to apply to the court for permission to dispose of

---

[20] s.29(2)(a) of the Insolvency Act 1986.

[21] The 23 powers are stated in full in Appendix 2.

[22] See *Joshua Shaw & Sons Ltd* [1989] B.C.L.C. 362, where the directors were not in breach of any duty to creditors because the assets were (at the material time) under the *control* of the administrative receivers; and *Gomba Holdings Ltd v. Homan* [1986] 1 W.L.R. 1301 at 1306, where it was stated that the primary duty of a receiver was to realise and manage the assets under his *control*.

[23] Sealy and Milman, *Annotated Guide to Insolvency Legislation* (4th ed., 1994), p. 92.

property that is subject to a prior charge. The disposal can be authorised if the court satisfies itself that it is likely to promote a more advantageous realisation of the company's assets than would otherwise be effected.

Another important feature of the definition of an administrative receiver is that a floating charge combined with a fixed charge can give rise to an administrative receivership. Many fixed charges are "supported" by a floating charge. In this way the creditor has the security of a definite fixed asset of the company, often land and buildings, together with the current assets of the company at the time when the floating charge crystallises. This is the most typical situation for a company with secured creditors and most companies with secured debt are therefore likely to have a creditor capable of appointing an administrative receiver.

Many treatments of the subject of receivership tend to cover receivership and administrative receivership together, only referring to administrative receivership separately when the two forms diverge: "In this chapter we will refer simply to receivers but this must be understood as including administrative receivers and where special rules apply to administrative receivers this will be made clear"[24] indicates the common approach taken to the subject. In *this* chapter the two sorts of receivership have been distinguished and dealt with in separate sections. This is because administrative receivership was created as part of the 1985 insolvency law reforms, which were implemented with a view to increasing the number of company rescues. In the context of this book it is the differences between ordinary receivership and administrative receivership that are all important; and it is fair to ask whether administrative receivership should be regarded as a *rescue* regime.

The problems with ordinary receivership (as a method of corporate rescue) were seen as twofold: the limited powers of receivers to keep the company running, and the fact that receivership was primarily designed to generate sufficient cash to repay the charge holder. Administrative receivership tackles the first problem by bestowing the 23 statutory powers, but does nothing about the second problem. As with an ordinary receiver, an administrative receiver owes a primary duty to the charge holder, a duty that will in most cases lead to asset realisation rather than company rescue. It will be remembered from the previous section that the duties owed by receivers are

---

[24] Farrar, Furey, Hannigan and Wylie, *Farrar's Company Law* (3rd ed., 1991), p. 675.

governed by the principles of equity rather than negligence and that the basic equitable obligation is for the receiver to act in good faith.[25] These principles apply equally to administrative receivers. There is no duty placed upon an administrative receiver to attempt to rescue the company. The principles outlined above have two consequences. First, secured creditors will find administrative receivership attractive; if they have the decision-making power (which they do), they will favour this option, as they can choose who to appoint[26] and know that the chosen person must act in their interests. Secondly, the decision making of the administrative receiver will be influenced by the fact that the primary purpose of the appointment is to realise assets on behalf of the secured creditors; a certain, quick sale of assets is likely to be preferable to a longer-term, risky rescue attempt, especially if a quick sale will raise sufficient cash for the secured creditors and a successful rescue will, therefore only benefit other claimants.

In the above analysis there is little to suggest that administrative receivership will promote corporate rescue. However, where asset realisation can be combined with the continuation of at least a part of the company's business, rescue can be achieved under administrative receivership. One way of realising the company's assets which is available to an administrative receiver is a "hive down." The powers given to administrative receivers include: the power to establish subsidiary companies; the power to transfer to subsidiaries of the company the whole or any part of the business and property of the company; and the power to sell or otherwise dispose of the property of the company. A hive down is a combination of these three elements: the creation of a newly formed subsidiary; the transfer of relevant assets to the new subsidiary; and the sale of the shares of the new subsidiary. The hive down has been described as "a favourite method of repackaging receivership assets for sale."[27] The power to continue trading while the details of a hive down are negotiated with the purchaser is also a vital factor in the success of such deals. The existing management are often potential purchasers of hived-down

---

[25] *China and South Sea Bank Ltd v. Tan Soon Gin* [1990] 1 A.C. 536; *Downsview Nominees Ltd v. First City Corporation Ltd* [1993] 2 W.L.R. 86.

[26] This is only limited by the fact that an administrative receiver must be a qualified insolvency practitioner (s.230(2) of the Insolvency Act 1986), cannot be a body corporate (s.30 of the Insolvency Act 1986), and cannot be an undischarged bankrupt (s.31 of the Insolvency Act 1986).

[27] Milman and Durrant, *op. cit.*, p. 59.

businesses, and management buy-outs during receivership are not unusual. Wright, Coyne and Mills in their detailed survey of U.K. MBOs found that about 5 per cent were of individual companies in receivership and a further 14 per cent were where the parent company was in receivership.[28] A hive down results in at least part of the distressed company's business continuing as a going concern. This is at least a partial rescue despite the fact that the original company may very well be liquidated. In so far as administrative receivership encourages hive downs rather than the breaking up of the company's business in a piecemeal sale of assets, it is encouraging the rescue of businesses.

6. Scotland

Receivership in Scotland differs from its counterpart in England and Wales in several ways. One of the reasons for these differences is that receivership as a remedy has only been available in Scotland since 1972[29] and it has not been easy to fit it into the existing framework of Scottish corporate insolvency law. In Scotland a receiver can be appointed by the holder of a floating charge over all or any part of the property of an incorporated company.[30] The circumstances that justify the appointment of a receiver include any events specified in the instrument creating the floating charge and a statutory list of grounds for appointments.[31] The powers of Scottish receivers are determined first by reference to the instrument creating the floating charge and secondly (in so far as they are not inconsistent with any of the provisions of the instrument) by reference to a list of 23 statutory powers.[32] The 23 powers are a Scottish version of the 23 statutory powers given to administrative receivers in England and Wales,

---

[28] Wright, Coyne and Mills, *Management Buy-outs* (1987).

[29] The remedy was first made available by the Companies (Floating Charges and Receivers) (Scotland) Act 1972. The main provisions are now to be found in c.II of Pt. III of the Insolvency Act 1986—Receivers (Scotland). Provisions concerning floating charges in Scotland are to be found in ss.462–466 of the Companies Act 1985. Additional provisions concerning receivers can be found in the Receivers (Scotland) Regulations 1986 (S.I. 1986 No. 1917 (S.141)) and the Insolvency (Scotland) Rules 1986 as amended.

[30] s.51 of the Insolvency Act 1986. The definition of a company for these purposes goes beyond the meaning of a company within the meaning of the Companies Act.

[31] s.52 of the Insolvency Act 1986.

[32] s.55 of the Insolvency Act 1986.

although they appear in a slightly different order.[33] These powers are granted to Scottish receivers only in relation to such part of the property of the company as is attached by the floating charge. Where a Scottish receiver is appointed by the holder of a floating charge which covers substantially the whole of the company's property, the receiver's powers will be exercised in respect of substantially the whole of the company's property. Such a receivership may be very similar to an administrative receivership in England and Wales. Where there is a smaller proportion of the company's property covered by the floating charge, the Scottish receiver's scope for action will be reduced. In addition to these powers Scottish receivers may apply to the court for permission to dispose of property that is subject to a prior security, interest, burden, encumbrance or diligence.[34]

It has been stated that the law of receivership in Scotland is separate from that applicable in England and Wales, is distinctive and is relatively new. Some of the features of Scottish receivership have been mentioned. In the context of this chapter, however, the important aspects of receivership law concern its potential to generate or obstruct corporate rescues. In this respect Scotland is little different from England and Wales. In Scotland, as in England and Wales, the person with most decision-making power is the holder of a floating charge and, in most of the circumstances in which a receiver may be appointed in Scotland, the appointment can be made directly by the holder of a floating charge without reference to the court.[35] The only circumstance where the appointment *must* be made by the court is where the holder of the floating charge claims that their position is likely to be prejudiced if no such appointment is made.[36] There is a parallel between Scottish charge holders being "prejudiced" and English charge holders being in "jeopardy." Both expressions mean that there is an immediate and substantial risk of the charge holder's security disappearing, or being dissipated, or falling substantially in value.[37] However, in most of the circumstances

---

[33] They are to be found in Sched. 2 of the Insolvency Act 1986—Powers of a Scottish Receiver (Additional to those Conferred on him by the Instrument of Charge).

[34] s.61 of the Insolvency Act 1986. This mirrors the power for administrative receivers in England and Wales to apply to the court regarding the disposal of property subject to a prior charge.

[35] s.51(1) of the Insolvency Act 1986.

[36] This is provided for by s.51(2) of the Insolvency Act 1986, which also *permits* appointment by the court in most of the circumstances where the charge holder can act directly.

[37] Pennington, *op. cit.*, p. 419.

that might give rise to a claim of prejudice or jeopardy, the charge holder will find that the company is in breach of one or more of its obligations under the terms of the loan and will be able to appoint a receiver without the trouble and expense of having to make such a claim before the court.

Once appointed, a Scottish receiver owes a primary duty to the charge holder. The granting of the 23 statutory powers to a Scottish receiver does not mean that they will be exercised in furtherance of a rescue attempt. In this respect the arguments which apply to administrative receivers in England and Wales apply equally to Scottish receivers. There is nothing here to suggest that receivership law in Scotland is any more favourable to corporate rescue than its English and Welsh counterpart.

7. Administration

The administration order was introduced in 1985 as a new legal rescue regime for the United Kingdom. It is being discussed under the heading of "decision making by secured creditors." This is because of the way in which the statutory provisions on administration have been drafted. An application for an administration order is made by petition to the court.[38] Section 9(2) of the Insolvency Act 1986 then provides: "Where a petition is presented to the court notice of the petition shall be given forthwith to any person who has appointed, or is or may be entitled to appoint, an administrative receiver of the company."

Notice of the petition gives time for an administrative receiver to be appointed and, when the application for an administration order comes before the court, it is the court's duty to dismiss the petition if there is at the time of the hearing an administrative receiver of the company. These provisions ensure that administrative receivership takes precedence over administration. As most companies with secured creditors are likely to have a person who "is or may be entitled to appoint an administrative receiver," this is yet another area where decision-making power has been given to the secured creditors. The position of a creditor who is able to appoint an administrative receiver contrasts sharply with the position of other creditors

---

[38] s.9(1) of the Insolvency Act 1986.

who have their rights suspended once a petition has been made.[39] In practice, petitions for administration orders will be made only where there is no possibility of an administrative receivership or where the secured creditors forbear to appoint an administrative receiver and so allow an administration to go ahead.

An administration order may be made only for the achievement of four statutory purposes:

"(a) the survival of the company, and the whole or any part of its undertaking, as a going concern;

(b) the approval of a voluntary arrangement under Part 1 [a CVA];

(c) the sanctioning under section 425 of the Companies Act of a compromise or arrangement between the company and any such persons as are mentioned in that section; and

(d) a more advantageous realisation of the company's assets than would be effected on a winding up."[40]

The court has to specify which purpose or purposes the order seeks to achieve. The order itself directs that during the period for which it is in force "the affairs, business and property of the company shall be managed by a person ('the administrator') appointed for the purpose by the court."[41] The main duty of the administrator is to make proposals for the achieving of the purpose or purposes specified in the order and this must be done within three months after the making of the order.[42] The administrator then has to seek the approval of the creditors for the proposals by summoning a creditors' meeting.[43] In order to fulfil this main duty the administrator has the general duty to take immediate control of all the property to which the company is or appears to be entitled.[44] Also, the administrator must manage the affairs, business and property of the company.[45] Section 14 of the Insolvency Act 1986 gives the administrator extensive powers. First, the administrator has a very general power to "do all such things as may be necessary for the management of the

---

[39] s.10(1) of the Insolvency Act 1986.
[40] s.8(3) of the Insolvency Act 1986.
[41] s.8(2) of the Insolvency Act 1986.
[42] Or such longer period as the court may allow; s.23(1) of the Insolvency Act 1986.
[43] s.24 of the Insolvency Act 1986.
[44] s.17(1) of the Insolvency Act 1986.
[45] s.17(2) of the Insolvency Act 1986.

affairs, business and property of the company."[46] Secondly, the 23 statutory powers listed in Schedule 1 of the Act apply equally to administrators and administrative receivers.[47] Thirdly, the administrator has the following "extra powers":

"(a) to remove any director of the company and to appoint any person to be a director of it, whether to fill a vacancy or otherwise, and

(b) to call any meeting of the members or creditors of the company."[48]

Finally, to make it quite clear that the administrator is in control, it is provided that the powers of the company or its officers cannot be exercised so as to interfere with the exercise of the administrator's powers except with the consent of the administrator.[49]

The effect of an administration order is also to place a moratorium on creditor actions. Under section 11(3) of the Insolvency Act 1986, while an administration order is in force:

"(a) no resolution may be passed or order made for the winding up of the company;

(b) no administrative receiver of the company may be appointed;

(c) no other steps may be taken to enforce any security over the company's property, or to repossess goods in the company's possession under any hire-purchase agreement, except with the consent of the administrator or the leave of the court and subject (where the court gives leave) to such terms as the court may impose; and

(d) no other proceedings and no execution or other legal process may be commenced or continued, and no distress may be levied, against the company or its property except with the consent of the administrator or the leave of the court and subject (where the court gives leave) to such terms as aforesaid."

This moratorium provides the breathing space for the formulation of the administrator's proposals.

An administration order can only be granted if the court is satisfied that the company is or is likely to become unable to pay its debts[50]

---

[46] s.14(1)(a) of the Insolvency Act 1986.
[47] They are given to administrators by s.14(1)(b) of the Insolvency Act 1986.
[48] s.14(2) of the Insolvency Act 1986.
[49] s.14(4) of the Insolvency Act 1986. Under s.14(4) the administrator may apply to the court for directions.
[50] s.81(1)(a) of the Insolvency Act 1986.

and considers that the making of an order would be likely to achieve one or more of the statutory purposes set out above.[51] A petition for an administration order can be made by the company, the directors, a creditor or creditors.[52] A member cannot petition for an administration order. If the directors make the petition it must be made by all the directors[53] and if the decision follows a board resolution it becomes the duty of all the directors including those who took no part in the deliberations of the board and even those who voted against the resolution, to implement it.[54] However, once appointed, an administrator does not act for the person or persons who petitioned for the administration order:

> "An administrator . . . like a liquidator, has no particular interest to which he may give priority. In the context of a sale of company property, a receiver may effect an immediate sale whether or not that is calculated to realise the best price, though he must take reasonable care to obtain whatever is the true market value of the property at the moment he chooses to sell it. But an administrator is under a duty to obtain the best price that the circumstances (as he reasonably perceives them) permit, and this means that he must take reasonable care in choosing the time at which to sell the property."[55]

In the context of rescue attempts more generally, an administrative receiver has no duty to attempt a rescue, whereas an administrator has a duty to formulate proposals for the achievement of the statutory purpose or purposes specified in the administration order. If the specified purpose is "the survival of the company, and the whole or any part of its undertaking, as a going concern," the administrator is under a duty to formulate a corporate rescue plan. In fact, the administrator has to formulate a proposal that includes the survival of *the* company—the survival of a part of its business in a hived-down subsidiary will not do.[56] An order made merely to achieve "a more advantageous realisation of the company's assets than would be

---

[51] s.8(1)(b) of the Insolvency Act 1986. Both of these aspects of administration have already been discussed in Part I of the book.

[52] s.9(1) of the Insolvency Act 1986.

[53] *Re International Electrical Services Ltd* (1988) 4 B.C.C. 301.

[54] *Re Equiticorp International plc* [1989] 1 W.L.R. 1010; (1989) 5 B.C.C. 599; see Sealy and Milman, *op. cit.*, p. 47.

[55] See Sealy and Milman, *op. cit.*, p. 65, where it is also pointed out that the conduct of an administrator is to be judged by the standards of a professional insolvency practitioner of ordinary skill, *Re Charnley Davies Ltd* [1990] B.C.C. 605.

[56] *Re Rowbotham Baxter Ltd* [1990] B.C.C. 113.

effected on a winding up" seems to impose less of an obligation to attempt a rescue, but does allow hive down type sales. In practice, combinations of the four statutory purposes often appear in petitions and administration orders. There is also a provision allowing the administrator to apply to the court for the administration order to be varied so as to specify an additional purpose.[57] The administrator's proposals must be considered by a creditors' meeting and once they have been approved the administrator must implement them. Once the proposals have been approved the administrator's duty is to manage the affairs, business and property of the company "in accordance with those proposals as from time to time revised."[58] This provision means that after the creditors' meeting the administrator's freedom to act is limited by the contents of the approved proposals.

8. Secured versus Unsecured Creditors

The starting point of this chapter was the scenario of a distressed company with secured creditors. Discussion has focused on the position of secured creditors when a corporate rescue might be attempted, which was said to depend first on the particular bargain struck between the company and the creditors. In section 2 of the chapter some characteristics of a typical creditors' bargain were set out. It was also pointed out that insolvency law also has an impact on the position of such creditors. Under U.K. law it is the secured creditors who can make the crucial decisions concerning potential rescues. In sections 3, 4, 5 and 7 of the chapter, four decision possibilities for the secured creditors were discussed: the decision to reschedule the debt; the decision to appoint a receiver; the decision to appoint an administrative receiver; and the decision to allow an administration order to be made by not exercising the option to appoint an administrative receiver. All these decisions are usually in the power of the secured creditors.

The essence of being a secured creditor is security; this is at the heart of the bargain that secured creditors make with the company. If the law strictly enforces creditors' bargains, some opportunities for corporate rescue will be lost. An alternative is for the law to state that

---

[57] s.18(1) of the Insolvency Act 1986.
[58] s.17(2)(b) of the Insolvency Act 1986.

creditors' bargains must be suspended (a moratorium on creditors' actions) in order to allow corporate rescues to be attempted. The creditors' bargain itself is then encroached upon by the insolvency regime. The position of secured creditors in the United Kingdom is a very strong one. The characteristics of receivership and administrative receivership make them far from ideal as rescue regimes. They are both designed primarily to facilitate the realisation of assets on behalf of the charge holders. Administration is the only true *rescue* regime, but administrative receiverships are much more usual. "Lightweight" floating charges are frequently written into creditor's bargains, not for the support they give in terms of valuable security, but to ensure that the secured creditors have the power to appoint an administrative receiver.[59] This chapter has the aim of showing how the secured creditors determine the course of a rescue attempt.[60]

The essence of being an unsecured creditor is exposure to risk, and the next chapter aims to show how unsecured creditors will be working to reduce their exposure to risk and how their actions may also have some influence over the course of a rescue attempt. There is one group of creditors who are difficult to place: Suppliers of goods who include retention of title clauses in their contracts are exposed to more risk than secured creditors who hold a charge over the company's assets, but they have more "security" than other truly unsecured creditors. Because the retention of title clause offers a form of "security" it will be discussed here, but in so far as creditors with a retention of title clause are in a similar position to other unsecured creditors they will also appear in the next chapter.

9. Retention of Title as a Form of Security

Retention of title clauses are also called *Romalpa* clauses after the leading case of *Aluminium Industrie Vaasen BE v. Romalpa Aluminium Ltd.*[61] In that case Aluminium Industrie Vaasen (AIV) sold foil to Romalpa. Clause 13 of AIV's general terms of sale provided: "The

---

[59] In *Re Croftbell Ltd* [1990] B.C.C. 781 the court reluctantly found a lightweight floating charge to be effective for the purpose of ensuring that an administrative receiver could be appointed.

[60] The secured creditors are also in a very strong position if the company goes into liquidations

[61] [1976] 1 W.L.R. 676.

ownership of the material to be delivered by AIV will only be transferred to purchaser when he has met all that is owing to AIV, no matter on what grounds." Romalpa owed a large amount to AIV when an administrative receiver was appointed. The Court of Appeal held: (a) that AIV were entitled to recover from Romalpa the foil still held by Romalpa' s receiver; (b) that following *Re Hallett's Estate*[62] AIV was entitled to trace the proceeds of foil lawfully resold by Romalpa during the course of business (the receiver had deposited these funds in a separate account, thus unwittingly facilitating the tracing exercise); and (c) that a fiduciary relationship existed between the parties and accordingly the implied power of resale given to Romalpa was a power to sell for AIV's account, not Romalpa's. The workings of a *Romalpa* clause can be seen as important to the course of a corporate rescue through the "security" the clause offers to an otherwise unsecured creditor. Three main points will be made here concerning *Romalpa* clauses and "security."[63] First, the operation of a *Romalpa* clause is far from certain; second, clauses covering all the company's obligations to a particular supplier can be valid; and thirdly, *Romalpa* clauses provide security, but not the same type of security as is afforded to charge holders.

(1) Uncertainty. The growing body of case law following *Romalpa* has clarified some points but revealed other difficulties.[64] No single formula for a retention of title clause has emerged as the best or most effective. It has been said that "it is of great importance to bear in mind that these [post-*Rompala*] cases have been concerned with different clauses, very often in materially different terms; that different cases have raised different questions for decision; and that the decision in any particular case may have depended on how the matter was presented to the court, and in particular may have depended on a material concession by counsel."[65] This means that any apparent security to be gained by the inclusion of a *Romalpa* clause could be challenged.

---

[62] (1880) 13 Ch.D. 696.

[63] As stated above, the similarities between unsecured suppliers of goods and unsecured lenders mean that retention of title also appears in the next chapter.

[64] The number of cases deciding issues arising out of the use of retention of title clauses is now large enough to preclude a thorough case-by-case presentation of the post-*Romalpa* story. See McCormack, *Reservation of Title* 2nd ed., 1995) for a thorough treatmet of the subject.

[65] *Per* Goff L.J. in *Clough Mill v. Martin* [1985] 1 W.L.R. 119 at 114.

(2) Scope. It is clear, first from the success of a retention of title clause in *Romalpa* and secondly from the wording of section 19(1) of the Sale of Goods Act 1979, that retention of title clauses are valid. Section 19(1) states:

> "Where there is a contract for the sale of specific goods or where goods are subsequently appropriated to the contract, the seller may, by the terms of the contract or appropriation, reserve the right of disposal of the goods until certain conditions are fulfilled; and in such a case, notwithstanding the delivery of the goods to the buyer, or to a carrier or other bailee or custodier for the purpose of transmission to the buyer, the property in the goods does not pass to the buyer until the conditions imposed by the seller are fulfilled."

More generally, at section 17(1) of the Sale of Goods Act 1979 there is the provision that in contracts for specific or ascertained goods, property passes to the buyer at such time as the parties to the contract intend it to pass. Both provisions are in line with the doctrine of privity of contract, and the approach of the courts to retention of title clauses included in contracts has generally been to construe them in such a way as to do as little "violence" to the contract as possible. Moreover, statute places no restriction on the nature of the conditions that may be imposed by the seller. In *Clough Mill v. Martin*[66] clause 12 of a contract for the sale of yarn was in dispute. It stated *inter alia*: "However, the ownership of the material shall remain with the seller, which reserves the right to dispose of the material until payment in full for all the material has been received by it in accordance with the terms of the contract. . . . Such payment shall become due immediately upon the commencement of any act or proceeding in which the buyer's solvency is involved."[67]

It should be noted that section 19(1) of the Sale of Goods Act 1979 permits the seller to "reserve the right of disposal of the goods until certain conditions are fulfilled [and] . . . the property in the goods does not pass to the buyer until the conditions imposed by the seller are fulfilled." A clause in which the seller retained title to *all* goods delivered to the buyer until *all* debts owed by the buyer to the seller were settled was held to be valid under sections 17(1) and 19(1) of the Sale of Goods Act 1979 in the case of *Armour v. Thyssen Edelstahlwerke A.G.*[68] In *Clough Mill v. Martin* the disputed clause 12

---

[66] [1981] 1 W.L.R. 111.
[67] *ibid*. at 113.
[68] [1990] 3 W.L.R. 810. This is a Scottish case; the references to s.17(1) and 19(1) of the Sale of Goods Act 1979 can be found in Lord Keith's judgment.

stated that the sellers were to retain title to *all* the material to which the contract related until the price of that material had been paid *in full*, and the judgment of Donaldson M.R. indicates (*obiter*) that this was a valid, if not unproblematic, condition.[69] Thus, the validity of clauses covering all obligations, sometimes referred to as "all-monies" or "current account" clauses, seems well established. This "security" looks rather similar to that afforded to charge holders as it does not matter that the value of the goods in which title is retained far exceeds the amount outstanding to the supplier. However, a retention of title clause is emphatically not the same as a charge over the company's assets.

(3)   The nature of the "security." The issue before the Court of Appeal in *Clough Mill v. Martin* was whether a retention of title clause created a charge that would be void for want of registration. The defendant claimed that, because the whole purpose of clause 12 of the contract was to give the plaintiff security for the payment of the purchase price, a charge was created by the buyer in favour of the plaintiff.

Oliver L.J. dealt with this claim in two steps: "In the first place, I question the correctness of the assumption that the whole purpose of the clause is to give the plaintiff security for the payment of the purchase price. No doubt that is a part, and an important part, of the purpose of the clause, but put in more general terms its purpose is to protect the plaintiff from the insolvency of the buyer in circumstances where the price remains unpaid."[70] Secondly, ". . . it is not a necessary incident of the seller's securing his position that he should pass the legal title. The whole question is, how has his position been secured? If in fact he has retained the legal title to the goods, then by definition the buyer cannot have charged them in his favour."[71]

This is a case where the retention of title clause "worked" and it seems that part of the reason for its success was the fact that the purpose of the clause went "well beyond a mere security for payment."[72] The clause was effective at least partly because it had protection of the seller from the insolvency of the buyer as its

---

[69] [1985] 1 W.L.R. at 125/6. This part of clause 12 was not determinative of the appeal but was referred to by Donaldson M.R. as "one other aspect which creates problems."

[70] *ibid.* at 122.

[71] *ibid.* at 123.

[72] *ibid.* at 122.

purpose. Thus, retention of title clauses are not only valid but have been explicitly endorsed as a method of gaining protection from insolvency; the nature of the security they afford, however, operates differently from that of a charge holder and is more uncertain.

Chapter 9

Possibilities for Unsecured Creditors

1. Introduction

The idea that a company's unsecured creditors voluntarily accept the risk of its insolvency has been put forward on many occasions.[1] However, the voluntary nature of this assumption of risk is far from obvious. The terms agreed between a company and its suppliers (of goods, services or finance) depend on a multitude of factors, not least the relative bargaining power of the parties. Suppliers of goods and services may be faced with the stark choice of supplying on credit or not at all. Suppliers of customer-specific goods may easily find themselves tied into a relationship with a particular customer, as they have nowhere else to sell their products. Decisions about whether to commence or continue supplying a company may involve an assessment of the risk associated with becoming or continuing to be an unsecured creditor. There are, however, various steps that potential unsecured creditors can take to improve their position. In this chapter such steps are called "queue-jumping", the queue in question being the ranking by priority of creditors in a winding up. Queue-jumping can be effected either by avoiding the queue altogether or by being at or near the head of the queue when it forms. Some methods of jumping the queue can be attempted by unsecured creditors at any time; however, a statutory super priority for lending during a moratorium is queue-jumping linked into the rescue itself.

This chapter begins with a "static" example in which it is assumed that a particular set of transactions have been made by the company

---

[1] For instance, ". . . unsecured creditors voluntarily accept the risk that the trustee bank might become insolvent and unable to discharge its obligations in full," *per* Lord Templeman in *Space Investments v. Canadian Imperial Bank of Commerce Trust Co. (Bahamas)* [1986] 3 All E.R. 75 at 77.

concerned either with or without effective queue-jumping man-oeuvres in place. The *Quistclose* trust[2] and the retention of title clause[3] are used in the example, which reveals that they operate in a similar way although they tend to be employed differently. Various queue-jumping devices are then considered in more detail in the context of rescues including the *Quistclose* trust and statutory super priority. The opening example, being "static," cannot give a full picture. Once queue-jumping is known to occur and to be taking place it is likely to have an impact on other transactions of the company. For instance, if more finance is made available to a company under a *Quistclose*-type arrangement, this may be the vital ingredient in a successful rescue. It may, however, encourage more trading by the company and simply increase the value of the claims of unsecured creditors when the company is finally put into liquidation.

Unsecured creditors generally have very little power and come off very badly if a rescue attempt fails. Because of their poor position they are likely to employ any method or strategy that may reduce the risk they bear. The aim of this chapter is to highlight the position of the unsecured creditors. Methods that they can, and do, use to try to improve their position are discussed. The proposal for statutory super priority, which has been dropped for the present, is also examined and compared with its U.S. counterpart.

2. A Static Example of Queue-jumping

In this section the effect of queue-jumping is examined in a "static" way, which assumes a particular set of transactions to have been made by the company concerned either with or without effective queue-jumping manoeuvres in place. Two queue-jumping man-oeuvres which have similar characteristics will be used to illustrate this basic effect. They are the *Quistclose* trust and the retention of title clause.

THE QUISTCLOSE TRUST

In *Barclays Bank Ltd v. Quistclose Investments Ltd*[4] Rolls Razor declared a dividend while in financial difficulty. Further financing by Barclays

---

[2] *Barclays Bank Ltd v. Quistclose Investments Ltd* [1970] A.C. 567.
[3] Or *Romalpa* clause; *Aluminium Industrie Vaasen BV v. Romalpa Aluminium Ltd* [1976] 1 W.L.R. 676.
[4] [1970] A.C. 567.

Bank was agreed subject to the payment of the dividend. Quistclose lent Rolls Razor £209,719 specifically for the purpose of paying the dividend. This money was paid into a separate account with a covering letter to Barclays informing them that it was for use only to pay the dividend. Rolls Razor was subsequently liquidated without the dividend having been paid.

The House of Lords approved a long line of "Bankruptcy Cases" and held that the funds had been impressed with a trust for Quistclose in the event of the primary purpose failing and that the bank, having had notice, was bound by the trust. This decision presents those who consider providing finance for an ailing company with the option of doing so without assuming all the risk of becoming an ordinary unsecured creditor. Much of the risk, of course, remains, as the "security" offered by a *Quistclose* trust disappears if the primary purpose of the trust is fulfilled. If the dividend had been paid, the assets of the trust would have been properly used and would not have been available for Quistclose to claim. As lenders will only need to rely on a *Quistclose* trust if better forms of security are unavailable, the majority of such arrangements are likely to occur in the context of emergency attempts to rescue failing companies.

RETENTION OF TITLE

A retention of title clause has been described as "a clause in an agreement whereby the party who is transferring property under that agreement seeks to reserve to itself the ownership of that property until certain specified conditions have been met."[5] Such clauses are sometimes called reservation of title clauses. They are also known as *Romalpa* clauses, after the leading case of *Aluminium Industrie Vaasen BV v. Romalpa Aluminium Ltd.*[6] The statutory basis for retention of title clauses can be found in section 19 of the Sale of Goods Act 1979, but it was the *Romalpa* decision which revealed their enormous potential to the business community and led to their inclusion in many standard form contracts. The parallels between the *Romalpa* and *Quistclose* situations have been neatly pointed out by Goodhart and Jones, who state:

---

[5] McCormack, *Reservation of Title* (2nd ed., 1995), p. 1.
[6] [1976] 1 W.L.R. 676. The operation of retention of title clauses as a form of security is discussed in Chap. 5, where a more detailed account of *Romalpa* also appears.

"If goods are sold on condition that the property in them does not pass until the price is paid in full but the customer has a right in the meantime to use or resell the goods in the normal course of business, the Sale of Goods Act produces a result which is in its practical consequences identical to the result in *Quistclose*. The goods are delivered into the possession of the customer for the primary purpose of being used or resold in the course of his business. If that purpose fails because the customer goes into liquidation . . . the supplier gets his [*sic*] goods back."[7]

Because of this similarity, both methods of jumping the queue are illustrated in the example given below. The significant difference between the two methods is that retention of title clauses are employed as a matter of routine whereas the terms that create *Quistclose* trusts are more often employed in a crisis situation. A supplier's decision to include retention of title clauses in standard form contracts is a general insurance. The terms of a *Quistclose*-type loan are more likely to be specially tailored to the borrower's circumstances and, therefore, offer a more specific type of insurance.

The possible effects of queue-jumping manoeuvres in a "static" situation can be seen in Table 9.1. It is assumed in this figure that queue-jumping could have occurred either through effective retention of title clauses or through a recent financing agreement for the specific purpose of paying off certain unsecured creditors in an attempt to save the company; the new finance was paid into a separate bank account and the purpose of the loan has failed. These assumptions apply in columns II and IV. Without the retention of title clauses and the *Quistclose* trust, the suppliers and lenders would be unsecured creditors; this position is shown in columns I and III. In the example shown in columns I and II the assets on liquidation are sufficient to cover all claims except those of the unsecured creditors. The effect of the retention of title clauses and the *Quistclose* trust is to lessen the assets available to the remaining unsecured creditors. In columns III and IV the assets available on liquidation are sufficient only to meet the costs of liquidation, the claims of the preferential creditors and part of the claims of the holders of the floating charge. The effect of the retention of title clauses and the *Quistclose* trust is to reduce the assets available to the holders of the floating charge. In both examples the benefit of an effective retention of title clause or *Quistclose* trust is a jumping of the queue.

---

[7] Goodhart and Jones, "The Infiltration of Equitable Doctrine into English Commercial Law" (1980) 43 *Modern Law Review* 509.

Table 9.1—Distribution of Assets with and without Queue-jumping (a "Static" Example)

Claims[a]:		I	II	III	IV
Subject to retention of title clauses	A	–	£0.3m	–	£0.3m
Held under a *Quistclose* trust	B	–	£0.3m	–	£0.3m
Costs of liquidation	C	£0.5m	£0.5m	£0.5m	£0.5m
Preferential creditors	D	£1.0m	£1.0m	£1.0m	£1.0m
Charges secured by a floating charge	E	£5.0m	£5.0m	£5.0m	£5.0m
Ordinary trade creditors	F	£3.0m	£2.4m	£3.0m	£2.4m
The company is in insolvent liquidation and there are assets valued at		£7.1m	£7.1m	£5.8m	£5.8m
Allocation[b]:		All of C, D and E. F receive 20p in the £1.	All of A, B, C, D and E. F receive nothing.	All of C and D. E receive £4.3m. F receive nothing.	All of A, B, C and D. E receive £3.7m. F receive nothing.

[a] Claims include various types of claim on the assets concerned including claims that the assets are not the property of the company and so not available to the liquidator.
[b] Allocation includes the returning of assets not available to the liquidator and the liquidator's distribution of the company's assets.

3. Queue-jumping Using a *Quistclose* Trust

The salient facts of *Quistclose* have been given above. The importance of the case can be judged by the fact that trusts arising out of similar circumstances are now referred to as *Quistclose* trusts. If a *Quistclose* trust is found, the insolvency queue is avoided because any money advanced is not the property of the borrower but is held on trust. Such money will not, therefore, be available to an administrator or liquidator of the borrower as a company asset. The decision in *Quistclose* both follows and approves a line of bankruptcy cases.[8] In all

---

[8] *Toovey v. Milne* (1819) 2 B. & Ald. 683; *Moore v. Barthrop* (1822) 1 B. & C. 5; *Edwards v. Glyn* (1859) 2 E. & E. 29; *Giber v. Gonard* (1884) 54 L.J. (Ch.) 439; *Re Rogers* (1891) 8 Morr. 243; *Re Drucker* [1902] 2 K.B. 237; *Re Watson* (1912) 107 L.T. 783; *Re Hooley* [1915] H.B.R. 181.

these cases the essential elements that prevented assignees in bankruptcy from keeping or recovering the sums involved were that the
money was held on trust for a specific purpose and that purpose had
failed. The issues concerning *Quistclose* trusts that may be important
to the decisions being made in a rescue situation are: how the
purpose of the trust fails; how far the principles in *Quistclose* can be
extended; who can enforce the trust; and the invisibility of such
arrangements to third parties. These features will now be presented
under the headings of failure of purpose, scope, enforcement, and
invisibility.

FAILURE OF PURPOSE

In order to find a *Quistclose* trust the courts usually have to imply
intentions from the facts; it is rare for them to be simply giving effect
to the express intentions of the parties. This can be seen in even the
earliest of the cases. In *Toovey v. Milne* money was borrowed to settle
with other creditors and thus avoid bankruptcy. When the borrower
nevertheless became bankrupt, he repaid what was left of the loan.
Millett has provided an analysis of this case which shows that the
definition of the purpose of the loan can be very important to the
finding that the purpose has failed.[9] If the purpose was simply the
payment of other creditors, then the purpose had not failed; the
payment could still have been made, and "a trust, unlike a power,
does not fail merely because the trustee refuses to perform it, but
only if it becomes unlawful or impossible to carry it out."[10] If,
however, the purpose of the loan was to save the borrower from
bankruptcy, then on the borrower's bankruptcy the purpose would
clearly have failed. This seems the only sensible interpretation of the
case.[11]

However, a simple promise to refund monies may not be sufficient
to raise a trust. In *Moseley v. Cressey's Co.*[12] a promise to refund
monies paid by share applicants if no allocation was made was
insufficient to raise a trust or lien in favour of the shareholders. This
case was distinguished in *Re Nanwa Gold Mines*,[13] where a company

---

[9] Millett, "The Quistclose Trust: Who Can Enforce It?" (1985) 101 L.Q.R. 271
[10] *ibid.*
[11] *Moore v. Barthrop* (1822) 1 B. & C. 5 is a similar case. *Edwards v. Glyn* (1859)
2 E. & E. 29 also illustrates failure of purpose.
[12] (1865) L.R. 1 Eq. 405.
[13] [1955] 1 W.L.R. 1080.

sought to raise further capital by a rights issue and applications for the new shares had to be accompanied by payment in full. The application form made clear the issue was conditional and contained the two conditions. It also stated: "Should either of these conditions not be fulfilled, application moneys will be refunded and meanwhile will be retained in a separate account." Most of the shareholders did not apply for new shares and the issue was abandoned without the stated conditions being fulfilled. The promise to keep the money in a separate account proved crucial. Harman J. in holding that the shareholders should be refunded said: ". . . here I have not only those words [the promise to refund], but the promise to retain the money 'in a separate account' . . . I cannot but think that the whole object of making such a promise was to indicate that it would be kept apart and separate, not mixed with the company's moneys, until the board saw whether the conditions were fulfilled."

Turning now to *Quistclose* itself, one purpose of the loan was quite clear in this case; it was to be used to pay the dividend which had already been declared. A separate bank account was opened and the bank had, on the facts, accepted the money with knowledge of the circumstances which made it, in law, trust money. One debatable point which has arisen concerns the failure of purpose in *Quistclose*. There is an assumption in the case that the purpose failed when the company was put into voluntary liquidation, but Millett has argued strongly that it is far from clear why this should be so.[14] Millett's argument is that, if the money is trust money and does not belong to the company, then statutory provisions that restrict the application of *the Company's* assets once a voluntary winding-up has commenced[15] cannot prevent a trustee from paying *trust money* to those beneficially entitled to it. If the purpose of the loan was simply to pay the dividend, it is argued, that purpose was not defeated by the passing of the resolution for voluntary winding up. A better way of viewing the case may be to find a wider purpose for the loan. The negotiation of the loan was part of the last desperate efforts to save the company; the purpose of the loan was "not merely the payment of the dividend, but the preservation of [Rolls Razor] as a going concern."[16]

---

[14] Millett, *op. cit.*, pp. 275–276.
[15] s.74(2)(f) of the Insolvency Act 1986 (previously s.212(1)(g) of the Companies Act 1948 and s.502(2)(f) of the Companies Act 1985) prevents a member's debt (*qua* member) from being paid in competition with other debts of the company being wound up by deeming it not to be a debt.
[16] Millett, *op. cit.*, p. 276.

This is a purpose that clearly failed on the commencement of the winding up.

Scope

One very important extension of the *Quistclose* trust is described below in the section dealing with customers of the company. Restricting the discussion at this stage to providers of financial assistance, there are two questions relating to scope which should be mentioned. First, there has been a suggestion that there should be a presumption raised against a trust unless explicit trust language is used.[17] This could be a restriction on the scope of *Quistclose* trusts. Bridge has said that it is in the area of cases where rigorous language is not used and the payer is not consciously mounting a corporate rescue effort that a "too-easy judicial inference of a trust could have disturbing implications for insolvency distribution."[18]

Secondly, *Quistclose* occurred in the context of an attempted corporate rescue and concerned the honouring of an existing commitment (the dividend had been declared before the finance was raised from *Quistclose*), so the extension of its principles to other situations including the payment of future as well as existing creditors may be an issue. *Re Northern Developments (Holdings) Ltd*[19] is a case in which *Quistclose* principles have been applied in a way which extends the scope of this type of trust. This case involved a subsidiary company, Kelly, which was in financial difficulties. One of the secured creditors exercised a power of sale over all sites charged to it. The danger was that if Kelly were wound up it might bring the whole group down with it. In an attempt to rescue Kelly, the parent company arranged a loan from various banks already dealing with the group. The money was paid into a special account in the name of the parent company for the express purpose of "providing moneys for Kelly's unsecured creditors over the ensuing weeks". When Kelly was put into receivership, some £350,000 remained. These circumstances differ from and extend *Quistclose* in two important ways. First, the use

---

[17] Rickett, "Trusts and Insolvency: The Nature and Place of the Quistclose Trust" in Waters (ed.), *Equity, Fiduciaries and Trusts* (1993), p. 332, following his previous in depth analysis "Different Views on the Scope of the *Quistclose* Analysis: English and Antipodean Insights" (1991) 107 L.Q.R. 608.

[18] Bridge, "The Quistclose Trust in a World of Secured Transactions" (1982) 12 O.J.L.S. 358.

[19] Unreported, decided on October 6, 1978.

of the money was not confined to Kelly's existing creditors. Kelly's secretary understood the fund was "as good as share capital" and money was withdrawn from the account when requested and paid in to Kelly's ordinary bank account. Secondly, Kelly's unsecured creditors were told of the existence, size and purpose of the fund, and this information could have affected their decision making.[20] Despite these differences, both of which appear to operate in favour of the unsecured creditors, it was the lenders who eventually benefited from the funding that had been arranged.

ENFORCEMENT

The facts of *Re Northern Developments Holdings Ltd* have been given above. The primary purpose of paying Kelly's unsecured creditors was still capable of being carried out, but had not yet been performed.[21] The question before the court was who was entitled to the £350,000 which remained of the fund. Millett has argued that the unsecured creditors should have been in a strong position: ". . . for on well-settled principles communication of the arrangements to C, followed by forbearance by C, raises an equity against A which prevents him from revoking the payments or otherwise intercepting payment to C."[22]

However, Megarry V.-C. held that the arrangements constituted a trust of the *Re Denley's Trust Deed*[23] type. He held that the trust was enforceable by the bank as lenders, Kelly (as the fund was set up for Kelly's benefit) and the unsecured creditors. This analysis leaves the beneficial interest in suspense until the payment is made. Despite the difficulties associated with this approach, it was followed in *Carreras Rothmans Ltd v. Freemans Matthews Treasure Ltd.*[24] The reasoning in *Re Northern Developments* has, however, been severely criticised, notably by Millett who believes the real problem with the judgment is the failure to explain the basis for enforcing the trust.[25]

---

[20] See Millett, *op. cit.*, pp. 278–279.
[21] An alternative argument would be that although the loan was to be used to pay the unsecured creditors, its ultimate purpose was the preservation of Kelly as a going concern, a purpose which has failed.
[22] Millett, *op. cit.*, p. 278.
[23] [1969] 1 Ch. 373.
[24] [1984] 3 W.L.R. 1016.
[25] Millett, *op. cit.*, p. 283.

INVISIBILITY

From the above analysis, it can be seen that *Quistclose*-type arrangements are attractive to those who provide loans in situations where they would otherwise become simple unsecured creditors. To the extent that funds provided for a particular purpose remain unused the providers of finance are able to avoid the insolvency distribution queue because the money never becomes the property of the borrower. The major problems with such arrangements are, first that the philosophical and doctrinal debates that continue in this area mean there is a degree of uncertainty involved, and, secondly, these trusts are usually invisible. They do not have to be registered and they are unlikely to be discoverable from the borrower's accounts. Given the short-term and emergency nature of most *Quistclose*-type loans, it may seem unlikely that a set of annual accounts including such a loan would be prepared and approved in time to influence an outsider's decision making, but they may be.

The way in which assets and liabilities must be identified for inclusion in the balance sheet under Financial Reporting Standard (FRS) 5 "Reporting the Substance of Transactions" means that a loan made subject to a *Quistclose*-type arrangement would create an asset (the money) and an equal liability (the obligation to repay the lender) in the accounts of the borrower. So the loan will appear to increase the pool of assets available for unsecured creditors generally.[26] Indeed, in *Re Northern Developments (Holdings) Ltd* the unsecured creditors were encouraged to believe that the loan was for their benefit. However, when the unsecured creditors need it most, at the point when the purpose of preserving the company as a going concern fails, the fund must be returned to the lender rather than being made generally available.

4. Customers and *Quistclose* Trusts

In a narrow set of circumstances customers can also be affected by a (*Quistclose*-type trust. There can only be an impact where customers can become creditors of the company, which usually arises only

---

[26] Rules concerning notes to the accounts make it unlikely that the status of the loan as a trust will be disclosed.

through customers paying in advance for goods or services. The leading case on the application of *Quistclose* principles to a relationship between a company and its customers is *Re Kayford Ltd.*[27] The facts were that Kayford carried on a mail order business. Customers paid either the full price or a deposit before receiving the goods they had ordered. Kayford's chief supplier (which Kayford had lent substantial sums of money) was in financial difficulty which in turn threatened the solvency of Kayford. On accountants' advice Kayford opened a separate customers' trust deposit account in which monies paid by customers for goods not yet received would be held. Kayford liquidated with £37,872 in the deposit account, and Megarry J. held that the money in the deposit account was held on trust for the customers and should not be treated as part of the general assets of Kayford.

The notable aspect of the Kayford case is that the trust was unilaterally declared by the company and no intention was communicated to the customers at any time. In coming to the decision Megarry J. relied on *Re Nanwa Gold Mines Ltd.*[28] However, the decision in *Re Kayford* extends *Quistclose* trusts to new territory. The unilateral *Quistclose* trust is explicitly endorsed in the judgement, where Megarry J. states:

> "No doubt the general rule is that if you send money to a company for goods which are not delivered, you are merely a creditor of the company unless a trust has been created. The sender may create a trust by using appropriate words when he sends the money . . . or the company may do it by taking suitable steps on or before receiving the money. If either is done, the obligations in respect of the money are transformed from contract to property, from debt to trust."[29]

It should be noted that this is not a unilateral declaration of a trust by the company over its *own* assets; the declaration must be such that the money is already subject to the trust when it is received by the company and equally must prevent the customers from ever becoming the company's creditors. Goodhart and Jones have argued that "[a]n analysis of the facts of *Re Kayford* suggests that it is very difficult to accept that the customers never became "creditors" of Kayford."[30] However, it is only because they never became creditors

---

[27] [1975], 1 All E.R. 604; [1975] 1 W.L.R. 279.
[28] [1955] 1 W.L.R. 1080.
[29] [1975] 1 W.L.R. at 282.
[30] Goodhart and Jones, *op. cit.*, at 496.

that the trust was effective against the company's (other) creditors. Had the customers become creditors, then the company's action could have constituted a preference invalidated by section 239 of the Insolvency Act 1986.[31] Also, any actual repayment of the customers on the company's insolvency could have been in breach of the general obligation under section 597 of the Companies Act 1985[32] for a company's property on winding up to be applied *pari passu* in satisfaction of its liabilities.[33]

The invisibility of a *Quistclose* trust held for the benefit of customers and the accounting issues that arise out of such a trust are similar to those arising out of trusts held for the benefit of lenders and discussed above in that context. Again it is likely that the requirement for the accounts to give a "true and fair view" would demand the inclusion of the assets and liabilities arising from the transaction, and it is possible that the queue jumping effect of the trust would not be detected by readers of the accounts. However, the *Quistclose* trust involving customers of the company has a limited application in that it is confined to situations where customers pay in advance. Also, *Re Kayford* involved customers who were consumers and may in the future be confined to consumer situations.[34] Megarry J. did remark that "[d]ifferent considerations may perhaps arise in relation to trade creditors."[35]

5. Statutory Super Priority

As stated earlier, statutory super priority (SSP) was merely a proposal, and one that was subsequently dropped. In October 1993 the

---

[31] Under s.240 of the Insolvency Act 1986 the preferential transaction would be voidable if done within six months of the insolvency and at a time when the company is unable to pay its debts.

[32] This is applicable to every voluntary winding up and was formerly s.302 of the Companies Act 1948.

[33] In *British Eagle International Air Lines Ltd v. Compagnie National Air France* [1975] 1 W.L.R. 758 a contractual agreement which would have allowed a particular set of unsecured creditors to jump the queue was held to be contrary to public policy because its implementation would have involved the company in a breach of its obligation under s.302 of the Companies Act 1948 (now s.597 of the Companies Act 1985).

[34] The only other case along similar lines is *Re Chelsea Cloisters Ltd* (1981) P. & C.R. 98, which involved a landlord and tenant relationship. It has been said that this case takes *Re Kayford* to the limits.

[35] [1975] 1 All E.R. at 607, [1975] 1 W.L.R. at 282.

Insolvency Service published its first consultative document proposing new procedures for company voluntary arrangements.[36]
Chapter 2 of this document consists of a discussion of barriers to the
use of CVAs and possible solutions. In the section on lack of funding
there is the following proposal:

> "One option for guaranteeing funding during a moratorium is to
> introduce the concept of statutory super priority so that providers of
> funding during this period can have priority over all existing creditors.
> This is a concept found in the USA Chapter 11 provisions and views on
> its suitability here, and on the particular form it might take, would be
> particularly welcome. Such super priority could be financed either from
> cashflow or (in England and Wales) by a lien over specific uncharged
> assets. There ought to be a requirement that such funds are used only in
> the ordinary course of business (for example to pay employees during
> the moratorium) and that any extraordinary items would have to be
> referred to the lender for authorisation. Views on this are sought."[37]

It can be seen that this proposal is expressly intended to allow
providers of capital during the moratorium to jump the queue by
giving them priority over all existing creditors. However, the proposal was not developed any further. Following the submission of
comments on the first consultative document, the proposal for
granting statutory super priority was withdrawn in April 1995 when
the Insolvency Service published its second consultative document,
Revised Proposals for a New Company Voluntary Arrangement Procedure.
Several reasons were given for the abandoning of SSP. First,
comments had suggested that "competition between lenders to
provide SSP funds (with repayment having priority over *all* existing
debts, including secured debts) might mitigate against the proper
consideration of the viability of the business by a lender—the proper
basis on which further funds should be advanced during a moratorium."[38] Here, at least, the decision-making processes of the
potential lenders and the fact that the proposed scheme would give
the wrong incentives to potential lenders is being recognised. Concern was also expressed about the availability of uncharged assets or
cash flow for the "financing" of the super priority. It was suggested

---

[36] The Insolvency Service, *Company Voluntary Arrangements and Administration Orders: A Consultative Document* (October 1993).

[37] *ibid.* para. 2.29

[38] The Insolvency Service. *Revised Proposals for a New Company Voluntary Arrangement Procedure* (April 1995), para. 2.2, p. 24.

that a company contemplating a CVA would probably have insufficient uncharged assets and that cash flow during the relatively short time period of the moratorium might not be adequate for these purposes.[39] A final objection to SSP was its permanence. In particular, the displacement of existing priorities would be irreversible in the event of the proposal (*i.e.* the rescue plan) failing. The Insolvency Service has now pulled back from SSP and is proposing that the nominee (the person who assesses the suitability of the company for a CVA and supervises the activities of the directors during the period of the moratorium) should be required to consider the availability of funding as part of his or her initial assessment as to whether there is a reasonable prospect of a successful CVA.[40]

The U.S. rules permitting super priority for post-petition lending are to be found in Chapter 3 of the Bankruptcy Code.[41] These rules allow a firm in bankruptcy to obtain credit, but super priority is the last resort, not the first. The first rule is that the court may authorise the obtaining of unsecured credit.[42] The second option is that the court may authorise the obtaining of secured credit with some (but not super) priority; this can only be sanctioned by the court if unsecured credit cannot be obtained.[43] The second option is found in paragraph 364(c), which permits the obtaining of credit:

"(1) with priority over any or all administrative expenses . . . ;

(2) secured by a lien on property of the estate that is not otherwise subject to a lien; or

(3) secured by a junior lien on property of the estate that is subject to a lien."[44]

It is the final option that includes the possibility of super priority in the sense of priority over *all* existing creditors. This rule (paragraph 364(d)) permits the obtaining of credit secured by a senior or equal lien on property already subject to a lien; this is sometimes called a "priming" lien. The court can only authorise this if the debtor in possession cannot obtain such credit otherwise and there is adequate

---

[39] *ibid.* para. 2.3, p. 24.
[40] *ibid.* para. 2.5, p. 24.
[41] 11 U.S.C. Chap. 3.
[42] 11 U.S.C. para. 364(b).
[43] 11 U.S.C. para. 364(c).
[44] *ibid.*

protection for the existing holder of the lien.[45] A priming lien under paragraph 364(d) is rarely granted. Finance is most often obtained in accordance with paragraph 364(c)(1) and (2), with the debtor in possession offering a post-petition lender a senior lien on unencumbered property and an overriding administration priority.[46] Westbrook states: ". . . the truth is that the Chapter 11 financing devices work because blanket liens are less common in the United States [than in the United Kingdom], leaving unencumbered assets available for pledge for post-petition financing."[47]

When new funding is negotiated it may be the existing loan creditors who provide it. Such creditors may have various incentives for providing extra funding. In particular, in making the new loan they may be able to renegotiate the terms of their existing loan. The obtaining of additional post-petition security for undersecured pre-petition loans in exchange for post-petition financing has been termed "cross-collaterisation" and has given rise to some concern in the United States.[48] The promise of fresh supplies in return for action on an existing contract is not unknown in the United Kingdom but has been seen in relation to the supply of goods rather than the supply of finance. This is discussed in the next section.

6. Bargaining Power in New Contracts

In a rescue situation in the United Kingdom unsecured creditors may be able use the threat of discontinuing supplies as a means of obtaining full payment on all pre-rescue contracts. The supplier's bargaining power is strongest where continued supplies are vital to the attempts of an administrative receiver or administrator to keep the company running and there is little hope of finding an alternative supplier in the short term. If the supplier is a monopoly, there will be no hope of obtaining an alternative supply. Generally, the abuse of monopoly power has been seen as a matter for public concern and government action. In the Insolvency Act 1986 the (then) monopoly

---

[45] 11 U.S.C. para. 364(d). The debtor in possession has the burden of proof on the issue of adequate protection.
[46] Westbrook, "Chapter 11 Reorganisation in the United States," Chap. 21 of H. Rajak (ed.), *Insolvency Law: Theory and Practice* (1993), p. 355.
[47] *ibid.* p. 354.
[48] *ibid.* p. 356.

power of suppliers of gas, electricity, water and telecommunications services was tackled. Section 233(2) of the 1986 Act states that, if an "office-holder" requests supplies of the named services, a supplier:

"(a) may make it a condition of the giving of the supply that the office-holder personally guarantees the payment of any charges in respect of the supplies but

(b) shall not make it a condition of the giving of the supply, or do anything which has the effect of making it a condition of the giving of the supply, that any outstanding charges in respect of a supply given to the company . . . are paid."

Administrative receivers are office-holders for this purpose but other receivers are not. In the ten years since the 1986 Act came into operation, there have been strenuous government efforts to enhance competition generally. These efforts have included action in respect of the suppliers named in section 233. As the provisions of section 233 were based on the "abuse of monopoly power" argument, they may now seem out of step with the competitive state of the named industries. If one telecommunications firm cuts off the company another supplier may now relatively easily be found. If ease of access to alternative suppliers had been the ground for statutory interference with a supplier's bargaining powers, the statutory provisions would have been drafted much more widely. The current statutory provision gives the company being rescued no protection from the bargaining powers of suppliers other than those in the four named categories. The position of other suppliers will now be discussed.

Two cases arose out of Leyland DAF's administrative receivership, in which bargaining powers, the request for continuing supplies and the existence of retention of title clauses interacted. An effective retention of title clause can mean that the supplier of goods can reclaim goods from the buyer. This depends in practice on either recognition by the receiver, administrative receiver, administrator or liquidator of the retention of title claim, or a court ruling that the claim is sound. However, even when a judicially sanctioned wording is used for the retention of title clause it cannot be assumed that it will "work" in all circumstances. It has been pointed out that "judges have neatly distinguished the facts in one ROT [retention of title] dispute from another, and therefore brought to nothing apparently watertight ROT claims"[49] The cases of *Leyland DAF Ltd v. Automotive*

---

[49] Elks "Retention of Title: The Leyland DAF Cases" (1994) 9 *Insolvency Law and Practice* 172.

Products plc[50] and *Lipe Ltd v. Leyland DAF Ltd*[51] show how a retention of title clause which gives the supplier a prima facie claim, may increase the bargaining position of the supplier.

In the case of *Leyland DAF Ltd. v. Automotive Products plc* the main source of the supplier's bargaining power came from the fact that Leyland DAF's receivers were attempting to sell part of the business as a going concern and so needed to continue producing vehicles. This in turn required a continued supply of parts which in the short term could only be provided by Automotive Products (AP). When the receivers were appointed, Leyland DAF owed AP £758,955. AP claimed to have a valid retention of title claim and refused to supply any more parts until they were paid in full. AP's solicitors wrote: ". . . our client cannot be forced to trade with your clients [Leyland DAF] and is reluctant to do so whilst your clients continue to prevaricate over our client's perfectly valid retention of title claim." The question before the court was whether AP's refusal to supply constituted an abuse of dominant position contrary to Article 86 of the Treaty of Rome.[52] The Court of Appeal held that there was no infringement of Article 86 and agreed that, as a matter of English law, AP were under no obligation to continue to supply Leyland DAF: "AP's position, *vis-à-vis* Leyland DAF, depends solely, E.C. law apart, on strength of will and strength of bargaining power."[53] The disputed retention of title clause formed a part of AP's bargaining power. Indeed, a retention of title claim which is prima facie valid, may be crucial to this type of bargaining. Paying off a retention of title claim is not the same as paying off an unsecured creditor which may fall foul of section 239 of the Insolvency Act 1986 (before the onset of insolvency) as a preferential transaction or section 597 of the Companies Act 1985, the rule that, in a liquidation, a company's property should be applied *pari passu* in satisfaction of its liabilities.

It appears, then, that where further supplies from a particular supplier are needed for a rescue attempt and there is a retention of title claim which is at least arguable, the supplier is in a very strong bargaining position. If *Leyland DAF Ltd v. Automotive Products plc* has

---

[50] [1993] B.C.C. 389.

[51] [1993] B.C.C. 385.

[52] Article 86 states: "Any abuse by one or more undertakings of a dominant position within the common market or in a substantial part of it shall be prohibited as incompatible with the common market in so far as it may affect trade between Member States."

[53] *Per* Dillon L.J. [1993] B.C.C. at 398.

shown this type of bargaining to be legitimate, another case arising out of Leyland DAF's administrative receivership, *Lipe Ltd v. Leyland DAF Ltd*[54] shows that there are limits to what can be achieved by a seller with a retention of title claim. A valid retention of title clause allows the supplier to repossess goods rather than have to prove in a liquidation as an unsecured creditor. In *Lipe Ltd v. Leyland DAF Ltd* the administrative receivers wanted, as part of the rescue attempt, to be able to sell the goods in question and, therefore, gave Lipe a type of personal undertaking which is now common enough to be described as "customary" in which they promised, if the retention of title claim was established, to either return the goods or pay Lipe the value of the goods. The Court of Appeal held that in these circumstances the supplier was not entitled to an injunction restraining selling or dealing with the goods. Hoffmann L.J. said:

> "If an injunction is granted, and in particular if others asserting an arguable claim to retention of title are encouraged to adopt similar tactics, the goods in question will be frozen and there will be a substantial risk of damaging the business which the receivers are trying to sell. The practical consequence is likely to be that the receivers will be forced to abandon their challenge to the retention of title clauses and pay the suppliers immediately on the sale of the goods in dispute. To force a party to abandon a bona fide defence by this kind of commercial pressure seems to me an injustice which outweighs any risk [that the receivers' personal undertaking is not fulfilled] which will have to be borne by Lipe."[55]

A retention of title clause theoretically allows repossession of goods.[56] Most suppliers would rather receive payment for the goods, and would rather have immediate payment than a receiver's promise to pay later if the retention of title claim is established. *Leyland DAF Ltd v. Automotive Products plc* shows how a threat to cut off supplies coupled with an arguable retention of title claim can legitimately be used to obtain immediate payment. *Lipe Ltd v. Leyland DAF Ltd*

---

[54] [1993] B.C.C. 385.

[55] *ibid*. at 387/8.

[56] Repossession of goods under a retention of title clause is not permitted during the period beginning with the presentation of a petition for an administration order and ending with the making of such an order except with the leave of the court, Insolvency Act 1986, s.10(1)(b), and while an administration order is in force except with the consent of the administrator or the leave of the court, Insolvency Act 1986, s.11(3)(c).

shows that the courts are unwilling to grant an injunction based on an arguable retention of title claim when the "practical consequence" would be immediate payment and the abandoning of the buyer's challenge to the retention of title claim. It appears that a retention of title clause can strengthen bargaining power that a supplier already has (the threat to cut off future supplies), but the courts will not allow the receivers to be held to ransom by the abuse of an injunction to increase that bargaining power.

7. Conclusion

The availability and interaction of the various queue-jumping methods that can be attempted by suppliers of goods or finance may be of importance to a company from two points of view. First, viewing the situation as a potential unsecured creditor, it seems sensible to attempt to jump the queue and the possibility of making such an arrangement may tip the balance in favour of making the loan or supplying the goods or not. Astute suppliers will, however, realise that others will be attempting similar manoeuvres and that the outcome of the attempt is far from certain. Secondly, from the point of view of the company, a loan subject to a *Quistclose* trust, or the continued supply of goods under retention of title clauses, may be crucial to the company's survival.

During a rescue attempt a much needed loan may only be made available subject to a *Quistclose* trust. Those in control of a rescue attempt (directors, administrative receivers or administrators) therefore need to be aware of the possibility of offering a potential lender some security in the form of a *Quistclose*-type arrangement. A rescue may only be able to proceed if the company can continue to trade. Those in charge of a rescue therefore need to be aware of the bargaining power of the unsecured creditors who will be asked to supply further goods during the rescue attempt. This chapter has shown that some unsecured creditors may be able to exert power during a rescue attempt despite having to operate from a position of relative weakness. In the next chapter the position of the company's employees is considered.

Chapter 10

The Position of Employees

1. Introduction

This chapter sets out the employment issues that arise out of corporate rescue. For the purposes of this book rescue is defined as *a major intervention necessary to avert the eventual failure of the company*. A major intervention implies that there will be changes for the company's employees. The primary concern of this work is with the law, but it must be remembered that, in dealing with employees, what is politically expedient and practically feasible may be as important as what is legally allowable. In a rescue attempt the company is likely to retain some employees, perhaps on new terms and conditions, and to dismiss others. The main points to be made here are first, that in dealing with employees during a rescue attempt it is important to understand the legal consequences of decisions to change working practices, to dismiss employees or to sell the business.[1] Secondly, in dealing with employees the legal position should not be considered in isolation; if the long-term survival of the business depends on the commitment and motivation of the continuing employees the political and motivational aspects of employment changes must be a part of the decision-making process.

Three types of employment changes are identified in this chapter: changes in ways of working; dismissals that result from a reorganisation or redundancy; and changes because the business or part of the business is sold as a going concern. In the first case the individual

---

[1] This chapter provides a broad coverage of the legal consequences; for more detail see Deakin and Morris, *Labour Law* (1995) and Duggan, *Business Reorganisations and Employment Law* (1992).

employee will have the same employer, but be required to work differently or for different hours or pay. In the second case some employees will be dismissed and may be entitled to some form of compensation; others will be retained. In the third case the employee may have a new employer, but their original employment contract, which would be terminated at common law, may be preserved by the Transfer of Undertakings (Protection of Employment) Regulations. If a company enters a formal rescue regime, the administrative receiver or administrator may seek to rescue the company by continuing to trade. The position of company employees who continue to work for such an office holder has been the subject of an important House of Lords decision and emergency legislation: the Insolvency Act 1994.

Before going into detail, a brief explanation of wrongful and unfair dismissal may be useful. Wrongful dismissal gives rise to a claim for breach of contract. Damages for wrongful dismissal are very rarely substantial because the employer usually has the right at common law to terminate the contract simply by giving notice and damages will be limited to a sum representing net salary for the notice period.[2] The inadequacy of the remedies for wrongful dismissal led to the introduction of the principle of statutory unfair dismissal. Tribunals deal with claims for unfair dismissal, and such claims are subject to separate time limitations. Most employees who are found to have been unfairly dismissed are awarded compensation rather than being granted one of the other statutory remedies of reinstatement or re-engagement.

2. Working Differently

The first way in which a rescue attempt may affect the employment relationship is if the employer wants to ask employees to work differently. The employer may be entitled to do this under the existing contract of employment and the employee is then bound to accept the change. There are two factors that work in favour of the employer, first the fact that the common law duty of obedience to the employer remains a central contractual obligation of employees. The

---

[2] For a discussion on this point and a summary of recent developments in remedies for wrongful dismissal, see Deakin and Morris, *op. cit.*, pp. 350–387.

duty of obedience has its origins in the Master-Servant Acts of the nineteenth century, but it has been carefully preserved in the modern contractual relationship as an implied fundamental term.[3] The second is the fact that express contractual terms are most often set unilaterally by the employer, who can introduce a degree of flexibility into the contract itself by the use of wide job descriptions and express flexibility or mobility clauses. There are, therefore, many changes an employer may be able to make as to what work their employees must do (where, when, how and for how long) under their existing employment contracts. There are, however, some factors working in favour of the employees. First there is the duty of the employer to maintain the mutual trust and confidence of the employment relationship, and secondly there is the overriding duty of the employer to take reasonable care to ensure the employee's safety and health. Some of these factors will now be examined in more detail.

EXPRESS AND IMPLIED FLEXIBILITY AND MOBILITY

Express flexibility and mobility clauses are often written into employment contracts. Many contracts appear to allow employers to move employees to other places of work or to transfer them to a different type of work. In general, employees are bound by the contract they have made. Cases where the court has been willing to imply terms that restrict the operation of express flexibility and mobility terms are rare. In *Nelson v. British Broadcasting Association*[4] Roskill L.J. stated: ". . . it is a basic principle of contract law that if a contract makes express provision in almost unrestricted language it is impossible in the same breath to imply into that contract a restriction. . . ."[5] When deciding issues relating to express flexibility and mobility clauses. the courts have adopted an approach that essentially applies the ordinary common law rules on the implication of terms into contracts. Under these rules terms can only be implied by the court to give business efficacy[6] to the contract and to give effect to the unstated intentions of the parties.[7]

---

[3] See Anderman, *Labour Law: Management Decisions and Workers' Rights* (2nd ed., 1993) p. 33.

[4] [1977] I.C.R. 469.

[5] In *Rank Xerox v. Churchill* [1988] I.R.L.R. 280 the EAT refused to imply a restriction on a mobility clause.

[6] *The Moorcock* (1889) 14 P.D. 64.

[7] In decisions on other aspects of employment contracts, implied terms do not always depend on the presumed intention of the parties but can be based on the "nature of the underlying transaction." See Deakin and Morris, *op. cit.*, p. 216 for further discussion.

However, express terms do not give employers unlimited power because, even under the tight common law rules, the courts do sometimes imply terms restricting an employer's discretion. In *United Bank Ltd v. Akhtar*[8] the contract of a junior bank clerk included the following: "the bank may from time to time require an employee to be transferred temporarily or permanently to any place of business which the bank may have in the UK for which a relocation allowance or other allowance may be payable at the discretion of the bank." Mr Akhtar had worked at the Leeds branch of the bank for several years when he was asked to relocate to Birmingham at very short notice. He first heard of the transfer on June 2; on Friday June 5 he had it in writing that he was to transfer as from Monday June 8. The industrial tribunal implied a term into the contract that reasonable notice should be given in the exercise of the employer's power and the bank's discretion should not be exercised so as to make the employee's performance a practical impossibility. The EAT upheld this decision, finding that the employer, by insisting upon immediate transfer, committed a fundamental breach of contract. The EAT stated that there was a clear difference between implying a term which negatives a provision which is expressly stated in the contract and implying a term which controls the exercise of discretion which is expressly contained in a contract.

United Bank Ltd v. Akhtar should not, however, be understood as implying a term that an employer should act reasonably, and in *White v. Reflecting Roadstuds Ltd*[9] it was stressed that when implying terms "the touchstone [for the court] is always necessity and not reasonableness." In *White* the employment contract stated: "The company reserves the right, when determined by requirements of operational efficiency, to transfer employees to alternative work and it is a condition of employment that they are willing to do so when requested." Mr White began working for the company in the despatch department and then asked for a transfer to the rubber mixing department. This was the highest paid department and involved the hardest work in physical terms. Following a deterioration in Mr White's attendance which affected team work in the mixing department, he was transferred to the pressing department and suffered a drop in pay. The question arose as to how the employer was allowed to exercise the discretion given in the express

[8] [1989] I.R.L.R. 507.
[9] [1991] I.R.L.R. 331.

contract term. *United Bank Ltd v. AkAtar* was interpreted as stating that the employer should not exercise discretion in such a way as to prevent the employee from being able to carry out their part of the contract, not as implying a term that the employer should act reasonably. The forced transfer to the pressing department did not prevent the employee from being able to perform the contract and the transfer was a legitimate use of the employer's discretion.

Where there is no express mobility or flexibility term in the contract the employer may still be able to require changes in the way work is done or where it is done. In *Courtaulds Northern Spinning Ltd v. Sibson*[10] there was no express mobility clause, but the court was willing to imply a term that the employer had the power to direct the employee to any place of work within a reasonable travelling distance of his home (partly because the employee was a lorry driver). The facts were as follows: The employee had been a union member but resigned from the union over a dispute concerning union funds. This led to other employees ostracising him. The employer requested him to transfer to another depot a mile away. The court held that the employer had been entitled to make this request and the employee should have acceded to it.

The employer may wish to change the way work is done by introducing a new technology. If the same work is to be carried out but in a different manner, this is likely to be a legitimate demand. The leading case is *Cresswell v. Board of Inland Revenue.*[11] The Inland Revenue sought to replace clerically maintained records with a computerised system. This change affected clerical assistants, tax officers and tax officers higher grade. Walton J. held that: "there can really be no doubt as to the fact that an employee is expected to adopt himself [*sic*] to new methods and techniques introduced in the course of his employment. . . . Of course in a proper case the employer must provide any necessary training or retraining."[12] This case shows how a job description can be interpreted as covering different ways of doing a job. It can also be seen as imposing a duty on employees to cooperate with employers.

---

[10] [1988] I.C.R. 451.
[11] [1984] I.C.R. 508; [1984] I.R.L.R. 190.
[12] [1984] I.R.L.R. at 195.

Employment as a Relationship of Mutual Trust and Confidence

A smooth move to new working arrangements with employees depends on maintaining a good relationship.[13] Any statement of what an employer is legally allowed to do will be based on decided cases which are, by definition, confrontational. However, the law itself recognises the particular nature of the employment contract. It acknowledges that it is a relationship of mutual trust and confidence. Moreover, the employer is under a duty not to destroy that mutual trust and confidence.

Ideally, when employment changes are part of a rescue plan the employer would put them to the employees and they would be accepted. If the employees agree to the changes, it does not matter whether they are ones which can be demanded under existing contracts or ones which amount to a variation of existing contracts. If the employees do not like the proposed changes, the employer is in a stronger position if it can be argued that the changes can be made legitimately under the existing contracts. Changes that amount to variations in existing contracts are discussed separately below. If the employer believes the changes can be demanded under the original contracts, they may be imposed on an unwilling workforce. Unhappy employees who then leave may be able to claim to have been constructively dismissed.

For an employee to be constructively dismissed the employer must have committed a fundamental breach of contract. Anything less than a fundamental breach will not allow an employee to leave and claim constructive and unfair dismissal. The leading case setting out a test for constructive dismissal is *Western Excavating (ECC) Ltd v. Sharp*.[14] Lord Denning M.R. stated the test as follows:

> "If the employer is guilty of conduct which is a significant breach going to the root of the contract of employment, or which shows that the employer no longer intends to be bound by one or more essential terms of the contract, then the employee is entitled to treat himself as discharged from any performance. If he does so, then he terminates the contract by reason of the employerss conduct. He is constructively dismissed. The employee is entitled in those circumstances to leave at the instant without giving any notice at all or, alternatively, he may give notice and say he is leaving at the end of the notice. But the conduct

---

[13] Of course, a smooth transition may not be possible.
[14] [1978] I.C.R. 221.

must in either case be sufficiently serious to entitle him to leave at once. Moreover, he must make up his mind soon after the conduct of which he complains for, if he continues for any length of time without leaving, he will lose his right to treat himself as discharged. He will be regarded as having elected to affirm the contract."

In *United Bank Ltd v. Akhtar* the court held that not only was there an implied term that the employee should be given reasonable notice, but also that the actions of the employer amounted to a fundamental breach of the general implied contractual duty of maintaining trust and confidence between employer and employee. This duty was discussed in *Woods v. WM Car Services (Peterborough) Ltd*[15] where Browne-Wilkinson J. stated: "It is clearly established that there is implied in a contract of employment a term that the employers will not, without reasonable and proper cause, conduct themselves in a manner calculated or likely to destroy or seriously damage the relationship of confidence and trust between employer and employee."

The duty to maintain the relationship of trust and confidence is an overriding one. This means that any express clause (such as the ones in *Akhtar* and *White*) must not be used by the employer in a way that destroys mutual trust and confidence. Even when employers do ostensibly have the power to impose changes they should take care over the way they exercise that power. The key to the maintenance of the relationship of trust and confidence is consultation. It was not the move *per se* but the lack of reasonable notice that caused the problem in *Akhtar*. Also, in *White* the court made the link between trust and confidence and "communication."

VARIATION OF THE EMPLOYMENT CONTRACT

The employer may recognise that the desired changes in employment arrangements mean a variation in the contracts of employment. Again, the best scenario is that the changes are proposed to the employees and accepted. So long as there is a clear indication of acceptance there should then be no problem. This can be oral[16] or written. It should be noted, however, that for an employer to simply issue a new statutory statement of terms and conditions[17] will not suffice.[18]

---

[15] [1981] I.C.R. 666; [1981] I.R.L.R. 347, EAT; [1982] I.C.R. 693, CA.

[16] *Simmonds v. Doughty Seals Limited* [1978] I.R.L.R. 211.

[17] As required under s.1(1) of the Employment Protection (Consolidation) Act 1978.

[18] *Jones v. Associated Tunnelling Co Limited* [1981] I.R.L.R. 477.

If the employees do not agree to the proposed variations they may be able to continue working under the original contract, "under protest" against the new terms. In *Rigby v. Feredo*[19] the employers were in severe financial difficulties and asked the workforce to take a cut in pay. They claimed that this was the only way in which the business could be rescued. Some employees objected to this, although they continued to work normally. They were paid the lower wages and brought an action for damages for breach of contract. The House of Lords found that the employees had made it quite clear that they were unwilling to accept, and never did accept, the new contractual terms. Faced with that situation Lord Oliver pointed out that the employer could have chosen to terminate their contracts with proper notice, but it did not do so. He stated:

> "[The employer] continued to employ them week by week under contracts which entitled them to a certain level of wages, but withheld from them part of that entitlement. . . . I can . . . see no basis upon which it can be argued that the continuing working by Mr Rigby *for the time being and under protest* of the wage that the appellant, with full knowledge of his lack of agreement, chose to pay him is to be constructed as an acceptance by him either of the repudiation by the appellant of the original continuing contract or of the new terms which the appellant was seeking to impose."

The main problem if employees continue working when a variation is imposed on them is to determine whether they have by their actions elected to affirm the new contract. If the proposed variation in terms concerns the place of work or the type of work, the employee may be able to try out the new job for a short period without being taken to have accepted the new terms. In *Shields Furnishing v. Goff*[20] working at a new factory for three weeks did not affirm the new contract. In *Sheet Metal Components Limited v. Plumridge*[21] two months work at a new factory did not amount to affirmation of the new contract. So long as the employees have not accepted the new terms (explicitly or impliedly), they may be able to treat the imposition of the terms by the employer as a repudiation of the original contract; they can leave and claim to have been constructively dismissed.

---

[19] [1988] I.C.R. 29.
[20] [1973] I.C.R. 187.
[21] [1974] I.C.R. 373.

It has already been stated that constructive dismissal requires there to have been a fundamental breach, in Lord Denning's words "a significant breach going to the root of the contract of employment." In determining whether there has been a fundamental breach, however, an industrial tribunal's function is to look at the employer's conduct as a whole. A series of incidents can be taken individually or collectively for this purpose. In *Woods v. WM Car Services (Peterborough) Ltd*[22] Woods was employed as "chief secretary and accounts cleric." The business was taken over and she was offered a job on terms that were to be no less favourable than those she had previously. The new employer sought to change her terms and conditions: She was asked to take a reduction in salary, increase her hours and change her job title (removing the word "chief"). She acceded to none of these. She had her work changed from mainly secretarial to mainly clerical and then had some duties transferred to another employee. She was sent an unjustified written warning. These incidents occurred over a four-month period, and the industrial tribunal did not consider that they amounted to a fundamental breach by the employer. The decision was upheld by the EAT, but Browne-Wilkinson J. expressed the view that an employer who persistently attempts to vary an employee's conditions of service may be destroying the relationship of trust and confidence and therefore be in fundamental breach. *He* would have found that the conduct did amount to a breach of the implied duty to maintain mutual trust and confidence, but did not consider that the EAT could interfere with the finding of the tribunal. On appeal the Court of Appeal held that the EAT was right not to interfere with the tribunal's decision.

Employers who attempt to vary terms of employment as part of a rescue attempt will be aware that they may meet with resistance. They should also be aware that they may be in fundamental breach of contract, which will allow the employee to leave, either immediately or after a short trial of the new terms, and claim to have been constructively dismissed. It may be better for the employer to formally dismiss the employees and re-engage them on new terms. Employment protection legislation allows employees who believe they have been unfairly dismissed to bring their claim before an industrial tribunal, and if the tribunal finds in their favour the employer will have to pay them compensation. However, there is nothing in the legislation to say that either a constructive dismissal or

---

[22] [1981] I.C.R. 666, EAT; [1982] I.C.R. 693, CA.

any other dismissal in which the employer acts in repudiatory breach of contract must be unfair. For a claim of unfair dismissal to succeed there must have been a dismissal; it is in this way that the law on constructive dismissal is important to such a claim. Unfair dismissal is considered in more detail in section 3 below.

EMPLOYER'S DUTIES REGARDING HEALTH AND SAFETY

In many rescue scenarios the employer will be asking the employees to accept the fact that there is less work to do. This may take the form of redundancy, laying off or short time working. However, the employer may want to extract more work out of the employees, and the question then arises as to whether there are any limits on what can be demanded. There are two recent important cases on this point. In *Johnstone v. Bloomsbury Health Authorities*[23] a junior hospital doctor had an employment contract which required him to work a basic 40-hour week and to be available for a further 48 hours overtime per week. He sought damages for ill health brought on by working excessive hours and a declaration that his contract did not require him to work hours beyond the point where his health was put in danger. The Court of Appeal found in favour of the employee, but with one of the judges dissenting. Leggatt L.J. would have struck out the claim as disclosing no cause of action because the express agreement to be available for up to 88 hours per week prevailed over any implied term protecting the employee's health and safety. The principle that express terms prevail is a strong one, and this is a principled, if harsh, judgment. The other two judges gave different reasons when finding for the employee. Deakin and Morris prefer the reasoning of Stuart-Smith L.J., who said that the express terms of the contract did not override the duty of the employer in both contract and tort to take reasonable care to ensure the employee's safety and health. They state:

> "There are a number of reasons for thinking that the judgement of Stuart-Smith L.J. is correct in principle, notwithstanding that he found himself in a minority of one in believing that the express term governing working hours was limited by the employer's implied obligations with regard to health and safety. Firstly, it would be odd if the employer's obligation, which is both an implied term in the contract

---

[23] [1991] I.R.L.R. 66.

and also a duty of care in tort, could be limited by an express contract term which did not take the form of a formal disclaimer or exclusion clause of the kind which would normally be needed to oust a tort duty of this kind. Secondly, if the contract term does limit the employer's duty of care in tort since that duty relates to the physical health and safety of the employee the term would be nullified by section 2(1) of the Unfair Contract Terms Act 1977."[24]

The other recent case on overwork is *Walker v. Northumberland County Council*.[25] In this case an employer overworked an employee to the extent that he suffered a foreseeable nervous breakdown and was unable to work thereafter. The local authority employer was held to be in breach of its duty of care and liable in negligence for a work-engendered psychiatric injury. Both *Johnstone* and *Walker* show that there are limits to what an employer can demand of employees. However, it has been pointed out that constraints are imposed "only at the outer reaches of managerial authority. In any but the more extreme cases, the employer's exercise of discretion in respect of hours of work, place of work, etc., will be non-repudiatory."[26]

CONCLUSIONS ON CHANGING WAYS OF WORKING

The above section on changing ways of working is long, and a summary of the main points may therefore be useful. Employees who have express flexibility and mobility clauses in their contracts of employment are generally bound by them. There is no implied term that an employer will act reasonably in exercising the discretion given by such clauses, but there is an implied overriding duty to maintain the relationship of trust and confidence. The employer also has an implied overriding duty in both contract and tort to take reasonable care to ensure the employee's safety and health. If new technology is introduced, employees are under an implied duty to adapt, so long as they are being asked to do the same work. Employees do not have to agree to variations in their contracts. If a variation is imposed upon them this may constitute a repudiation by the employer. Employees may be able to leave, either immediately or after a short trial of the new terms, and claim to have been constructively and unfairly

---

[24] Deakin and Morris *Labour Law* (1995), pp. 218–219.
[25] [1995] 1 All E.R. 737.
[26] Anderman, *op. cit.*, p. 56.

dismissed. If employees are able to continue working whilst objecting to the new terms, the employer may be liable for damages for breach of contract. The employer may dismiss employees who do not agree to a variation in their contracts, but may then be subject to claims for unfair dismissal.

3. Dismissals Resulting from Reorganisation or Redundancy

Corporate rescue often involves a decrease in the number of employees through cut-backs, downsizing, rationalisation, reorganisation or plant closure. A successful rescue depends on a good plan of how, where and what operations the company should undertake in the future. It can also depend on good management of the transition which, by definition, is a major change for the company. If there are to be dismissals, the employer is likely to have two objectives: to incur the minimum cost and to retain the best employees. The most obvious costs of dismissing employees are the amounts payable in compensation, which are usually either redundancy payments or compensation for unfair dismissal. These could be classified as the direct costs of dismissing employees. The company is also likely to incur indirect costs in terms of disruption to production. Employee time spent discussing the dismissals and negotiating terms, the opportunity cost of the management time devoted to effecting the dismissals, and any general drop in productivity due to falling morale in the workforce would contribute to the indirect costs. A dispute over the dismissals which leads to industrial action is likely to be even more costly.

An employee who is dismissed fairly and is not redundant will not be entitled to compensation. An employee who is dismissed for redundancy will be entitled to statutory redundancy pay calculated as a function of the age, weekly pay and length of service.[27] This calculation currently produces a maximum sum of £6,450.[28] Where an employee is dismissed unfairly the court will award compensation in two parts: a basic and a compensatory award. The basic award is calculated in the same way as a statutory redundancy payment. The

---

[27] Sched. 4 of the Employment Protection (Consolidation) Act 1978.
[28] The amount is fixed by Order from time to time. This figure has applied from September 1995.

compensatory award under section 74 of the Employment Protection (Consolidation) Act 1978 is "such amount as the tribunal considers just and equitable in all the circumstances having regard to the loss sustained by the complainant in consequence of his dismissal in so far as that loss is attributable to action taken by the employer." The object of this part of the award is to compensate fully but not to award a bonus,[29] but it is subject to an upper limit of £11,300 (except in cases where dismissal amounts to sex or racial discrimination, where the upper limit has been removed). As the compensatory award is made over and above the basic award, compensation for unfair dismissal will be more costly than a statutory redundancy payment in almost every case.[30] The median award of compensation for unfair dismissal in 1993–94 was £2,773.[31]

The direct costs of dismissal will depend on whether the employee is redundant and whether the dismissal was fair. In order to qualify for redundancy payments an employee must have had two years' continuity of employment up to the "relevant date," and for this purpose only continuity over the age of 18 is counted. For most claims of unfair dismissal an employee must have had two years' continuity of employment at the time of the dismissal, which is termed the "effective date of termination" and is defined under section 55 of the Employment Protection (Consolidation) Act 1978. There are, however, some reasons for dismissal or for selection for redundancy that are automatically unfair and for which there is no qualifying period of employment. Automatically unfair reasons include reasons related to the employee's membership or non-membership of an independent trade union or participation in union activities and reasons connected with pregnancy or maternity. Problems that can arise out of the selection of employees for dismissal or redundancy are considered in more detail below. In terms of direct costs, a fair dismissal (other than for redundancy) incurs the least cost, a fair dismissal for redundancy involves a redundancy payment, and an unfair dismissal is the most costly outcome. It is therefore safe to assume that employers will seek to dismiss fairly whenever possible. It should be noted that this area of the law is complex and

---

[29] *Norton Tool Co. Ltd v. Tewson* [1972] I.C.R. 501.

[30] The court may reduce the compensatory award under s.74(6) or may award nothing under s.74(1) on the grounds that this is just and equitable. The total award would then equal the basic award, which would in turn equal the statutory redundancy payment.

[31] Deakin and Morris, *op. cit.*, p. 445.

cannot be discussed fully here. This section aims simply to highlight the important issues for an employer attempting a corporate rescue. These include the potential costs; the risk of a dispute with an ex-employee; and some procedural aspects of dismissal.

The company, as employer, is obliged to give the employee a written statement of the reasons for dismissal[32] which must contain a simple statement of the essential reasons for dismissal.[33] If an employee claims that dismissal was unfair, it is for the employer to show to the industrial tribunal what the reason was for the dismissal and that the reason falls under one of the five categories of fair reason set out in section 57 of the Employment Protection (Consolidation) Act 1978. In the context of a rescue attempt, the alternatives open to the company as employer are to dismiss the employee on the grounds that they are redundant or to claim that the dismissal falls into the category of "some other substantial reason." Either of these are *potentially* fair reasons for dismissal; however, there is a further requirement in section 57 that the employer's conduct is reasonable in the circumstances.[34] The reasonableness test states: "the determination of the question whether the dismissal was fair or unfair, having regard to the reasons shown by the employer, shall depend on whether in the circumstances (including the size and administrative resources of the employer's undertaking) the employer acted reasonably or unreasonably in treating it as sufficient reason for dismissing the employee."[35] The correct way for an industrial tribunal to test the reasonableness of the employer's actions is ask whether they fall within the range of reasonable employer responses. Reasonableness is a matter of fact for the industrial tribunal, and a decision will not be changed on appeal unless the industrial tribunal applied the wrong test or applied the test incorrectly. It is possible that different tribunals will reach different decisions on essentially similar facts and none of the decisions will be interfered with on appeal. This aspect of the law on unfair dismissal increases the uncertainty faced by employers.

---

[32] s.53 of the Employment Protection (Consolidation) Act 1978.
[33] *Horsley Smith and Sherry Ltd v. Dutton* [1977] I.C.R. 594.
[34] The burden of proof is on the employer to show the reason for the dismissal, but is neutral as between the parties when considering the reasonableness of the employer's conduct.
[35] s.57(3) of the Employment Protection (Consolidation) Act 1978.

Redundancy

Under section 81(2) of the Employee Protection (Consolidation) Act 1978 a dismissal is taken to be by reason of redundancy if it is attributable wholly or mainly to:

"(a) the fact that the employer has ceased, or intends to cease, to carry on the business for the purposes of which the employee was employed by him, or has ceased, or intends to cease, to carry on that business in the place where the employee was so employed; or

(b) the fact that the requirements of that business for employees to carry out work of a particular kind, or for employees to carry out work of a particular kind in the place where he was so employed, have ceased or diminished or are expected to cease or diminish."[36]

Plant Closure

Under section 81(2)(a) redundancy is caused by a cessation of business. A corporate rescue plan can often involve the cessation of business at one particular plant or site. If the company has no work to offer the employees affected by the closure, they will be redundant.[37] Redundancy payments may not have to be paid to all these employees, however, if the company has work to offer at a different plant or site.

The first way in which redundancy may be avoided is if the employer can claim that the employee must relocate to a different plant under the terms of their contract. The workings of mobility clauses have already been discussed above. However, mobility clauses as a method of avoiding redundancy are not without problems. In *Bass Leisure Ltd v. Thomas*[37a] the contract included the following term: "The company reserves the right to transfer any employee either

---

[36] Anderman interprets these statutory circumstances as three basic managerial decisions: (i) the closure of a business or part of a business; (ii) a decision that an employee, or group of employees, is surplus to the requirements of the business at a particular place of work; and (iii) a decision to move a business or part of a business to a new location, Anderman, *op. cit.*, p. 157.

[37] In *Moon v. Homeworthy Furniture (Northern) Ltd* [1977] I.C.R. 117 the EAT held that it was not the tribunal's task to inquire into management's motives for the closure of a factory. The employees claimed that the closure was a response to a bad industrial relations record.

[37a] [1994] I.R.L.R. 104.

temporarily or permanently to a suitable alternative place of work and to change the terms and conditions of employment in order to meet the needs of the business. Domestic circumstances will be taken into account in reaching a decision if relocation is involved." When Bass closed their Coventry depot they offered Mrs Thomas, a driver, relocation to the Erdington depot 20 miles away. Family commitments made work in Erdington impossible. The EAT held that Mrs Thomas had been constructively dismissed since the offer of alternative work had not, objectively speaking, taken adequate account of her domestic circumstances. It also held that she was dismissed for redundancy, on the basis that her "place of work" was the Coventry depot. The employee's normal place of work should be ascertained on a factual test, regardless of whether the contract required the employee to move from one "place" to another.

The second way in which redundancy payments may be avoided is if employees are made an offer of suitable alternative employment. If the employer makes an offer of a new contract of employment *before* the ending of the employee's old contract, and the new contract is for either the same work or suitable alternative employment, the employee will not be entitled to a redundancy payment if the offer is unreasonably refused.[38] Where the terms of the new contract differ wholly or in part from the old contract the employee can try out the new job for up to four weeks. An employee who turns down the offer of alternative work, either at the outset or during the trial period can still claim to have been made redundant from the original job, but the refusal of the alternative job may be found to be unreasonable. An employee who continues to work in the alternative job beyond the statutory four-week period loses the right to claim that he or she was made redundant from the original job. The statutory trial period operates without prejudice to an employee's claim to have been constructively dismissed by the imposed variation in contract terms.[39] The question of whether an offer of suitable employment has been unreasonably turned down is a matter of fact for the tribunal. The suitability of the job refers to "the objective characteristics of the job itself"[40] whereas the reasonableness of the refusal "seems to allow for subjective considerations relating to the

---

[38] s.82 of the Employment Protection (Consolidation) Act 1978.
[39] *Shields Furnishing v. Goff* [1973] I.C.R. 187 and *Sheet Metal Components Limited v. Plumridge* [1974] I.C.R. 373. Also *see* section 2 above under "Variation of the Employment Contract."
[40] G. Pitt, *Employment Law* (2nd ed., 1995), p. 184.

employee's personal circumstances to be taken into account."[41] The provisions concerning an offer of suitable alternative work are not confined to situations where there is a cessation of business. They apply to any potential redundancy and are extended by section 94 of the Employment Protection (Consolidation) Act 1978 to cover offers of employment made when there is a change in the ownership of the business. The provisions of section 94 (change of ownership) overlap with the provisions of the Transfer of Undertakings (Protection of Employment) Regulations 1981, which are discussed in more detail below.

Reorganisation and Rationalisation

Dismissals associated with reorganisation or rationalisation have been termed "economic dismissals." However, the definition of redundancy has been construed narrowly and not all economic dismissals will amount to redundancy. Under section 81(2)(b) redundancy is caused by the diminishing requirements of the business. There seems to be little difficulty in establishing that there is redundancy where *the amount of work required by the business has fallen.* In many corporate rescue scenarios, falls in the company's sales and production are symptoms of the overall problem. Dismissals are made in line with the consequent diminishing requirements for production workers will be redundancies. Corporate rescue may also involve a significant reorganisation of the way in which work is done. A reorganisation in which *the same amount of work is done, but more efficiently,* may be exactly what is required to achieve a successful rescue. The line of reasoning in the earlier cases was that if there is no reduction in the overall amount of work which is required to be done there is no redundancy.[42] Later cases place more emphasis on the requirements of the business for employees to carry out the work and thus find that the dismissed employees are redundant.[43] Another scenario is that *tasks are reorganised on the grounds of economic efficiency.* Many of the cases on this point involve a reorganisation of work which the employees find unacceptable; when they are dismissed (or constructively dismissed) they claim a redundancy payment based on

---

[41] *ibid.*
[42] *Delanair v. Mead* [1976] I.C.R. 522.
[43] *Carry All Motors Ltd v. Pennington* [1980] I.R.L.R. 455; *McCrea v. Cullen & Davidson Ltd* [1988] I.R.L.R. 30.

197

the fact that their job no longer exists. In *Johnson v. Nottingham Combined Police Authority*[44] the working hours of two civilian clerks were reorganised from a five-day week to a shift system and a six-day week. When they refused to accept these changes, they were dismissed and replacements were taken on. It was held that they were not redundant as the work remained the same and the fact that it was at different hours did not change its nature. In *North Riding Garages Ltd v. Butterwick*[45] the workshop manager of a garage had his job reorganised so that he had to do less engineering work and more paperwork, which he did not do well. When he was dismissed it was held to be for incompetence, not redundancy. The work for which he was employed remained essentially the same, as both the vehicle workshop and the requirement for a workshop manager remained. Occasionally, a reorganisation does involve a change in the nature of the work and a genuine redundancy. In *Murphy v. Epsom College*[46] a plumber who worked on a heating system was dismissed when a new heating system was installed which was electronically controlled. The employer required a heating technician who could deal with electrical and plumbing work rather than a general plumber. This was held to be a redundancy.

DISMISSAL FOR "SOME OTHER SUBSTANTIAL REASON"

The category of "some other substantial reason" (SOSR) is another potentially fair reason for dismissal. Deakin and Morris state:

> "Whereas the statutory definition of a 'redundancy' has been narrowly confined by case-law, the residual SOSR category has been greatly expanded to cover most economic dismissals which do not fall into the category of redundancy. The effect is that an economic dismissal will not be unfair just because it cannot be classified as redundancy; it will most likely fall into the SOSR category."

In order to fall into the SOSR category the employer has only to put forward a "sound, good business reason."[47] To be fair, not only

---

[44] [1974] 1 All E.R. 1082; [1974] I.C.R. 170.
[45] [1967] 2 Q.B. 56; [1967] 1 All E.R. 644.
[46] [1984] I.R.L.R. 271; [1985] I.C.R. 80.
[47] *Hollister v. National Farmers' Union* [1979] I.C.R. 542. *Orr v. Vaughan* [1981] I.R.L.R. 81 is an exceptional case where a tribunal found that objectively speaking no good business reason existed for the reorganisation and dismissal.

does a dismissal have to fall into a category of potentially fair reasons, but the actions of the employer must also pass the reasonableness test which has already been described. In *Evans v. Elementa Holdings Ltd*[47a] the employee was offered new terms as part of a reorganisation which would have required him to work overtime, unpaid, up to an unspecified number of hours per week. When he resigned and claimed constructive dismissal[48] the EAT held that the unreasonableness of the terms on offer made the dismissal unfair. This is an example how an employer that tries to force through variations in employment contracts can find itself having to pay compensation to employees. However, the dismissal in *Evans* was only held to be unreasonable because the demands of the employer were excessive.

Unfair Redundancy

Although it is usually fair to dismiss an employee for redundancy, employees often seek to claim that the dismissal was unfair in order to obtain the higher level of compensation which is attracted by an unfair dismissal. As stated above, under section 57 the fairness of a dismissal depends upon it being for a potentially fair reason and reasonable in the circumstances. The three main ways in which employees may be able to establish that the employer acted unreasonably in dismissing for redundancy are: the use of an unfair selection procedure; the failure to warn or consult employees; and the failure to consider offering alternative employment.[49]

Selection on the basis of union membership or non-membership is automatically unfair and in such cases the employee has the right to receive an enhanced "special award" of compensation.[50] If the method of selection for redundancy amounts to sex or racial discrimination, there is no upper limit set on the amount of compensation that the employee may be awarded. In *Clarke v. Eley (IMP) Kynoch Ltd*[51] it was held that selection of part-time workers before full-time workers amounted to indirect sex discrimination, as the majority of part-time staff were female. It is good industrial

---

[47a] [1982] I.R.L.R. 143.
[48] Constructive dismissal due to the unilateral variation of terms of employment is discussed in more detail in section 2 above.
[49] *Polkey v. A.E. Dayton Services Ltd* [1988] I.C.R. 142; [1987] I.R.L.R. 503.
[50] s.152 of the Trade Union and Labour Relations (Consolidation) Act 1992.
[51] [1983] I.C.R. 165.

relations practice for an employer to establish criteria for selection which as far as possible do not depend on the opinion of the person making the selection but can be objectively checked against such things as attendance record, efficiency, experience or length of service. In *Williams v. Compair Maxam Ltd*[52] the company's failure to use objective criteria for selection led to a finding of unfair dismissal. The company should also ensure that a record is kept of how the chosen selection criteria were applied. In *Paine and Moore v. Grundy (Teddington) Ltd*[53] a failure to ascertain reasons for absence when applying a selection procedure involving attendance records made the dismissals unfair.

Good industrial relations practice requires consultation with the redundant employee so that the employer can find out whether the needs of the business may be met in some other way than by dismissal, and, if not, what other steps the employer can take to ameliorate the blow to the employee.[54] Omission of this procedural step will only be found to be fair if the employers can reasonably conclude, in the light of the circumstances known to them at the time of the dismissal, that consultation or warning would be utterly useless.[55] An employer may also be under statutory obligations to consult and/or inform trade unions and the government. Under section 188 of the Trade Union and Labour Relations (Consolidation) Act 1992 an employer who proposes to make one or more employees redundant[56] has an obligation to inform and consult about such a decision with a trade union that has been recognised for collective bargaining for that grade of employee. The consultation must begin at the earliest opportunity and in any case in accordance with statutory minimum periods; which vary depending on how many employees the employer proposes to dismiss. Employers are also required to notify the Department of Employment when they propose to dismiss ten or more employees for redundancy.[57]

Whilst the employer cannot be under a duty to *find* alternative employment, redundancy has been found to be unfair where an

---

[52] [1982] I.C.R. 156.

[53] [1981] I.R.L.R. 267.

[54] *Grundy (Teddington) Ltd v. Plummer* [1983] I.R.L.R. 98.

[55] *Polkey v. A.E. Dayton Services Ltd* [1988] I.C.R. 142; [1987] I.R.L.R. 503.

[56] For this purpose the definition of redundancy has been widened by s.34 of the Trade Union Reform and Employment Rights Act 1993 to cover effectively all economic dismissals.

[57] s.193 of the Trade Union and Labour Relations (Consolidation) Act 1992. Failure to notify is punishable by a fine.

employer has failed to take *reasonable steps* to find alternative employment.[58] As stated above, the correct way for an industrial tribunal to test the reasonableness of the employer's actions is ask whether they fell within the range of reasonable employer responses. Thus, an attempt to find alternative employment that was limited to the employee's "section" was thought to be too narrow to be reasonable,[59] but an attempt that extended to the whole of a company but not to other companies in the group was found to be within the range of reasonableness.[60]

4. The Transfer of a Business

Many corporate rescue scenarios include the sale of the business or part of the business. If shares in the troubled company are sold, control of the company may pass into different hands and the new owners may wish to change the way in which the company's employees work. This scenario does not change the identity of the employer. The company as a separate legal person remains in existence. A change in corporate control has no direct effect on the employment contracts which have been made between the company as employer and its employees. If the new owners of the company wish to change the way employees work or the size of the workforce, sections 2 and 3 of this chapter provide the appropriate framework for considering the implications of such decisions.

The sale of a hived-down business is a different matter. A hive down involves the creation of a new subsidiary company and the transfer of relevant assets to the new company. The whole idea of a hive down is to be able to offer for sale a business which is not encumbered. The value of the hived-down business will be greater if it can be freed from the liabilities of the original company and will be smaller if it is required to take on the commitments of the original company. When the business is transferred from the troubled parent to the newly formed subsidiary it is very important to know whether the parent company's commitments to the employees of the business are also transferred. As employment is a personal relationship, at

---

[58] *Vokes Ltd v. Bear* [1974] I.C.R. 1; *Modern Injection Moulds Ltd v. Price* [1976] I.C.R. 370.

[59] *Thomas & Betts Manufacturing Ltd v. Harding* [1980] I.R.L.R. 255.

[60] *MDH Ltd v. Sussex* [1986] I.R.L.R. 123.

common law any change of employer amounts to a termination of the original contract and entering into a new one. At common law, the subsidiary company would be able to make a fresh start picking the best of the original worlkforce and offering them fresh contracts. The parent company would be responsible for making any payments associated with the termination of the original contracts. This position has been radically changed by the Transfer of Undertakings (Protection of Employment) Regulations 1981 (TUPE Regulations). The effect of the regulations is set out in regulation 5(1):

> "A relevant transfer shall not operate so as to terminate the contract of employment of any person employed by the transferor in the undertaking or part transferred but any such contract which would otherwise have been terminated by the transfer shall have effect after the transfer as if originally made between the person so employed and the transferee."

There is a statutory novation of the contracts of employment so that it is as though the transferee has always been the employee. Hive downs by receivers or administrators may, however, be different because they are specifically provided for in the TUPE Regulations. In a hive down, the transfer of the business from the parent to the new subsidiary occurs in advance of the sale of the subsidiary to new owners. Under regulation 5(3)[61] contracts are novated for employees of the business who were so employed "immediately before the transfer." Under this regulation employees of the insolvent parent would be transferred to the new subsidiary along with the viable business being rescued via the hive down. However, where a receiver, administrator or liquidator transfers a business from the insolvent parent to a wholly owned subsidiary special rules under regulation 4 apply. The transfer from the parent to the subsidiary is deemed not to have been effected until the subsidiary is sold or the business of the subsidiary is sold to *another person*. It is also deemed to be effected as one transaction only. This provision seemed to give receivers and administrators an opportunity to free the new subsidiary from any obligations to the existing employees of the business, using the following procedure:

(1) The receiver or administrator creates a wholly owned subsidiary. The business is transferred to the subsidiary.

---

[61] Transfer other than by a receiver, administrator or liquidator.

Under regulation 4 the transfer does not happen at this point.

(2) Employees are retained by the parent company and provided to the subsidiary to keep the business going.

(3) The employees who are technically employed by the parent company, but de facto working for the subsidiary company, are dismissed by the parent prior to (4) below. The new owner of the business may offer them employment on different terms.

(4) The share capital (or the business) of the subsidiary is sold. Under regulation 4 the transfer is deemed to happen at this point as a transfer from the parent to the subsidiary (or from the parent to the new owners of the subsidiary's business).

The receiver or administrator may therefore dismiss the employees before the point at which the TUPE Regulations bite, so that they never enter the subsidiary's employment and so cannot be transferred to the ultimate purchaser of the business. The validity of this procedure and of regulation 4 itself is, however, in doubt. The TUPE Regulations implement the E.C. Acquired Rights Directive,[62] but they do not do this very well. As a result there has been litigation concerning the interpretation that should be given to the Regulations when they are read in the context of the Directive. In *Lister v. Forth Dry Dock & Engineering Co. Ltd*[63] the transferor (Forth Dry Dock; insolvent) which was in receivership dismissed its employees one hour before the transfer of the business to the transferee (Forth Estuary; solvent). The employees were not taken on by Forth Estuary and so made a claim for holiday pay and damages for wrongful and unfair dismissal against Forth Estuary. The House of Lords had the task of interpreting the phrase "immediately before the transfer" used in regulation 5(3). It was held that this phrase should be read as applying; both to an employee actually employed immediately before the transfer and to one who "would have been so employed if he had not been unfairly dismissed in the circumstances described in

---

[62] E.C. Directive 77/187.
[63] [1989] I.R.L.R. 161.

regulation 8(1)", that is dismissals which have as their reason or principal reason "the transfer or a reason connected with it." The effect of *Lister* is that the transferee will inherit the pre-existing liabilities of the transferor towards its dismissed employees. It is not yet clear how the ruling in *Lister* will affect the workings of regulation 4, but it may mean that hived-down businesses under receivership or administration become less attractive to potential purchasers as there is a risk of a claim from the dismissed employees of an insolvent parent company.

5. Administration, Administrative Receivership and Employment Contracts

Both administrators and administrative receivers are given extensive powers. These powers include the power to carry on the business of the company and the power to employ and dismiss employees. In order to continue running the business as a going concern, some, if not all, of the existing employees are likely to be needed. Employees are unlikely to work without regular payment, so, in practices wages and salaries will be paid to the employees who are not dismissed immediately by the relevant office holder. If they continue to work and to be paid, employees may not question whether they are employed under their old contract of employment or under a new one made by the office holder as agent of the company. However, this issue becomes important if and when the employees want to obtain statutory or contractual entitlements accrued under the old contract. The position of employees was considered to be of sufficient importance for special provisions to be made concerning contracts of employment in the Insolvency Act 1986. All receivers appointed under debentures[64] were made personally liable on contracts of employment which they "adopted," but with a right of indemnity out of the assets of the company.[65] In administration the consequence of "adopting" a contract of employment was that

---

[64] The appointment of a receiver by the court automatically terminates existing contracts of employment because employment is a personal relationship and the appointment of a receiver by the court substitutes a new party in place of the company. Receivers are rarely appointed by the court.

[65] Administrative receivers under s.44 and other receivers under s.37 of the Insolvency Act 1986.

employee claims were ranked in priority above the administrator's remuneration and expenses.[66] All three categories (receiver, administrative receiver and administrator) had 14 days in which to decide whether to adopt a contract of employment because nothing done or omitted to be done within the 14 days after appointment was to be taken as adopting the contract.

The framing of these provisions meant that adopting employment contracts was potentially burdensome to all three categories of office holder and ways were sought of avoiding "adoption." Decisions in the cases of *Nicoll v. Cutts*[67] and *Re Specialised Mouldings Ltd*[68] led many insolvency practitioners to believe that the adoption of employment contracts could be avoided by writing to the employees, saying that their contracts of employment would be continued on the same basis as previously, that the receiver (or administrative receiver or administrator) would not be adopting the contract, and that they (the administrator, receiver or administrative receiver) would assume no personal liability in relation to the employee's employment. The writing of such letters became common practice. The Court of Appeal decision in the case of *Powdrill v. Watson Re Paramount Airways Ltd*[69] made it clear that such letters are ineffective. Dillon L.J. in the Court of Appeal decision said that "the mere assertion by an administrator or receiver that he is not adopting the contract is mere wind with no legal effect, because adoption is a matter not merely of words but of fact."[70] Browne-Wilkinson L.J., in a House of Lords judgment that affirmed the Court of Appeal decision, found that "For the purpose of section 19 and section 44 [of the Insolvency Act 1986] an employee's contract of employment is 'adopted' if he is continued in employment for more than 14 days after the appointment of the administrator or receiver."[71]

The *Powdrill v. Watson* decisions meant that many administrative receivers were personally liable for the accrued holiday pay and pension rights of ex-employees of dissolved companies. Administrators were also affected where they had assumed that the priority

---

[66] s.19 of the Insolvency Act 1986.
[67] [1985] B.C.L.C. 322.
[68] Unreported.
[69] [1994] I.R.L.R. 295.
[70] *ibid*. at 299.
[71] [1995] 2 W.L.R. 312 at 352. The House of Lords decided on three appeals: *Powdrill v. Watson* (Paramount Airways Ltd), which was concerned with administration; and *Talbot v. Cadge* and *Talbot v. Grundy* (Leyland DAF Ltd and Ferranti International Plc), which were concerned with administrative receivership.

ranking of liabilities to employees only applied to current liabilities and had made final distributions of the company's assets on that basis. An outcry from insolvency practitioners following the Court of Appeal decision resulted in emergency legislation being introduced to save administrative receivers and administrators from what were seen as the problems of the ruling in *Paramount*. The Insolvency Act 1994 amended the Insolvency Act 1986 by limiting the claims by employees under "adopted" contracts to "qualifying liabilities" which are defined as wages, salaries and occupational pension contributions. Holiday and sickness payments are included only in respect of services rendered wholly or partly after the adoption of the contract, and (where services are rendered only partly after the adoption of the contract) the portion of the qualifying liability which represents payment in respect of services rendered before the adoption of the contract is to be disregarded. Under the new statutory provisions administrators and administrative receivers can retain the services of employees in the knowledge that their commitment is restricted. However, the Insolvency Act 1994 did not operate retrospectively; it only applies to contracts of employment adopted on or after March 15, 1994. The appeals to the House of Lords were not affected by the new provisions. The 1994 Act also left the position of "ordinary" receivers unchanged.

In summary: Before the Court of Appeal decision in *Paramount*, administrators, administrative receivers and receivers retained the employees they needed to run the business in the belief that they could limit their liabilities to them by a simple letter. The Insolvency Act 1994 was introduced following the Court of Appeal decision. It has the effect of officially limiting the liabilities of administrative receivers and the priority claims that can be made by employees in an administration. For administrators and administrative receivers the consequences of retaining employees to keep the business running in the hope of achieving a rescue are now both known and limited. It is difficult to assess whether rescue attempts will have been encouraged by the extra certainty, or discouraged by the knowledge that adoption of employment contracts cannot be avoided by a simple letter. For ordinary receivers, *Paramount* coupled with the failure to include receivers in the emergency legislation means that the potential personal liabilities which can arise out of retaining employees beyond 14 days are now much larger than was believed pre-*Paramount*. Rescue attempts by ordinary receivers will have been discouraged.

6. Conclusion

This chapter has demonstrated that the legal position of employees must be considered very carefully when mounting a rescue attempt whether within a legal rescue regime or not. The legal position is not, however, everything; political and motivational aspects of employment relations are also very important.

In the context of retrenchment, Hardy states:

"Long-term survival depends on the commitment and motivation of the continuing employees. Unfortunately, the personnel reductions involved in these [retrenchment] decisions can lead to resentment, fear, union hostility, industrial action, and unfavourable publicity. Given the problems that led to the need for cutbacks in the first place, management can ill afford to allow productivity to fall, strikes to occur, unfavourable publicity to deter customers, or people with much needed skills to leave. Managers have, nevertheless, often ignored these human implications of downsizing, because they fail to see the link between them and the survival of the enterprise. . . . Many of the adverse effects of retrenchment—for both employees and organizational survival—can be avoided with a retrenchment program that takes into account the needs of both the departing and the continuing employees, as well as the unions and other interest groups which are involved. It will allay many of the fears associated with the cutbacks, and help employees to view retrenchment as a challenge rather than a threat, enabling them to respond positively to the changes demanded of them."[72]

In the broader context of the management of change, Carnell states:

"To manage change effectively involves the ability to create a new synthesis of people, resources, ideas, opportunities and demands. . . . People must be influenced, departmental boundaries crossed or even 'swallowed up', new ideas accepted, new ways of working embraced and new standards of performance and quality achieved. The politics of the organization are crucial. Support must be mobilized, coalitions built and supported, opposition identified and considered. People need help to cope with the stress, anxiety and uncertainties of change. Continuity and tradition must be overturned, in part, as the old is replaced by the new. Yet, continuity and tradition provide people with stability, support and meaning and should not needlessly be destroyed. The effective management of organizational change demands attention to all these somewhat conflicting issues and challenges."[73]

---

[72] Hardy, *Strategies for Retrenchment and Turnaround: The Politics of Survival* (1989), p. 2.
[73] Carnell, *Managing Change in Organizations* (2nd ed., 1995), p. 113.

The concept of corporate rescue has been given a wide meaning in this book. It includes *any major intervention necessary to avert the eventual failure of the company*, but another constant element within the idea of rescue is that it is a response to a *crisis*. The advice given above about the management of a retrenchment program, or a major structural and strategic change is good, but requires time. In some rescue situations there may be time to plan and act appropriately. However, many potential rescue situations arise out of sudden financial crisis. In a sudden and severe crisis, managers may themselves feel in need of "help to cope with the stress, anxiety and uncertainties of change," but they are unlikely to have the time or resources to organise such help for themselves or their employees. Also, what is possible in a large company may be impossible in a small one.

Chapter 11

Conclusion

1. Summary

It is now time to look back over the material that has been presented and to recapitulate some of the arguments. This is done under three headings: concepts; approaches; and law.

CONCEPTS

In Part I the aim was to concentrate on the conceptualising of corporate rescue. The starting point for all the arguments which follow was that corporate rescue, as an activity, should be defined broadly. In particular it should include activity both within and outwith[1] legal rescue regimes. The definition of corporate rescue employed throughout this volume is *a major intervention necessary to avert the eventual failure of the company*. In Chapter 2 the scope of the chosen definition was discussed and some of the problems arising out of it were addressed. Questions were posed concerning both the beginning and ending of corporate rescue: When does the day-to-day management of a business change in character and become a rescue attempt? And when is a rescue completed, or (put slightly differently) what constitutes a successful rescue?

Chapters 3 and 4 of the book explored the route to eventual failure more closely. Financial distress is usually seen as a step on the road to

---

[1] The bulk of this book has been written during my first year's residence in Scotland. The discovery of the use of the word "outwith" has been a delight. I hope its appearance here is seen as a celebration of its usefulness and appropriateness and not as an attempt on my part to establish my Scottish credentials.

eventual failure. In Chapter 3 the concept of financial distress was discussed as a warning signal; as a hurdle; and as a trigger. The material presented in Chapter 4 was based on the premise that, once a company is financially distressed, it can proceed in one of two ways: it can fail or not. The techniques that have been used to distinguish failures from non-failures were presented. The development of prediction of failure models was discussed and their limitations were pointed out. The chapter also indicated some of the practical applications of the results of such models. The focus for the discussion in Chapter 5 was the going concern concept. A short non-technical treatment was followed by a more technical explanation of how accountants define and apply the going concern concept and the implications of this for corporate rescue. Part I of the book closed with Chapter 6, on the design of legal rescue regimes. The chapter began by pointing out that the task of judging the success or failure of a rescue regime is far from simple. Even at a theoretical level, criteria for comparing the comparative efficiency of rescue regimes produce hazy rather than clear-cut results. A taxonomy of rescue regimes highlighted their advantages and disadvantages. Chapter 6 also included discussions about the process of decision making and about uncertainty. Whether a company is rescued or not will depend on both the law and the decisions taken by various "players" (directors, creditors, etc.) given the legal possibilities. The Cork Report, the new rescue possibilities introduced in 1985, concerns about the low up-take of the CVA procedure, and the drafting of further reforms all suggest that there is not enough corporate rescue in the United Kingdom. In designing (or re-designing) a rescue regime the aim is to produce a system that operates in such a way that the "right" companies (and only the "right" companies) are rescued. The major problem, of course, is knowing which are the "right" companies. Another design problem is the difficulty of predicting how a technically sound regime will work in practice. If designers are to predict the response to a regime correctly, they need to understand the way in which the relevant "players" make their decisions. Chapter 6 concluded that decision making under adversity and uncertainty (the norm for a company in crisis) may be more difficult to predict than routine decision making.

Overall, Part I of the book demonstrated the complexity of the problem of designing and implementing a rescue regime. The issue is complex because definitions are not clear-cut, because criteria for judging success or failure[2] are not obvious, and because the impact of existing concepts in law[3] and accounting[4] cannot be ignored.

APPROACHES

Chapter 2 not only explored the basic concept of corporate rescue, but also introduced the reader to the two-fold pattern of approach employed throughout the book. The first characteristic of this book is its multidisciplinarity. For me it makes no sense to attempt an evaluation of the workings of the law in isolation. In the context of a distressed company, all decisions are informed by the law, but in some decisions the law is the determining factor and in others it has a lesser part to play. Legal expertise may be a necessary ingredient of corporate rescue, but legal skills alone will not be sufficient. In a successful rescue, legal, managerial, accounting, economic and other competencies are likely to be combined; thus, at a practical level, the law does not stand alone. At a theoretical level, a discussion of companies in decline, by its very terminology, encourages a multi-disciplinary approach. This book's multidisciplinarity is, of course, connected with the broad definition of corporate rescue which was adopted. A narrower definition, confined to formal legal rescue, would have neither demanded nor allowed the degree of multi-disiplinarity that has been employed here.

The second feature of the book is its use of the United States as a comparator. The United States was a natural choice because it provides a contrast in terms of its insolvency regime (*i.e.* the contrast between a creditor- and a debtor-based regime) but offers similarity in its corporate governance system, at least in respect of the largest companies. In the British and U.S. corporate governance systems external long-term finance is mostly raised on an active (and some claim efficient) stock market. Shares are relatively widely owned, there are few large controlling shareholdings and the threat of takeover is seen as the main way of disciplining management. In this type of system, banks make their decisions as *outsiders*. In Germany

---

[2] *i.e.* criteria for judging either an individual rescue attempt or the operation of a regime as a whole.

[3] For instance, the statutory definitions of insolvency and the provisions concerning wrongful trading.

[4] For instance, the going concern concept and accounting-based definitions of distress.

and Japan, in contrast, banks often make decisions as *insiders*, as they supply most of the external finance and demand seats on the board of directors.

LAW

Part II of the book focused on the law and attempted to show how the legal position of the various players in a rescue scenario permitted or restricted decision making and thus affected the course of the rescue itself. Chapter 7 tackled the position of directors seeking to rescue their company by making either formal of informal arrangements with creditors. A large part of the chapter was concerned with the renegotiating of loans and the raising of extra finance. These activities are often the most crucial element of a corporate rescue.

In Chapter 8 the position of the company's secured creditors was revealed as extremely strong. A secured creditor holding a floating charge over the whole, or substantially the whole of the company's property, is in the strongest position, as this form of security brings with it the ability to appoint an administrative receiver who must act primarily in the interests of the charge holder. "Lightweight" floating charges can be coupled with fixed charges so that it is the fixed charge which provides the security in terms of asset value, whilst the floating charge provides the charge holder with the statutory right to appoint an administrative receiver. The courts have reluctantly held in *Re Croftbell Ltd*[5] that the device of a lightweight floating charge did operate in this way. The appointment of an administrative receiver not only operates *in favour* of secured creditors, because it takes precedence, but also operates *against* more pure forms of rescue such as the administration order.

In Chapter 9 the position of the company's unsecured creditors was considered. The idea that unsecured creditors voluntarily accept the riskiness of their position was questioned. Unsecured trade creditors use retention of title clauses as a way of escaping the consequences of their unsecured status. Indeed, retention of title can be viewed as a form of security.[6] In the course of a corporate rescue, a retention of title clause can also be used as part of the bargaining power of unsecured creditors, who may be asked to continue to

---

[5] [1990] B.C.C. 781.
[6] This aspect of retention of title clauses was considered briefly at the end of Chap. 8.

supply the company so that it can continue to trade. Unsecured suppliers of finance demand high interest payments; higher returns compensate for higher risks. However, these creditors also seek to minimise their risks and in a rescue scenario may only be willing to advance money if it is made subject to a *Quistclose* trust, so that, if the purpose of the advance is not achieved, any balance will return to the particular creditor and not enter the general pool available for all creditors. The idea of offering a statutory super priority to creditors who advance money during a rescue attempt was also discussed. This proposal has recently been put forward by the DTI, but then abandoned. The advantage of a statutory super priority is that distressed companies may be able to raise funds more easily. One of the disadvantages is that lenders may find this market too attractive and be discouraged from making advances in more normal circumstances. Overall, Chapter 9 concluded that unsecured creditors were likely to make use of every opportunity that might improve their position either during a rescue or in the event of the company's liquidation. These activities all potentially affect rescue attempts.

In Chapter 10 it was the turn of the employees to be considered. Like the unsecured creditors, the employees of a distressed company are often perceived as having little power. However, in a rescue attempt the company is likely to retain some employees, perhaps on new terms and conditions, and to dismiss others. Contractual obligations and employment protection law together mean that management's discretion in these matters is not unlimited. If a rescue plan includes the sale of the whole or a part of the company's business, the TUPE regulations need particular attention. If the TUPE regulations apply, they will preserve employees' employment contracts through the transfer so that the buyer of the business becomes the employer. The efficacy of a procedure that has regularly been used by administrators and administrative receivers to avoid the transfer of employee-related obligations to the buyer of a company's business is in some doubt following a recent European decision. Overall, in a rescue situation, the legal position of employees may be strong and their capacity to contribute to a smooth and successful rescue or to become a stumbling block should not be underestimated.

2. Unfinished Business

This book has probably raised more questions than it has answered. In conclusion, I want to highlight some of its unfinished business in three areas: U.K. law reform, Europe and empirics.

UNITED KINGDOM REFORM

This is necessarily an area of unfinished business. This chapter of the book is being written during the final run up to a general election.[7] Whatever the character of the new government, it is unlikely that the reform of U.K. insolvency law will be high on the agenda. However, the Insolvency Service's work on the drafting of the provisions for a 28-day moratorium scheme, at least for small companies, continues and may be taken up by the new Government.

EUROPE

This is by way of being unstarted business rather than unfinished business. The European Union has not harmonised its insolvency regimes. No attempt has been made in this volume to deal with the insolvency regimes that operate in other European countries.[8] The E.C. Convention on Insolvency Proceedings should, however, be mentioned. This is not a harmonisation measure, rather its aim is to simplify the administration of insolvency cases that have cross-border aspects.[9] Under the convention, jurisdiction to open insolvency proceedings is given to the contracting state in which the debtor's centre of main interests is situated.[10] Once insolvency proceedings have been opened, the convention gives them automatic recognition and enforcement rights in all contracting states. The corporate insolvency proceedings covered by the convention include, *inter alia*, CVAs and administration, but not receivership. Where a debtor has

---

[7] The result, of course, was a Labour victory following 18 years with the Conservatives in power.

[8] Rescue procedures in France, Germany and Ireland are described in Brown, *Corporate Rescue: Insolvency Law in Practice* (1996).

[9] Cross-border problems and conflict-of-laws rules under private international law are beyond the scope of this book.

[10] "Centre of main interests" is not defined, but there is a rebuttable presumption that it is situated at a company's registered office.

an establishment[11] (not its centre of main interests) in a contracting state, the convention also covers secondary insolvency proceedings opened by "local" creditors of the establishment. Such proceedings are recognised by other contracting states but only in respect of the debtor's assets situated in the "local" establishment's state.

EMPIRICS

There are many empirical questions about corporate rescue in the United Kingdom that have not been answered in this book. The empirical results that have been reported mostly relate to the United States. A *full* assessment of the workings of the Insolvency Act 1986 would include empirical results. Tests of the levels, trends and effectiveness of rescue activity in the United Kingdom would be appropriate. Comparisons of the costs of informal and formal procedures would be helpful. Unfortunately, data that are readily available in the United States are not obtainable in the United Kingdom. This explains the lack of U.K. empirical studies that employ the sorts of statistical and econometric modelling so familiar in the U.S. work. One of the reasons for a lack of information is confidentiality. This makes empirical work that requires information on a large number of individual rescues almost impossible. The only empirical indicators of rescue activity for the United Kingdom are the overall statistics on the numbers of CVAs, administration orders, etc., and the anecdotal reports that arise out of research based on interviews. Access to data would only be a first step towards good statistical empirical research. The problems concerning the underlying theory, modelling, methodology and interpretation of the results would be immense. However, a complete lack of data means that virtually nothing empirical can be said about the effectiveness of the Insolvency Act 1986 in terms of rescuing the "right" companies (however defined). Before 1985 it was claimed that too few companies were being rescued. It is still being claimed that too few companies are being rescued and further reform is thought necessary. With access to the right sort of data, the results of empirical research could make a significant contribution to the debate.

---

[11] "Establishment" is defined as "any place where the debtor carries out a non-transitory economic activity with human means and goods."

Appendix 1

Insolvency Rules 1986, Rule 1.3

1.3(1) The directors' proposal shall provide a short explanation of why, in their opinion, a voluntary arrangement under Part I of the Act is desirable, and give reasons why the company's creditors may be expected to concur with such an arrangement.

1.3(2) The following matters shall be stated, or otherwise dealt with, in the directors' proposal—

    (a) the following matters, so far as within the directors' immediate knowledge—

        (i) the company's assets, with an estimate of their respective values,

        (ii) the extent (if any) to which the assets are charged in favour of creditors,

        (iii) the extent (if any) to which assets are to be excluded from the voluntary arrangement;

    (b) particulars of any property, other than assets of the company itself, which is proposed to be included in the arrangement, the source of such property and the terms on which it is to be made available for inclusion;

    (c) the nature and amount of the company's liabilities (so far as within the directors' immediate knowledge), the manner in which they are proposed to be met modified, postponed or otherwise dealt with by means of the arrangement, and (in particular—

        (i) how it is proposed to deal with preferential creditors (defined in section 4(7)) and creditors who are, or claim to be, secured,

        (ii) how persons connected with the company (being creditors) are proposed to be treated under the arrangement, and

(iii) whether there are, to the directors' knowledge, any circumstances giving rise to the possibility, in the event that the company should go into liquidation, of claims under—

section 238 (transactions at an undervalue),
section 239 (preferences),
section 244 (extortionate credit transaction), or
section 245 (floating charges invalid);

and where any such circumstances are present, whether, and if so how, it is proposed under the voluntary arrangement to make provision for wholly or partly indemnifying the company in respect of such claims.

(d) whether any, and if so what, guarantees have been given of the company's debts by other persons, specifying which (if any) of the guarantors are persons connected with the company;

(e) the proposed duration of the voluntary arrangement;

(f) the proposed dates of distributions to creditors, with estimates of their amounts;

(g) the amount proposed to be paid to the nominee (as such) by way of remuneration and expenses;

(h) the manner in which it is proposed that the supervisor of the arrangement should be remunerated and his expenses defrayed;

(j) whether, for the purposes of the arrangement, any guarantees are to be offered by directors, or other persons, and whether (if so) any security is to be given or sought;

(k) the manner in which funds held for the purposes of the arrangement are to be banked, invested or otherwise dealt with pending distribution to creditors;

(l) the manner in which funds held for the purpose of payment to creditors, and not so paid on the termination of the arrangement, are to be dealt with;

(m) the manner in which the business of the company is proposed to be conducted during the course of the arrangement;

(n) details of any further credit facilities which it is intended to arrange for the company, and how the debts so arising are to be paid;

(o) the functions which are to be undertaken by the supervisor of the arrangement; and

(p) the name, address and qualifications of the person proposed as supervisor of the voluntary arrangement, and confirmation that he is (so far as the directors are aware) qualified to act as an insolvency practitioner in relation to the company.

Appendix 2

Insolvency Act 1986, Schedule 1: Powers of Administrative Receivers

1. Power to take possession of, collect and get in the property of the company and, for that purpose, to take such proceedings as may seem to him expedient.

2. Power to sell or otherwise dispose of the property of the company by public auction or private auction or private contract.

3. Power to raise or borrow money and grant security therefor over the property of the company.

4. Power to appoint a solicitor or accountant or other professionally qualified person to assist him in the performance of his functions.

5. Power to bring or defend any action or other legal proceedings in the name and on behalf of the company.

6. Power to refer to arbitration any question affecting the company.

7. Power to effect and maintain insurances in respect of the business and property of the company.

8. Power to use the company's seal.

9. Power to do all acts and to execute in the name and on behalf of the company any deed, receipt or other document.

10. Power to draw, accept, make and endorse any bill of exchange or promissory note in the name and on behalf of the company.

11. Power to appoint any agent to do any business which he is unable to do himself or which can more conveniently be done by an agent and power to employ and dismiss employees.

12. Power to do all such things (including the carrying out of works) as may be necessary for the realisation of the property of the company.

13. Power to make any payment which is necessary or incidental to the performance of his functions.

14. Power to carry on the business of the company.

15. Power to establish subsidiaries of the company.

16. Power to transfer to subsidiaries of the company the whole or any part of the business and property of the company.

17. Power to grant or accept a surrender of a lease or tenancy of any of the property of the company, and to take a lease or tenancy of any property required or convenient for the business of the company.

18. Power to make any arrangement or compromise on behalf of the company.

19. Power to call up any uncalled capital of the company.

20. Power to rank and claim in the bankruptcy, insolvency, sequestration or liquidation of any person indebted to the company and to receive dividends, and to accede to trust deeds for the creditors of any such person.

21. Power to present or defend a petition for the winding up of the company.

22. Power to change the situation of the company's registered office.

23. Power to do all other things incidental to the exercise of the foregoing powers.

Bibliography

Aghion, P., Hart, O. and Moore, J. (1992) "The Economics of Bankruptcy Reform", *Journal of Law Economics and Organization*, 8, (3), 523–546.

Altman, E.I. (1968), "Financial Ratios, Discriminant Analysis and the Prediction of Corporate Failure", *Journal of Finance*, 23, 589–609.

Altman, E.I., Haldeman, R. and Narayanan, P. (1977) "Zeta Analysis, A New Model to Identify Bankruptcy Risk Corporations", *Journal of Banking and Finance*, 1, 29–54.

Anderman, S.D. (1993) *Labour Law: Management Decisions and Workers' Rights* (2nd ed., Butterworths, London).

Arnold, J., Hope, T., Southworth, A. and Kirkham, L. (1994) *Financial Accounting* (2nd ed. Prentice Hall, New York and London).

Bannock, G. and Doran, A. (1991) *Venture Capital and the Equity Gap* (National Westminster Bank, London).

Barnes, P. and Hooi, D. (1987) "The Strange Case of the Qualified Success", *Accountancy*, November 32–33.

Belcher, A. (1991) "Predicting Company Failure", *Insolvency Law and Practice*, 7, (2), 64–67.

Belcher, A. (1993) "The Economic Implications of Attempting to Rescue Companies" in Rajak, H. (ed.) *Insolvency Law, Theory and Practice* (Sweet and Maxwell), 235–249.

Belcher, C.A. (1994) "Company Reporting of Research and Development Expenditure: A Study of the Decision to Disclose and the Market's Reaction to Disclosure", Ph.D. thesis University of Manchester.

Belcher, A. (1995) "Techniques for Evaluating Regulatory Change", *European Journal of Law and Economics*, 2, 211–226.

Berry, R.H., Crum, R.E. and Waring, A. (1993) *Corporate Performance Evaluation and Bank Lending Decisions* (CIMA, London).

Betker, B.L. (1995) "An Empirical Examination of Prepackaged Bankruptcy" *Financial Management*, 24, (1), 4.

Bolton, J.E. (1971) *Report of the Committee of Inquiry on Small Firms* Cmnd. 4871 (HMSO, London).

Bowman, R.G. (1983) "Understanding and Conducting Event Studies", *Journal of Business Finance and Accounting*, 10, 561–584.

Brealey, R.A. and Myers, S.C. (1996) *Principles of Corporate Finance* (5th ed., McGraw-Hill, London and New York).

Bridge, M. (1992) "The Quistclose Trust in a World of Secured Transactions", *Oxford Journal of Legal Studies*, 12, 358.

Brown, C., Hamilton, J. and Medoff, J. (1990) *Employers Large and Small* (Harvard University Press, Cambridge, Mass. and London).

Brown, D. (1996) *Corporate Rescue: Insolvency Law in Practice* (John Wiley & Sons, Chichester).

Bublitz, B. and Ettredge, M. (1989) "The Information in Discretionary Outlays: Advertising, Research and Development", *Accounting Review*, 64, 108–124.

Carnell, C.A. (1995) *Managing Change in Organizations* (2nd ed., Prentice Hall International, Hemel Hempstead).

Cooke, T.E. and Hicks, A. (1993) "Wrongful Trading–Predicting Insolvency", *Journal of Business Law*, 338–350.

Cork Gully on Insolvency Judgments 1980–1990 (Longman, 1991).

Cork, K. (1982) "Insolvency Law and Practice: Report of the Review Committee" Cmnd. 8558.

Coyne, J. and Wright, M. (eds.) (1986) *Divestment and Strategic Change* (Philip Allan; Oxford).

Cressy, R.C. *Small Firm Debt Rescheduling Versus Insolvency: The Bank's Decision Problem*, SME Centre, Warwick Business School.

Cross, M. (1983) "Small firms in the United Kingdom" in D.J. Storey (ed.) *The Small Firm: An International Survey* (Croom Helm, Kent).

Deakin, E.B. (1972), "A Discriminant Analysis of Predictors of Business Failure", *Journal of Accounting Research*, 10, (1), 167–179.

Deakin, S. and Morris, G.S. (1995) *Labour Law* (Butterworths, London, Dublin and Edinburgh).

DeAngelo, H., DeAngelo, L. and Skinner, D.J. (1994) "Accounting Choice in Troubled Companies", *Journal of Accounting and Economics*, 17, 140.

DeAngelo, L. (1986) "Accounting Numbers as Market Valuation Substitutes: A Study of Management Buyouts of Public Stockholders", *The Accounting Review*, 67, 77–96.

DeFond, M.L. and Jiambalvo, J. (1994) "Debt Covenant Violation and Manipulation of Accruals", *Journal of Accounting and Economics*, 17, 145.

Dixon, R. (1991) "Venture Capitalists and the Appraisal of Investments", *Omega*, 19, (5), 333–44.

Duggan, M. (1992) *Business Reorganisations and Employment Law* (Longman, London).

Dunne, P. and Hughes, A. (1992), "The Changing Structure of Competitive Industry in the 1980s" in C. Driver and P. Dunne (eds.) *Structural Change in the U.K. Economy* (Cambridge University Press, Cambridge).

Easterbrook, F.H. (1990) "Is Corporate Bankruptcy Efficient?" *Journal of Financial Economics*, 27, 411.

Elks, L. (1994) "Retention of Title: The Leyland DAF Cases", *Insolvency Law and Practice*, 9, (6), 172.

Farrar, J.H., Furey, N.E., Hannigan, B.M. and Wylie, P. (1991) *Farrar's Company Law* (Butterworths, London, Dublin and Edinburgh).

Fletcher, I.F., (ed.) (1990) *Cross-Border Insolvency: Comparative Dimensions*, UKNCCL.

Flood, J., Abbey, R., Skordaki, E. and Aber, P. (1995) (*The Professional Restructuring of Corporate Rescue: Company Voluntary Arrangements and the London Approach*, ACCA Research Report No. 45 (Certified Accountants Educational Trust, London).

Flood, J. & Skordaki, E. (1995) "Insolvency Practitioners and Big Corporate Insolvencies", ACCA Research Report No. 45 (Certified Accountants Educational Trust, London).

Floyd, R.E. (1995) "Corporate Recovery: The London Approach" *Insolvency Law and Practice*, 11, (3), 82.

Foster, G. (1986) *Financial Statement Analysis* (2nd ed., Prentice Hall, Englewood Cliffs).

Franks, J.R. and Torous, W.N. (1989) "An Empirical Investigation of U.S. Firms in Reorganization", *Journal of Finance*, 44, (3), 750.

Franks, J.R. and Torous, W.N. (1992) "Lessons from a Comparison of U.S. and U.K. Insolvency Codes", *Oxford Review of Economic Policy*, 8, (3), 70–82.

Frost, A.J. and Hager, D.P. (1990) *Debt Securities* (Heinemann Professional Publishing, Oxford).

Gilson, S. (1989) "Management Turnover and Financial Distress", *Journal of Financial Economics*, 25, 241–262.

Gilson, S.C. (1990) "Bankruptcy, Boards, Banks and Blockholders", *Journal of Financial Economics*, 27, 355–387.

Gilson, S.C., John, K. and Lang, L.H.P. (1990) "Troubled Debt Restructurings: An Empirical Study of Private Reorganization of Firms in Default", *Journal of Financial Economics*, 27, 315–353.

Goldberg, W.H. (1983) *Mergers: Motives, Modes, Methods* (Gower, Aldershot).

Goldston, M.R. (1992) *The Turnaround Prescription: Repositioning Troubled Companies* (The Free Press, New York).

Goodhart, W. and Jones, G. (1980) "The Infiltration of Equitable Doctrine into English Commercial Law", *Modern Law Review*, 43, 509–510.

Goudie, A.W. (1987) "Forecasting Corporate Failure: The Use of Discriminant Analysis within a Disaggregated Model of the Corporate Sector", *Journal of the Royal Statistical Society*, 150, (1), 69–81).

Gould, S.J. (1977) *Ever Since Darwin* (Norton, New York).

Grinyer, P.H., Mayes, D.G. and McKiernan, P. (1988) *Sharpbenders: The Secrets of Unleasing Corporate Potential* (Basil Blackwell, Oxford and New York).

Hahn F. (1984) *Equilibrium and Macroeconomics* (Basil Blackwell, Oxford).

Hardy, C. (1989) *Strategies for Retrenchment and Turnaround: The Politics of Survival* (Walter de Gruyter, Berlin and New York).

Hill, S. (1990) "Company Voluntary Arrangements", *Insolvency Law and Practice,* 6, (2), 47–58.

Hudson, J. and Cuthbertson, C. (1991) "A Rising Tide of Bankruptcies", *Insolvency Law and Practice,* 7, (1), 138–139.

Hurst, D.K. (1995), *Crisis and Renewal: Meeting the Challenge of Organizational Change* (Harvard Business School Press, Boston).

Innes, J. (1990) "External Management Auditing of Companies: A Survey of Bankers", *Accounting, Auditing and Accountability*, 3, (1), 18–37.

The Insolvency Service (1993) *Company Voluntary Arrangements and Administration Orders: A Consultative Document*, October.

The Insolvency Service (1995) *Revised Proposals for a New Company Voluntary Arrangement Procedure*, April.

Jones, B. (1993) "Insolvency and the Balance Sheet", *Insolvency Law and Practice* 9, (5), 136.

Kent, P. (1993) "The London Approach", *Bank of England Quarterly Bulletin*, 33, (1), 110.

Kent, P. (1994) "The London Approach: Distressed Debt Trading", *Bank of England Quarterly Bulletin*, 34, (2), 172.

Khanna, N. and Poulsen, A.B. (1995) "Managers of Financially Distressed Firms: Villains or Scapegoats?" *Journal of Finance*, 50, (3), 919–940.

Kharbanda, O.P. and Stallworthy, E.A. (1985) *Corporate Failure: Prediction, Panacea and Prevention* (McGraw-Hill, Maidenhead).

Kharbanda, O.P. and Stallworthy, E.A. (1988), *Takeovers, Acquisitions and Mergers: Strategies for Rescuing Companies in Distress* (Kogan Page, New Jersey).

Langlois, R.N. (1986) (ed.) *Economics as a Process* (Cambridge University Press, Cambridge), 226.

Lau, A.H. (1987), "A Five-state Financial Distress Prediction Model", *Journal of Accounting Research*, spring, 127–138.

Lev, B. (1974) *Financial Statement Analysis: A New Approach* (Prentice Hall, Englewood Cliffs).

Limmack, R.J. (1992) "Corporate Mergers and Shareholder Wealth Effects 1977–1986", *Accounting and Business Research*, 21, 184–221.

Lingard, J.R. (1989) *Corporate Rescues and Insolvencies* (2nd ed., Butterworths, London).

Lipe, R.C. (1986) "The information Contained in the Components of Earnings", *Journal of Accounting Research* (Supplement), 37–64.

Littlechild (1986) "Three Types of Market Process" in Langlois, R.N. (1986) (ed.) *Economics as a Process* (Cambridge University Press, Cambridge).

Manne, H.C. (1965) "Mergers and the Market for Corporate Control", *Journal of Political Economy*, 73, 110–120.

McCormack, G. (1995) *Reservation of Title* (2nd ed., Sweet & Maxwell, London).

Meeks, G. (1977) *Disappointing Marriage: A Study of the Gains from Merger* (Cambridge University Press, London).

Millett, P.J. (1985) "The Quistclose Trust: Who Can Enforce It?" *Law Quarterly Review*, 101, 271.

Milman, D. and Chittenden, F. (1995) *Corporate Rescue: CVAs and the Challenge of Small Companies*, ACCA Research Report No. 44 (Certified Accountants Educational Trust, London).

Milman, D. and Durrant, C. (1994) *Corporate Insolvency: Law and Practice* (2nd ed., Sweet and Maxwell, London).

Mitchell, F., Reid, G.C. and Terry, N. (1994) "Post Investment Demand for Accounting Information by Venture Capitalists", University of St Andrews C.R.I.E.F.F. discussion paper No. 9424, 10.

Nelson, P.B. (1981), *Corporations in Crisis* (Praeger, New York).

Nelson, R.R. and Winter, S.G. (1982) *An Evolutionary Theory of Economic Change* (Harvard University Press, Cambridge).

Nueno, P. (1992) *Corporate Turnaround: A Practical Guide to Business Survival* (Kogan Page, New Jersey), 160.

Ohlson, J.A. (1980) "Financial Ratios and the Probabilistic Prediction of Bankruptcy", *Journal of Accounting Research*, 18 (1), 109–131.

Ormrod, P. and Cleaver, K.C. (1993) "Financial Reporting and Corporate Accountability", *Accounting and Business Research*, 23, No. 91A.

Peck, S.W. (1996) "The Influence of Professional Investors on the Failure of Management Buyout Attempts", *Journal of Financial Economics*, 40, (2), 267–294.

Pennington, R.R. (1991) *Pennington's Corporate Insolvency Law* (Butterworths, London, Dublin and Edinburgh).

Perry, S.E. and Williams, T.H. (1994) "Earnings Management Preceding Management Buyout Offers", *Journal of Accounting and Economics*, 18 (2), 157–179.

Piesse, J. and Wood, D. (1992) "Issues in Assessing MDA Models of Corporate Failure: A Research Note", *British Accounting Review*, 24, 33–42.

Pitt, G. (1995) *Employment Law* (2nd ed. Sweet & Maxwell, London).

Platt, H.D. and Platt, M.B. (1990) "Development of a Class of Stable Predictive Variables: The Case of Bankruptcy Prediction", *Journal of Business Finance and Accounting*, 17, (1), 31–51.

Pratten, C. (1991) *Company Failure*, Paper prepared for the Financial Reporting and Auditing Group of the Institute of Chartered Accountants in England and Wales.

Ravenscraft, D.J. and Scherer, F.M. (1987), *Mergers, Sell-offs & Economic Efficiency* (Brookings Institution, Washington).

Reid, G.C. (1991) "Staying in Business" *International Journal of Industrial Organization*, 9, 551.

Reid, G.C. (1994) "Fast Growing Small Entrepreneurial Firms and their Venture Capital Backers: An Applied Principal-Agent Analysis", University of St Andrews, C.R.I.E.F.F. discussion paper No. 9421, 3.

Reid, G.C., Jacobsen, L.R. and Anderson, M.E. (1993) *Profiles in Small Business: A Competitive Strategy Approach* (Routledge, London and New York).

Rickett, C.E.F. (1991) "Different Views on the Scope of the *Quistclose* Analysis: English and Antipodean Insights" *Law Quarterly Review*, 107, 608–648.

Rickett, C.E.F. (1993) "Trusts and Insolvency: The Nature and Place of the Quistclose Trust" in D.W.N. Waters (ed.) *Equity, Fiduciaries and Trusts*.

Sealy, L.S. and Milman, D. (1994) *Annotated Guide to Insolvency Legislation* (4th ed., CCH, Bicester).

Slatter, S. (1984) *Corporate Recovery* (Penguin, Harmondsworth).

Storey, D.J. (ed.) (1983) *The Small Firm: An International Survey* (Croom Helm, Kent).

Storey, D.J. (1994) *Understanding the Small Business Sector* (Routledge, London and New York).

Storey, D.J. and Johnson, S. (1987) *Are Small Firms the Answer to Unemployment?* (Employment Institute, London).

Strong, N. (1992) "Modelling Abnormal Returns: A Review Article", *Journal of Business Finance and Accounting*, 19, 533–553.

Taffler, R. (1983) "The Z-score Approach to Measuring Company Solvency", *The Accountant's Magazine*, 87, (921), 91–96.

Taffler, R. (1984) "Empirical Models for the Monitoring of U.K. Corporates", *Journal of Banking and Finance*, 199–227.

Taffler, R. (1992) *Applications of the Z-score Approach in Financial Analysis*, paper read to the British Accounting Association.

Tashjian, E., Lease, R.C. and McConnell, J.J. (1996) "Prepacks: An Empirical Analysis of Prepackaged Bankruptcies", *Journal of Financial Economics*, 40, 135–162.

Thomas, R.E. (1986) "Parent-to-parent Divestment", in J. Coyne and M. Wright (eds.) (1986) *Divestment and Strategic Change* (Oxford; Philip Allan).

Watts, R.L. and Zimmerman, J.L. (1986) *Positive Accounting Theory* (Prentice Hall, Englewood Cliffs).

Webb, D. (1991) "An Economic Evaluation of Insolvency Procedures in the United Kingdom: Does the 1986 Insolvency Act Satisfy the Creditors' Bargain?" *Oxford Economic Papers*.

Westbrook, J.L. (1991) "Chapter 11 Reorganisation in the United States", in H. Rajak (ed). (1991) *Insolvency Law: Theory and Practice* (Sweet and Maxwell, London).

White, M.J. (1989) "The Corporate Bankruptcy Decision", *Journal of Economic Perspectives*, 3, (2), 129–151.

Wright, M., Coyne, J. and Mills, A. (1987) *Management Buy-outs* (Woodhead-Faulkner, Cambridge).

Wruck, K.H. (1990) "Financial Distress, Reorganization, and Organizational Efficiency", *Journal of Financial Economics*, 27, 419–444.

Zimmerman, F.M. (1991) *The Turnaround Experience: Real-world Lessons in Revitalizing Corporations* (Mcgraw-Hill, New York).

Zmijewski, M.E. (1984) "Methodological Issues Related to the Estimation of Financial Distress Models", *Journal of Accounting Research*, 22, supplement.

Author Index

(All references are to page number)

Abbey, R., 72, 110, 117–118, 123
Aber, P., 72, 110, 117–118, 123
Aghion, P., 89
Altman, E.l., 59–60, 64–65
Anderman, S.D., 183, 191, 195
Anderson, M.E., 130
Arnold, J., 45

Bannock, G., 130
Barnes, P., 80
Belcher, A., 3, 43
Berry, R.H., 130–131
Betker, B.L., 123, 125
Bolton, J.E., 130
Bowman, R.G., 97
Brealey, R.A., 138
Bridge, M., 168
Brown, C., 128
Brown, D., 214
Bublitz, B., 43

Cadbury, 79
Carnell, C.A., 207
Chittenden, F., 108, 110–111, 128
Cleaver, K.C., 50
Cooke, T.E., 53
Cork, K., 72, 76–77
Coyne, J., 12, 27–29, 149
Cressy, R.C., 129, 142
Cross, M., 127
Crum, R.H., 130–131
Cuthbertson, C., 61

Deakin, E.B., 64
Deakin, S., 181–183, 191, 193, 198
De Angelo, L., 30, 50
De Angelo, H., 50

De Fond, M.L., 50
Dixon, R., 132
Doran, A., 130
Driver, C., 126–127
Duggan, M., 181
Dunne, P., 126–128
Durrant, C., 52, 144, 148

Easterbrook, F.H., 89, 93–94
Elks, L., 176
Ettredge, M., 43

Farrar, J.H., 16, 46, 147
Fletcher, I.F., 45
Flood, J., 22, 72, 110, 117–118, 121, 123
Floyd, R.E., 119
Foster, G., 40–41
Franks, J.R., 17–19, 51, 88, 92
Frost, A.J., 138
Furey, N.E., 16, 147

Gilson, S.C., 17, 22, 39–40, 116–117, 125
Goldberg, W.H., 33
Goldston, M.R., 20–21
Goodhart, W., 164, 171
Goudie, A.W., 68
Grinyer, P.H., 19

Hager, D.P., 138
Hahn, F., 95
Haldeman, R., 60
Hamilton, J., 128
Handy, C., 48
Hannigan, B.M., 16, 147

Index

(All references are to page number)